ON THE ROAD TO

CO-OPERATIVE

ON THE ROAD TO
CO-OPERATIVE

a memoir about a place and time

CHARLES DAN WORLEY

Word Wise Publishing
Indianapolis, Indiana

On the Road to Co-operative
a memoir about a place and time

Copyright ©2023 by Charles Dan Worley

All rights reserved. No part of this publication may be reproduced, distributed, or transmitted in any form or by any means, electronic or mechanical, including photocopying, recording, or by any information storage and retrieval system, without the prior written permission of the author, except the inclusion of brief quotations in critical reviews and certain other non-commercial uses permitted by copyright law.

Permission requests can be sent to
Charles Dan Worley at
charlesdanworley@yahoo.com

Facebook: @charlesworley

Published in the United States by
Word Wise Publishing Inc.
Indianapolis, Indiana

Front Cover Photo—Co-operative, Kentucky, December 1975—Courtesy of Robert Mercer
Back Cover Photo—Co-operative, Kentucky, October 2022—by Charles Dan Worley

Cover Design by Noosha Ravaghi

ISBN 978-1-952784-06-4 (paperback)
ISBN 978-1-952784-07-1 (hardcopy)
ISBN 978-1-952784-08-8 (ebook)

I dedicate this book to two special people:

RL TERRY
and
BRANDON WORLEY

RL TERRY
(1933–2021)

Other than family, once in a lifetime a friend comes along with whom you share similar memories and love of a place (Co-operative), even though you grew up at different times. RL Terry's memory of his young years in Co-operative was solid and he willingly shared his memories with me. I can still hear his soft voice as he told the stories. Telling me gave him the opportunity to relive them.

    As I look back, there was no way for either of us to know the end was so near. RL, my friend, was a joy to be with, and he looked for the good in everyone he met. So dedicating this book to him was an easy decision for me. RL was a man of high morals, and he stood firm on what he believed. I'm saddened he's gone, and I'm blessed to count myself RL's friend.

                        May he rest in peace.

BRANDON WORLEY & DRACO

I dedicate this book also to a man who has come through a lot of adversity and many years of struggles of one sort or another. At one point, it was questionable whether he would survive. But now on this side of the mountain, Brandon Worley has found peace without the trappings of this world and he can rest again.

I've witnessed Brandon go from near death to having two hobbies he is passionate about. With each passing day, he adds to the many others, a huge building block that keeps growing. Brandon's journey is a success story and could be therapy for others to emulate. His strong will and never giving up at his weakest point of life, I admire. I'm blessed to have Brandon as my son.

CONTENTS

Dedication   v
Contents   ix
Foreword: Samuel Perry   xiii
Foreword: Nathan Nevels   xxi
Introduction   xxiv

Chapter 1 Early 1900s	1
Chapter 2 Early Years	10
Chapter 3 1932	21
Chapter 4 1933	29
Chapter 5 1933 Continued	38
Chapter 6 1934	45
Chapter 7 1935	50
Chapter 8 1936	59
Chapter 9 1937	68
Chapter 10 1938	84
Chapter 11 1939	94
Chapter 12 1940	110
Chapter 13 1941	124
Chapter 14 1942	137
Chapter 15 1943	148
Chapter 16 1944	160
Chapter 17 Uncle Roy	171
Chapter 18 The Co-operative Prince	180
Chapter 19 1945	186
Chapter 20 Dynamite Fist—Beginning	194
Chapter 21 1946	207
Chapter 22 1947	220

Chapter 23 Armless Wonder	236
Chapter 24 1948	248
Chapter 25 1949	261
Chapter 26 1950	276
Chapter 27 Black Spider	289
Chapter 28 1951	297
Chapter 29 1952	307
Chapter 30 1953	320
Chapter 31 1954	330
Chapter 32 1955	339
Chapter 33 Dynamite Fist—Conclusion	348
Chapter 34 1956	358
Chapter 35 1957	366
Chapter 36 1958	374
Chapter 37 1959	381
Chapter 38 The Life & Times of Jack Smith	390
Chapter 39 1960 & Boris Haynes	401
Chapter 40 Walter Dixon Jr. & Damon Gibson	415
Chapter 41 Faron Clark & The Music	441
Gratitude List	453
Additional Names of Teachers	459
Worley's Published Books	461
Coming Soon	461
About the Author	462

LIST OF PHOTOS & DRAWINGS

Co-operative, 1975	Front Cover
RL Terry	vi
Brandon Worley	vii
Jeff and Eva Marcum Kidd	9
Jewell Bell Kidd and Neil Kidd	16
Co-op Boardinghouse	95
Dr. Simpson	100
Yamacraw Train Bridge	123
Co-op School	126
Co-op Upper Camp	138
Co-op Coal Tipple	166
Uncle Roy Dobbs	172
Don Dixon	195
Co-op Coal Tipple (top view)	228
Tommy Strunk	237
Co-op Lower Camp Drawings	252, 253
Co-op Bathhouse	264
Tommy Roundtree	288
Co-op Company Store	310
Jack Smith	391
Boris Haynes	400
Damon Gibson & Walter Dixon Jr.	414
Faron Clark	440
Jewell Kidd & Jewell Kidd's Grocery	448
Jewell Kidd's Grocery	450
The Road in Co-op, 2022	463 & Back Cover

FOREWORD
by Samuel D. Perry

On a sultry day in August 1961, I drove my father's 1952 Chevy sedan down a narrow road that threaded its way beneath pine and oak shrouded hills that lifted their rocky heads over a stream tinted orange by acid runoff from coal mines. Clouds of white dust from crushed limestone billowed behind me as the car bounced over "wash boarded" inclines and threatened to stall if I did not shift into a lower gear. I carried with me a recently acquired Bachelor of Arts degree, a teaching certificate from the State of Kentucky, and a head full of ideas that I would use to bring enlightenment to boys and girls living in one of the most isolated regions of McCreary County, Kentucky. I was twenty-two years old, and I had been tasked by the Superintendent of Schools of McCreary County with serving as Principal-Teacher of Co-operative Elementary School.

Co-operative Elementary School was located in a small community that had been built by the Stearns Coal and Lumber Company to house employees who labored in one of the Company's numerous coal mines that dotted the region drained by the Big South Fork River. The community's main feature was a great tipple of steel that belched clouds of black dust as it separated the bituminous mineral into grades of marketable fuel, destined for the industrial jungles of the North and East. Although the tipple was gone by the time I arrived there, and the mine had closed, Co-operative, or Co-op as it was more commonly called, remained home to dozens of families who contin-

ued to depend upon the Company for their livelihood. The school existed to serve the children of those employees as well as children whose parents lived elsewhere in the vicinity but were not in the employ of the Company. At the last count, 123 students were enrolled there. Four teachers were assigned to the school, three of whom I would supervise. Even though the others had forgotten more about the teaching profession than I would ever know, I had been tapped to serve as Principal solely because I was the only one possessing a four-year college degree.

Almost immediately before coming to an empty building that had been the Company Store, I turned left onto a wooden bridge that spanned a stream grown sluggish in the dog days of August. A sharp right turn after crossing the bridge and going about a quarter of a mile brought me to a field overgrown with broom sedge, goldenrod, ragweed, and blackberry brambles. I had arrived at Co-operative Elementary School.

To the left of the field and at the base of a wooded hillside, I could see two long, shuttered buildings. Each was sheathed in clapboard, its white paint faded by decades of exposure to the elements. Both buildings were trimmed in the Kelly green favored by the Company. Perched on top of the north building was a belfry containing a large, cast-iron bell that had become dislodged from its hanger. I had been told that the school consisted of two such buildings, each of which contained two spacious rooms where the students studied.

Reluctant to drive my car into the field lest I damage it on something hidden in the vegetation, I parked it and walked toward the school buildings. A sturdy telephone pole onto which had been attached a wooden backboard for a basketball goal told me that I was walking through what must have been the school playground, although it bore little resemblance to one at the time.

The August heat was intense and the humidity of the creek bottom was almost overpowering, yet the field was alive with grasshoppers that jumped away from me. Honeybees flitted among late-blooming flowers that painted the field in hues of blue, gold, and red. From the hillsides overlooking the school, the drone of cicadas served as a backdrop to the call of a wood thrush, sounding ever so much like a flutist practicing his notes in the forest. It was an incredibly pastoral and peaceful setting and an environment made to order for contemplation and meditation. But it was hardly a place for a school. Or so it seemed to me.

The Superintendent had given me keys to the buildings, so I made my way slowly to the one over which rose the belfry and unlocked the door. Upon entering, I found myself in a small foyer containing two doors opposite each other. Each door opened into a classroom. I chose the one on the right, walked in, and flipped the light switch.

To say that my new classroom was dismal would be to make the understatement of the century. It was dark and forbidding, in spite of the dim glow coming from bare lightbulbs on the high ceiling. The shuttered windows, six of them, blocked any natural light that might have entered the room. The oaken floor was almost black from decades of refinishing with oil to keep down the dust. Desks of the type seen only in history books extended from the front of the room to an elevated, and enclosed, structure at the back that served, I presumed, as some sort of stage for theatrical plays and performances. On the left side of the room stood an enormous potbelly stove, an iron colossus, with a rusty pipe disappearing into the side of the wall. On the floor sat a coal scuttle, still partially filled. Nearby was a small table upon which had been placed an enamelware bucket and an aluminum dipper. I could only presume that it was a water bucket.

My desk was a study one of oak and contained drawers of varying sizes. One contained sharpened pencils and an old stapler that had seen better days. Behind the desk, and screwed to the wall, was the chalkboard. It was cracked in several places and the black paint had chipped away on the edges. Pieces of white chalk in random sizes lay in a tray beneath the board along with some dusty erasers.

A refrigerator stood beside the door to the classroom. It was unplugged and the door was open. I had been instructed to keep it stocked with cartons of milk that I was to obtain each morning at the old Perkins General Store building in Whitley City for resale to students at minimal cost, but only if they could afford to buy them.

For a long time, I stared into the dim recesses of the classroom. I began to have second thoughts about the wisdom of having accepted the Superintendent's offer to serve as Principal. Depressed at the thought of having to work in such an environment, I sat down at the desk. The classroom in which I had found myself was not what I had expected. It was so unlike the one at London High School, where I had done my student teaching. There, the brightly illuminated classrooms with their fluorescent lights and color-filled walls, restrooms with flush toilets, and water fountains in the hallways, had made the teaching profession an inspirational endeavor, one for which I truly believed I had been created. Now, I was not so sure.

A noise coming from outside the building interrupted my reverie and I got up to look. At the bottom of the steps leading up to the main entrance stood a young man in his early teens. He stared at me from bright blue eyes and beneath a shock of wavy, cornsilk hair. "Who are you?" he asked. I introduced myself and expressed my concern about the physical appearance of the school, especially the playground. The young man was silent for a long time. Then, he turned and walked away, replying as he went, "I will be right back." I went back into the classroom to resume my self-pity.

I did not mourn for long, however. Soon, more noise, this time much louder than before, interrupted me.

I went to the door again and saw half a dozen, or more, boys in the field. They were armed with sling blades, sickles, rakes, and hatchets, and were busily chopping down the brambles and weeds that had enveloped the playground over the summer. The young man I had talked to earlier seemed to be leading and directing them.

I stood in awe and amazement at the work being done on the playground. Perspiring in the hot August sun, the boys worked diligently and in joyful camaraderie to push the encroaching vegetation away from the school buildings.

Almost immediately, my depression went away, disappearing like dew in the morning sun. If those boys valued education to the extent they were showing me, I reasoned, what right did I have to feel sorry for myself? I recalled reading somewhere that a school consisted of a teacher, a pupil, and a log upon which to sit. If the boys I saw laboring in the heat of a summer day were willing to provide the log and willing to serve as pupils, how could I refuse to provide the other third of the triad? I could not. So, I went back into the classroom, opened the windows, and pushed back the dark green shutters, filling the room with the sunlight of a bright summer day. I walked over to the refrigerator, closed the door, and plugged it into the electric outlet. Almost immediately, it began to hum. Seeing a broom leaning against a corner of the room, I picked it up and started sweeping the floor.

That was my introduction to Co-operative Elementary School. It was a day I will never forget. It was the first of many days that would serve as a crucible for the development of my own philosophy of education, a philosophy that sustained me through twenty-nine years as an educator. I can say without hesitation that the time I spent at the school was the most enjoyable of my teaching career and, very likely, the most rewarding, for Co-operative Elementary School turned me into a true teacher.

I served only one school year at Co-operative Elementary School. Compulsory military service interrupted my work there. When I hung up my uniform, two years later, the school had been closed and its students transferred to another school, where they could enjoy the amenities offered by more modern educational facilities.

I never lived in Co-op, so I never got to know most of the men and women who resided there, but I knew their children and through them I was not long in learning that the children at Co-operative Elementary School came from hardworking, decent, and honorable people. By the standards of today, most of them were poor. Some were impoverished. Although the Co-operative Mine had closed, many of the breadwinners remained dependent upon the Stearns Coal and Lumber Company for their livelihood. Each day, they went into the depths of other mines with picks, shovels, and dinner buckets filled with leftovers from previous meals. When they left home, there was no guarantee of their safe return. Many did not come back. Others did, but with broken limbs and shattered lungs that rendered further employment by the Company impossible. Life was not easy for those families and the struggles they endured were reflected in their offspring.

After more than sixty years, the names of many of the students who attended Co-operative Elementary School during that term I have forgotten, but their faces remain indelibly etched in my memory. I can see them now, staring back at me from the classroom, eagerly absorbing the words of wisdom a bumbling, young, greenhorn teacher would share with them. The trust I saw in their eyes was humbling. Their eagerness to learn was infectious. The sadness I shared with them when word came that a loved one had passed away was real and sobering. The joy and excitement I witnessed as they came to understand that they were part and parcel of a world immensely greater than the one they lived in was gratifying. Through the stories they told as they stood at my desk during recess, I was admitted into the inner circle of their domestic life. In impromptu counseling sessions on the steps of the schoolhouse and in the shade of the great black oak where we tossed horseshoes on Friday afternoons, I heard their laments about the present and their hopes for the future.

Nine months is but a blip on the radar screen of recorded history. It is also the human gestation period for new life. Nine months is the length of time I spent with the children of this place called Co-op. The nine-month school term I spent at Co-operative Elementary School, however, was much more than a blip to me. That term served as a professional gestation period for me, and it convinced me that in choosing to enter the teaching profession I had made a wise decision. The nine months at Co-operative Elementary School had, in essence, given me new life. I had come among them in August as a stranger; I departed the following May believing that I had become part of a great extended family. The years after I left them were not always good ones for me. Some were, indeed, horrific. Yet, throughout the challenges and difficulties that confronted me, I was strengthened and inspired by the memory of those young people I had known and come to love. They inspired me to do my best in my chosen profession. They strengthened me when I was weak and tempted to give up and find an easier job. They gave me courage when I feared the future.

The English philosopher John Locke observed that "No man's knowledge can go beyond his experience." I would like to think that when my career as an educator came to an end, I had become somewhat knowledgeable about what it takes to be a good teacher. If that, indeed, is true, it is, in no small part, because of the experience I had while serving at Co-operative Elementary School.

Danny Worley, the author of this book, was a fifth grader in Rebecca Logan's class, in the room adjoining mine, so I cannot say that I knew him well. I saw him only on the playground during recess and when Ms. Logan and I exchanged classrooms, which we did each day in the interest of providing a well-rounded educational experience for the most students. From all reports, and I did, indeed, receive reports from my fellow teachers, he was a good student and a good boy, one of those kids all teachers yearn to have in their classrooms. His tenure at Co-operative was cut short by circumstances beyond his control, but his early life in the little mining camp always remained a part of who he was and who he continues to be. He is a man of many gifts and talents, but he is, also, one of those rare individuals to whom the voices of the past cry out for attention. From the dim recesses of the mines, from the front porches of houses up and down the creek, and from the playground of Co-operative Elementary School, those voices plead with him that they not be forgotten, that they not be permitted to fade into obscurity and erased from collective memory of those living today. Danny Worley hears those voices and he listens and he responds to those supplications through the written word. We are all the better for it.

Samuel D. Perry
Retired Educator

Principal & Teacher
Co-operative Elementary
1961-1962

FOREWORD
by Nathan Nevels

I was the last principal at Co-operative Elementary School. I was assigned to Co-operative School in 1963, and I was told that when the new addition at Smithtown Elementary was completed, which would be soon, we would be consolidated.

I had taught one year in a two-room school at Beulah Heights in 1961. I had an Agronomy Degree from University of Kentucky (U.K.). I went back to U. K. in 1962 and got a teaching Degree in Biology. At the time, I lived in my grandparents' old house that did not have running water. We had an outside toilet and carried water from my mother's well. I had a new house under roof but did not get it finished until August 1964.

Co-operative Elementary had been a four-room school in two buildings, with two grades in each of the four classrooms. The four teachers were Becky Logan, Carolyn Ball, Joyce Wood, and me. On the first day of school, someone from the McCreary County Board of Education office came and told us Co-operative would need only three teachers because of the small number of students. Becky Logan was chosen to go to Whitley Elementary.

I had 6th, 7th, and 8th grades in one of the two rooms in the upper building. The room with the stage was used as a playroom when the weather kept the students indoors.

We had a big potbelly stove which burned coal for heat. In cold weather, we paid one of the older boys to come early and build fires in the three stoves. On really cold mornings, we would place desks in a circle around the stove to keep warm.

There were two outside toilets in the woods behind the school.

We carried drinking water from a well at the church close by.

Each teacher had about 25 students. Some of them lived close enough to walk and some of them rode the high school bus. They were good children, plenty smart, and well behaved.

Rayma Dean Clark lived across the road from the schoolhouse. She could sing just like Loretta Lynn. She loved singing to the class.

Billy Jay Kidd asked if he could drive his car to school. I said sure, just park on the side of the road. Don't bring it onto the playground. I tried to spark his sister Joyce in high school but she had a boyfriend who had a car.

We had a big Halloween party at school on a Friday. When we went back to school on Monday, there was a lot of vandalism. The wood steps to my building were torn down and both toilets were turned over and demolished. The older boys helped me put the girls' toilet back together and the boys went to the woods.

In October 1963, I took the boys who wanted to go camping to Great Meadows, a new forest service campground several miles past the school. Most of the boys brought shotguns and went squirrel hunting Saturday morning.

The Co-operative school moved to Smithtown in the middle of the 1963-1964 school year during Christmas break. I was happy to have a good room in a heated building with an indoor bathroom and a cafeteria.

All that's left of the Co-operative Coal Camp is the Baptist Church, which is still being used today and is well kept.

Co-operative School is a wonderful memory to thousands of children and dozens of teachers.

Nathan Nevels
Retired Educator

Last Principal of
Co-operative Elementary
Fall 1963

INTRODUCTION

Co-operative, Kentucky, the place of my birth, continues to be in my thoughts because of a happy childhood. The time was so different from today.

I've written this book not as a continuation of *CO-OP: Coal, Community, & House 52*, my memoir published in 2020, even though it's about the same community. The focus of this book is not on my family, but I will insert memories throughout the book. Some of the details I intend to share I've only recently uncovered; good or bad, I will shed light on these and other stories, giving an overall visual picture of the life before, during, and after my time in the place I hold dear, Co-operative, Kentucky, and the surrounding communities.

After publishing *CO-OP: Coal, Community, & House 52*, I was asked by many "When are you going to write another book?" or "Do you plan to write another book on Co-operative?"

Some time ago I was at Radio Station WHAY (Hay 98) on the "Lucky Dog Show" promoting my first book. (Lucky Dog, or Larry Davis, will forever be Little Elvis to me). The next day while talking with my friend Roger Terry, I learned he'd listened to the radio show. He said "I heard you announce you're going to write another book." Roger continued, "What I think happened, you got caught up in the excitement of being on the radio, and with one slip of the tongue, you made this big announcement about writing another book. But the question now is what are you going to do?" Of course, he laughed after he said it.

After doing preliminary research, I found a wealth of information and stories still to be told. That's the main reason I'm not ready to let go of the story of Co-operative. My life has been so touched by my upbringing of living in Co-op, I'm not willing to let these stories and the community of Co-operative die. I also could not wait to contact people who still have memories because when they're gone, so are their stories.

By capturing a small part of the story of Co-operative in print, we can preserve the innocence and the essence of a time of simple pleasures, mixed with the grandeur of a company forging its way into the unknown, what we now call Daniel Boone National Forest. The people who chose to come along also carved a way of life that resulted in a meager existence. Still, it was a way for poor people to live and raise their families with dignity, without complaint or apology. Their children, while young, were insulated from the hardships their parents endured. The children, with little if any begging, were satisfied to get one toy their whole life; some never received any.

But our upbringing wasn't about getting stuff; we were taught the important things in life—love, friendship, good morals, and hard work to succeed in life. Having good neighbors didn't necessarily mean they lived next door; they could live anywhere in the mining community. Developing those friendships almost always lasted a lifetime.

We must remember that people, no matter the circumstances, don't always get along. Through misunderstandings, some people ended up in violent situations; some lost their lives.

Even though I personally viewed the time of growing up in Co-operative the best of times, still others were having a rougher time and reacted far differently. What I mean is some families lost their husbands and dads as a result of accidents inside the coal mines, putting a heavy burden on the widow and children. Those moms were forced to raise their children alone and without help from the state. Older children had to drop out of school. Those young people had to make money by whatever means, even if it meant making moonshine, which was illegal. Widows with young children had to turn to other relatives for means of survival.

Saying it was a simple time doesn't fully inform the young people of today, yet it was a simple time. And there was also a mystical, somewhat magical, feel that is often hard to put into words. By no means am I diminishing the hardships, pain, loss of loved ones, and struggles our parents endured, and I will continue to tell those difficult stories where possible. This is only my personal perspective: As a child, I grew up in a time of simple pleasures, where friendships and hours of playing marbles or playing a softball game won the day.

I highlight several of the families I mentioned in *CO-OP: Coal, Community, & House 52* in more detail. Although Co-operative is my focus, I also recognize other areas such as Gregory, Fidelity, White Oak Junction, Bell Farm, Bald Knob, and Rattlesnake Ridge. These places were working communities before Co-operative was developed, and before these early communities began to die, Co-operative was born and thriving. So as Stearns closed a coal mine in one community, the miners went looking for work in the other nearby communities. When houses became empty in that new community, the miners moved their families closer to their work. If a house wasn't available close to the mine, the miner had to walk to work; sometimes they had to walk long distances such as to the other side of a mountain.

The Stearns Company developed these mining communities complete with housing for the miners and their families, a resident doctor, a Company Store, school buildings, and other amenities. Co-operative, for example, had two coal mine entrances and a tipple for distributing the different sized coal in separate coal gons. Co-operative also had a bathhouse for the coal miners to clean up after their shift, a boarding house for Company officials and potential buyers of Stearns Company coal, and a Company Store equipped with everything from clothes to grain to food to gasoline. The Company Stores in the mining camps, as with Co-operative, owned by Stearns Coal and Lumber Company, also housed the U. S. Post Office and an office for the Stearns Company paymaster. If the families needed anything during the week, they could charge items at the Company Store and the amount would be deducted from the miners' next paycheck, and if they needed cash, the paymaster would issue scrip also deducted from the miners' next paycheck. The scrip could be used at Stearns Company stores in full. If the scrip was used anywhere else outside the Stearns Company, it would be traded ninety cents to the dollar.

Everything in the community was within walking distance. This convenience was a necessity because only a rare few could afford the luxury of a car.

When the need arose to go to the town of Stearns, the resident would have to hire someone with a car to take them or ride the train. Riding the train was not the most convenient since it ran only early mornings and afternoons. The train was for the convenience of getting miners back and forth to the different mining operations and delivering the harvested coal out to Stearns to be dropped off. Still, it was an inconvenience most residents had little choice but to tolerate and at the same time to appreciate. The community of Co-operative was self-sustaining for everyday living, so leaving the community was not a regular occurrence or necessity for the residents.

The information and stories shared in this book are not only from my memory but from the many friends and family I've talked with, and although I will thank you by name in the Gratitude List, I want to collectively thank all of you here for your patience with me. You all were so gracious with my relentless pursuit of answers to my questions, trying to find the next nugget of information I felt was vital to the story. I value each one of you. Although some of you may have thought you had nothing of importance to share, you did. And I so appreciate your willingness to share with me. I thank you from the bottom of my heart. Because of you, these stories of Co-operative will live on.

Also, I must acknowledge the tremendous contribution of the *McCreary County Record* housed in the Digital Archives of the McCreary County Public Library in Whitley City. I spent countless hours poring over the many years of the *Record*. Most, if not all, of the early facts and stories in this book came from the *Record*. Thank you, Kay Morrow, for all your patience and help. I could not have done it without your guidance.

Every time I called the McCreary County Museum in Stearns, Kentucky, Dawn Strunk, you were always ready to help. Even if you were at home, you would take the time to meet me at the Museum to help with the questions I was concerned with. Thank you so much.

To my readers, thank you for taking the time to read this book. I hope it helps you understand the times and people who lived and died in these communities. Our parents worked backbreaking jobs, never wasting time dreaming they could be rich or famous. Their dream was the hope their children would have a better life than they did. I dreamed and I was allowed to dream and reach for the stars because of my parents; I was able to build and create what I wanted.

This dream gives me great joy to relive and to give the people that lived in these coal camps their place in history. Many people I was unable to mention for a number of reasons, and I regret that I couldn't, but the absence does not diminish the importance of their help in building and shaping these communities.

Though many I've written about in this book have left this life and will not get to see their names on these pages, it pleases me to know I've contributed to their names living on. That the place of Co-operative, Kentucky, lives on is my dream.

Charles Dan Worley

Note: If I have misspelled a name, left out a name, or gotten the details of a story wrong, it was unintentional and I sincerely apologize.

CHAPTER 1

Early 1900s

In the Big South Fork area, three men were asked to go into the heart of the virgin forest to determine the feasibility of harvesting the timber. They found out very quickly the many hollers and mountains would make maneuvering the great distances from cliff to cliff a challenge. Would a 400-plus-foot skidder cable span a particular gulf to secure the logs?

It was a December day and almost dusk; the men stopped on what looked to be an old logging road. Thinking of finding a campsite, it was there they met her cantering on her pony, and both parties were surprised to see the other, the crew more surprised to see the young woman in a practical wilderness at that time of day. She informed the men she was a schoolteacher, and the schoolhouse was approximately two miles behind her.

In further conversation, she said she made the trip morning and night, nearly nine miles each way to and from the schoolhouse, which was located on the opposite side of the Big South Fork River. She said the schoolhouse had been recently built because the old one went down river after an extremely high rainfall. The young woman was Elizabeth Blevins. Elizabeth was a small woman, weighing not much over a hundred pounds, and was twenty years old. She had graduated with honors from Louisville Girls High School and taken a three-year post-high-school course in Tennessee, enabling her to secure a four-year certificate to teach in compliance with the laws of the State of Kentucky.

Learning all this about the young woman, who could not admire the job she was doing under such trying circumstances? The men had known her ten years earlier when she was a child living in Stearns, where her father was the former head of the Stearns Coal and Lumber Company Timekeeping department.

That night, the three men stayed with a family that lived across from the schoolhouse. It was there they learned Elizabeth was beloved by all the children who attended the school. When the river was fordable, she assisted some of the smaller children across on her pony, sometimes carrying two or three kids each trip. If the river was swollen by heavy rains, Elizabeth tied her pony to a tree on the opposite bank from the schoolhouse, and the schoolmarm paddled her way across in a flat bottom boat.

Whatever emergence arose, Elizabeth was ready to meet it. For example, one evening she was on her way home and encountered a rattlesnake in the path that her pony refused to pass. Elizabeth tied off her pony. She then took a club and whaled the snake to death. All in a day's work for this enterprising young woman.

Along the road for seven miles after crossing the river, there were only two mountain cabins, and then the road wound down through a gap in the cliff some several hundred feet below to the valley to which she traveled twice each day. During the winter months, she was permitted to shorten the lunch hour to give her more time to negotiate this lonely route before dark. When extremely bad weather occurred, Elizabeth stayed with one of her pupils' family, an event which brought pleasure to teacher, students, and parents.

Elizabeth's story is one of many in the early 1900s in the Kentucky mountains. Teachers rode mules and horses and some got up around 2:30 a.m. to reach their destinations on time. These were dedicated educators who loved teaching and loved to see young people learn.

∞

Stearns Company knew it had to have a way to get the vast riches of timber to the sawmill in Stearns, and that way had to be close to the timber being harvested. So began the Stearns Company's venture into building railroads. As Stearns Company continued to explore for other minerals, it found black gold—or coal—and started building coal mining camps.

Stearns Company capitalized on the discovery of coal and developed communities and opened mines: one at Barthell, two at Worley, and two at Yamacraw (and opened a third community at Yamacraw that lasted only a year). Expansion continued with the company's sights set on White Oak Junction. The company had already discovered coal there and had determined that the supplies needed to open a mine and start a community could be brought in on rail. The next order of business was housing for the miners and their families, a company store, and a schoolhouse.

Stearns Company continued to expand its coal mines and communities and railroads. Crossing Bridge 11 and beyond about a half of a mile up the tracks was Mine 15; in another half of a mile was Exotus, a small area with only one coal mine entrance. A short distance beyond was the area of Fidelity. Interestingly, in this area, there were several families already scattered out along those mountains. Also, there was a graveyard, and since the opening of Fidelity around 1916, it had been called Fidelity Graveyard, but further investigation uncovered tombstones dating back to the middle of the 1800s. The post office was known as Shoopman Post Office even though Stearns Company called the area Fidelity. Was the post office already there when Stearns Company built Fidelity Mine? I assume it was, for it to keep a different name.

When Stearns Company built the Fidelity community, it was the largest Stearns Company coal camp with an estimated seventy-two houses (the number taken from maps drawn by surveyors at the time). Fidelity would remain the largest for only a few years. Another coal camp was on the horizon that would exceed the number of homes in Fidelity. The Fidelity mining community was scattered on both sides of the creek, complete with a company store, boardinghouse, bathhouse, schoolhouse with grades 1–12, and two tipples.

The next community, called Gregory, about a half of a mile from Fidelity, was one of the smaller communities with a few houses scattered along the tracks and across the creek where Jeff Kidd lived and operated a grocery store.

Beyond Gregory, the area of Bell Farm also had a school, small store, and post office. Oren Spradlin was postmaster from 1931 to 1975. The store, post office, and barbershop were all in the same building. Stearns Company also had its Company Store; the store manager was Sherman Blevins. Bell Farm was a place with a lot of logging activity and soon would be the home of a Civilian Conservation Corps (CCC) program. This program, established during the Great Depression by President Franklin D. Roosevelt as part of the Emergency Conservation Work Act of 1933, was a government program that provided jobs for unemployed, single, young men.

∞

Jeff Kidd learned logging from his dad in the foothills around Bell Farm and Shoopman. The art of hewing logs with an extra elongated blade called a hewing axe was a skill he would carry on into his adulthood. He watched his dad take a log and hew the bark off, and when he was finished, the log had four sides. With this style of cutting, he helped his dad build a new cabin and later a new barn. Jeff and his dad started branching out to sell the logs to other farmers in the area and new families as they began moving into the area. By the time Stearns Company started developing the area with the railroad, Jeff was ready to contract with Stearns Company, selling his hewed logs, which the company badly needed for its railroad. This lucrative business for Mr. Jeff Kidd allowed him to expand and build his sawmill close to the area of Bell Farm.

One morning a gentleman came to Jeff's sawmill and ordered some lumber but with the stipulation that Jeff's crew deliver it. On the day it was to be delivered, Jeff couldn't spare any workers from his sawmill, so he delivered the order himself. Reaching the farm, he waited for just a minute, looking around hoping to see somebody outside. Not seeing anyone, Jeff got off his horse-drawn wagon and started up the steps to the front porch when a voice said, "He's not in there." Jeff looked around and saw Eva Marcum who had come from somewhere behind the house. Eva continued, "Dad's out in the field."

"I just need to know where he wants the lumber put," Jeff said.

Eva said, "By the barn, but don't block the door." From this encounter, Jeff knew he'd be back to see Eva.

∞

MARRIED IN THE EARLY YEARS

Pete and Della Winchester, 1916
Children: Arnold, Arlin, Geneva, Starlin, Thelma, Conley, Dester, Faye, and Kaye

Sheridan Cooper and Eva Jane Waters, 1919

John Bolin (Bo) and Louvada Clark, 1922
Children: Fount, Ledford, Bonnie, Fred, William Gene, and Goman

Albert and Mertie Dobbs, 1923
Children: Sylvester, Odell, Clinton, Harold, Roger, Jewell, and Sherry

Virgil (Pete) Lewis and Minnie Jones, 1926

Orville (Bug) Shoopman and Bessie Murphy, 1927
Children: Mildred, Viola, Vonda, Ed, Elmer, Eugene, Junior, and Linda

Carroll Denton Rose and Mable Bledsoe, 1927
Children: Clarice Lee, Carroll Jr., and Diane

Harrison Dixon and Rosie Mae Flynn, 1927
Children: Cecil, Hobert, Donald, Clara, James Lonnie, Roy Gene, Betty, Hershel Lee, and Junior

∞

BORN IN THE EARLY YEARS

Cornelius (Neil) Kidd (1910)
Ernest Bowden (1912)
Okley Bowden (1914)
John N. Worley & Ruby Jewell Bell (1916)
Arnold Winchester (1917)
Arlin Winchester (1918)
Charlie Bowden (1919)
Josh Cooper (1920)
Don Bowden (1921)
Lexie M. Jones, Geneva Winchester, &
Sylvester Dobbs (1922)
Fred Lee Slaven & Fount Clark (1923)
Kenneth Marcum, Thelma Jo Cooper,
Starlin Winchester,
Frank Slaven, & Odell Dobbs (1924)
Ruby Cooper (1925)
Bill Marcum, Junior Slaven, & Clinton Dobbs (1926)

Thelma Winchester, Lela Lewis,
Buddy Cooper, & Bonnie Clark (1927)
Cecil Dixon, Sheila Marcum, Burman Slaven,
Harold Dobbs, Ledford Clark,
& Leroy Waters (1928)
Conley Bell, Mildred Shoopman, Lester Watson,
& Othea Lewis (1929)

JEFF KIDD AND EVA MARCUM KIDD
PHOTOS COURTESY OF REBA KIDD.

CHAPTER 2

EARLY YEARS

After a short courtship, Jeff Kidd and Eva Marcum were married. Jeff had built, and began living in, a one-room cabin with the lumber from his sawmill. It was here Jeff brought his wife. Jeff had to get busy expanding the cabin because the family grew with the births of Bethanie, Ned, Guy, Cornelius (Neil), Curtis, Rose, Jean, Sandra, and Ruth. Neil was born in 1910. Six years later, Stearns Company built its railroad near the front of their home. A year later Neil started school.

William (Bill) Bell married Nettie Miller and in the early days lived higher up the mountain from the Kidds. Born in this marriage were Estil (nickname Eck), Ruby Jewell, Dorthia (who died young), Opal Christine, and Betty Lois. Ruby Jewell Bell was born in 1916, the same year Stearns Company opened Fidelity Mine. The way Ruby Jewell's birthday fell, she was almost eight years old by the time she started school. Before Ruby Jewell started school, her family moved down into a house next door to the Jeff Kidd family.

And Stearns Company kept building its railroads, moving into parts of Tennessee. The mining communities continued to grow as the many families who worked for Stearns Company moved into the areas. Also, the home of Jeff Kidd expanded to accommodate his family and the grocery store he opened. Jeff converted part of his home into a store and Eva, his wife, was a big asset in the store business. The enterprising Jeff Kidd now had three businesses operating: the sawmill, a separate crew for hewing crossties, and the grocery store. Quite an accomplishment for someone during those times. As the older boys grew, they helped their mom in the store and were increasingly given more responsibility. Guy and Neil took a liking to the store business, more so than the other boys.

One evening at the supper table, Jeff told Eva the Stearns Company was opening a new area that spurred off from White Oak Junction. He added, "I've heard the place will be called Co-operative, and they want every crosstie I can make." He looked around the table and said, "I'm expecting you boys to help your mom all you can around the house and store because I'm going to be busy for a good while." At this point Neil was ten years old.

∞

As Co-operative was being built, down in Oneida, Tennessee, to the west, was a place called Grave Hill. In Grave Hill, Joseph Castello Slaven, known as either J. C. or Cack (some spelled it Kack), married Betty Thomas. They were among the first to move to Co-operative when Stearns Company opened Co-operative Mine.

∞

After Guy and Neil Kidd finished the eighth grade, they continued to work at the family grocery store while also helping at their sawmill. By now it was 1924, and the oldest Kidd brothers, Bethanie and Ned, began working for Stearns Coal and Lumber Company.

Around 1926, Neil began paying attention to Ruby Jewell Bell and would try making conversation with her when she came to the store. She was still young and shy; she was a big boned girl and tall for her age and very pretty. He made little progress at this time.

∞

Meanwhile, Harvey Terry and his wife and young son Paul lived on Lower Shirt Factory Road, but in those days, the place was likely called Revelo. Harvey worked at Fidelity Mine. To get to work, he walked to the Stearns Depot and rode the Kentucky & Tennessee (K & T) Railway, and when his shift was over, he rode the train back to Stearns and walked home. Early in 1927, Harvey's wife died trying to give birth to their second child; sadly, the baby died as well. Months later, Harvey met Hattie Nichols. Little is known about how they met, but they got married in 1928. When a house came open in Fidelity, Harvey moved Hattie and son Paul, by his first wife, to Fidelity.

∞

Harrison Dixon grew up in Wayne County; as a young man, the only job he could find was riding logs down the river to market at Cripple Creek, Tennessee. Those men who did this job for Stearns Coal and Lumber Company were called Devils and as they arrived close to the rough rapids at Blue Heron, they'd jump off, hence the name Devils Jump. Harrison and his first wife had two children—a son, Auston, and a daughter, Laura. His wife and their third child both died during childbirth. His wife's family wanted the two children, and Harrison agreed to let them take the two young kids, realizing it would be hard for him to work and raise two babies without help.

When Rosie Mae Flynn's mother died, Rosie moved to Wolf Creek to stay with her uncle John Flynn. John and wife Mollie owned a grocery store for a while and also ran a boardinghouse and washed clothes for people. Rosie helped Mollie with some of her workload, which Mollie appreciated.

Harrison Dixon stayed at the boardinghouse, and one day when he wasn't working, he met Rosie. They began talking and taking walks. Harrison Dixon and Rosie Mae Flynn were married in 1927. When they got married, they moved to Wall Town, and it was there their first child, Cecil, was born in 1928. For a short time, the Dixon family lived in Paint Cliff before moving to White Oak Junction and eventually to the Lower Camp at Co-operative. (Lower Camp was not an official name. It was the name we called the area east of the Co-operative tipple. Upper Camp lay west of the tipple.)

∞

Back in Gregory, in 1929, Ruby Jewell Bell was raised to be a good person and she loved people. So as Neil Kidd continued talking with her when she came to the Kidd store, she was nice to him and began responding. She was changing, becoming a little more outgoing. The relationship was beginning.

In front of the Kidd store was a storage building high off the ground. When Neil's dad, Jeff, decided to raise pigs, he fenced in that storage building. The building overlooked the railroad tracks and was a little distance away from the store. Jeff would sell the pigs, but those that didn't sell, he fattened up and killed in the fall. He then butchered them and sold the meat in the store.

∞

Guy and Neil Kidd loved walking over the mountain to Co-operative; they made the trip so many times they had their own path they followed. Going straight up the mountain behind their home place, they would reach the top in Hickory Knob. At the time, Columbus King owned all of Hickory Knob. They would walk through a field that years later would be Steam Boat Freeman's farm and go down the other side of the mountain. Reaching the bottom, they would be in Co-operative. There, they'd cross White Oak Creek where Dobbs Mountain bottomed out. Guy noticed a particular spot on one of his trips without Neil that he especially liked.

On one of their later trips together, Guy said to Neil, "This place is what I wanted to show you." The place was covered with underbrush and a few scattered trees. They both saw the potential.

"I like the place," Neil said.

Guy said, "Neil, you know if we ask Dad, he'll help us with lumber from the sawmill."

The Kidd brothers agreed this was the place they would start their own business, and it would be called Kidd Brothers' Grocery. The brothers were able to acquire the property and began clearing the ground. They used the smaller trees, six to eight inches in diameter, to cut the length they needed. These were used to brace the subfloor. Most of the lumber they needed came from their dad's sawmill.

It was natural for Mr. Kidd's boys to want their own place, growing up in a business environment. The brothers built a typical country store—a huge room with a potbelly stove in the center of the room. When you walked into the store through the front door, there was a counter running down both sides that connected in the rear with a short counter space and meat cooler. There was a small break in the rear counter space for walking into the customer space from behind the counter when the stove needed more wood or coal.

The main gravel road passed in front of the store. Looking out the front door of the store, the road east winded down through Copin Camp, Sawmill Camp, and on into the heart of Co-operative. Back at the Kidd Brothers' Store, the road west immediately winded up Dobbs Hill, leading to the top of Dobbs Mountain.

In these beginning days and months, Guy and Neil would leave the store and walk home by going up the mountain behind the store. At the top of the mountain, they'd walk across Hickory Knob and down the other side of the mountain to their home in Fidelity. Each evening, the brothers would hide the day's money in various places along the path. Ev-

JEWELL BELL KIDD AND CORNELIUS (NEIL) KIDD
PHOTOS COURTESY OF REBA KIDD.

ery morning, the Kidd brothers would pick up their money on the way back to the store to open for the day. The year was 1930.

The Kidd Brothers' Store sold a variety of food items and some dry goods. In those days, stores often allowed credit, which meant you could walk into the store and pick out your items with the promise you would pay later. The store clerk would write the items down under your account and you'd walk out with your items. The store relied on its customers' honesty to come back and pay the charges on their next payday.

∞

Well into 1931, the Kidd Brothers' Store was doing good business, but Guy had a bigger aspiration, his own store. Guy had a place in mind at White Oak Junction. He'd been there several times looking it over. Guy told his brother Neil what he wanted to do, so Neil bought Guy's share of the Kidd Brothers' Store.

Neil Kidd and Ruby Jewell Bell began courting, but they didn't have a lot of time now that Neil was a sole business owner. They enjoyed their walks together to and from church. Sometime early in 1932, Neil asked Ruby Jewell to be his wife. She accepted his proposal and later that year they were married. Neil brought his sixteen-year-old bride back across the mountain to his one-room store where they slept on a cot in the rear corner of the store.

In White Oak Junction, Guy built and opened his store. He, too, was very successful on his own. White Oak Junction was well populated and even though Stearns Coal and Lumber Company also operated a Company Store at White Oak Junction, there were enough families to support both stores.

Neil renamed his store after his beautiful wife. From that point on, the store became Jewell Kidd's Grocery. Both Neil and Jewell worked together managing the store, and the young Jewell had good business sense. Jewell thought it better, instead of having everything they sold mixed together, to have like items grouped together, so she began separating and organizing the whole store.

Walking into the store, you would see dry goods on the left side, and in the rear left corner, Neil installed shelves for displaying shoes. On the right side were groceries and the cash register. In the rear, on the right side, Jewell called that space the "notions" side; this area included medicines, deodorants, jewelry, and women's personal items. Neil began almost immediately adding rooms to the store for living space, building one room per year, on average.

The first room he added was at the rear of the store; this room became their first bedroom, and off the back of that room, he built a porch. The bedroom housed a bed, dresser, chest of drawers, and two chairs. On the porch is where they took baths in a wash tub; the wash tub they also used to wash clothes. Neil would later install a water pump on the porch. On the east side of the store, he added one room at a time for a total of six rooms that matched the length of the store. Over the doorway in the rear of the store separating the living area, Jewell hung a curtain.

∞

MARRIED IN THE EARLY YEARS

Harvey Terry and Hattie Nichols, 1928
Children: Paul (Harvey's first marriage), RL, Fayrene, JT, and Wanda

Walter and Bertha Watson, 1928
Children: Luke, Jess, Chet, and Lester

Les Hall and Ruth Frady, 1929
Children: Helen, Clara, Ruby, Alma Jo, John, Nelson, Roger, Leroy, Lena, Joyce, and Carol Sue

Leamon Stephens and Gladys Vanover, 1929
Children: Clarence, Clara, Lois, Lawrence, Bobby, and Shirley

Virgil Freeman and Emma Worley, 1929
Children: Dennis, Norman, Oma, Judy, Betty, and Teresa

Stobert McGuffey and Lessie Chitwood, 1929
Child: James

Oscar Ball and Lida Smith, 1931
Children: Vandon, Ronald, Varieta, Irma, Patricia Darrell, and Kevin

Wilburn Coffey and Roxie Gregory, 1931
Children: Ruby, Bob, Neil, and Randall

Cornelius (Neil) Kidd and Ruby Jewell Bell, 1932
Children: Joyce, Bob, Lindell, Billy Jay, and Jack

BORN THESE YEARS 1930 and 1931

Glenn Freeman (1930)
Estes Gregory (1930)
Wilma Cooper (1930)
Tommy Strunk (1930)
George Shepherd (1930)
Cleatus Slaven (1930)
Conley Winchester (1930)
Barbara Marcum (1930)
Clarence Stephens (1930)
Roger Dobbs (1930)
Hobert Dixon (1931)
Wilma Duncan Marcum (1931)
Earl Bell (1931)
Denzil Wilson (1931)
Chester Watson (1931)
Mildred Lewis (1931)
Helen Hall (1931)
Clara Jones Watters (1931)
Marie Dixon (1931)

CHAPTER 3

1932

Claude Frady moved into the area of Fidelity after securing a job with Stearns Coal and Lumber Company. The Frady family moved into the house vacated by C. D. Hurst.

∞

In Co-operative, Miss Ann Fleenor, beauty specialist, spent Wednesday, May 11, 1932, and Thursday, May 12, 1932, giving permanent waves to ladies in the area. These permanent waves were the newest sensation in the beauty business—for those who could afford it. Among those who gave it a try were Mrs. Eli Logan, Mrs. Herman Strunk, Mrs. Bertha Lewis, Mrs. C. D. Rose, Mrs. Morris Blevins, Mrs. Myrtle Wilson, Miss Kizzie Troxell, and Miss Cumie Howard.

∞

The new price of a marriage license in the county became $5.50. After the price increased, not one marriage license was issued for months. The county clerk pleaded, "Surely love is worth $5.50 even if we are in a depression." Of course, numbers picked up again. Even though at the time it seemed the price increase kept people from getting married, it likely had nothing to do with it.

∞

While these activities were happening, Amelia Earhart, an American aviator, flew solo across the Atlantic, the first woman to accomplish the feat. Amelia Earhart left Newfoundland, and about four hours later, she saw flames spitting out of the exhaust, but she didn't let that stop her. After a hazardous trip, conquering storm, fog, and fire, she landed in a green countryside field. Amelia was married to George P. Putnam.

∞

While celebration was in order for Amelia, tragedy struck the home of Charles Augustus Lindbergh. Mr. Lindbergh, also an American aviator, military officer, author, inventor, and activist, won the Orteig prize for making a nonstop, solo flight from New York to Paris. Mr. Lindbergh's son Charles Augustus Jr., less than two years old, was kidnapped one evening. When one of the household staff checked on the infant, she found a note instead of the baby. The note, pinned to one of the window curtains, demanded $50,000 ransom for the baby's return.

Investigators uncovered footprints, indicating a man and a woman were involved. They surmised a man entered the home and carried the baby outside to the woman who was waiting. Mr. Lindbergh agreed to pay the ransom to the kidnappers on the safe return of his son, while the desperate search continued. Two and a half months later, young Charles Augustus Jr. was found three miles from the Lindbergh home, dead. This was after the New York state police announced they had no concrete information leading to an arrest in the Lindbergh case.

∞

Back in Co-operative, the school year of 1932 got under way with the addition of a new teacher, Mr. Kenneth Larmee. The community welcomed him and wished him the best.

∞

At the depot in Stearns, three men, guests of the Stearns Coal and Lumber Company, got off the Southern Railway. They were coal salesmen from the State of Ohio: W. H. Hodges of Mechanicsburg, Ohio; D. H. Yoder of West Liberty, Ohio; and Mr. Howser of Troy, Ohio. They were established customers and had been selling Stearns coal for several years and would tour the communities of Co-operative and Worley.

∞

On the medical front, whooping cough was on the rise. The Kentucky State Board of Health urged mothers to assume their kids would get the disease and the sooner the better. The Board warned whooping cough was a serious disease and at the first signs of a cold accompanied by sneezes and sniffles to send for the doctor. The year before, in 1931, out of 9,000 cases reported, 180 died.

∞

Jeff Kidd of Gregory made a business trip to Stearns for the purpose of advising friends and others about raising hogs and the problem of cholera. Jeff had been raising hogs for years and his expertise was invaluable. Mr. Kidd stated we all had to work together to get rid of cholera or it would ruin the hog business for everyone.

∞

The following Saturday, citizens of Whitley City, Kentucky, were startled during their noon meal when gunshots rang out. News of a gunfight spread faster than a forest fire. It was rumored that Shorty Davis, a barber, had borrowed a set of clippers from Mrs. Bert Litton, a cook at Wilson's Restaurant. After a short time, Mrs. Litton called Mr. Davis and requested he return the clippers, which he did. There had not been enough time for Mr. Davis to use them to know if he liked them. Mr. Davis dwelled on the situation and became mad, thinking Bradley Wilson, the restaurant owner, must have said something about him to Mrs. Litton. Mr. Davis went to the restaurant and accused Mr. Wilson of telling Mrs. Litton that he was a crook. Mr. Davis and Mr. Wilson argued until it escalated into a fight and Mr. Wilson ordered Mr. Davis to leave his restaurant. Mr. Davis left and walked across Main Street (also Highway 27).

One report said that Mr. Davis began yelling obscenities across the street at Mr. Wilson. Another report said Mr. Wilson was yelling across the street at Mr. Davis. No eyewitnesses came forward, so it was not determined which one of the men fired first. But both had guns. Green Barnett was sitting in his car when the shooting began. Mr. Wilson shot three times and all three hit Mr. Davis. Mr. Davis shot twice. Both men began retreating when they started shooting. Mr. Davis ducked down behind a car that was close to where he was standing. Mr. Wilson hunkered down behind Green Barnett's car.

When the shooting stopped, Mr. Davis was wounded in three places, his left hand, a flesh wound on the chest, and one bullet through his left lung. Mr. Wilson was not hit by any bullets. Mr. Davis was taken to Somerset General Hospital where he was expected to be okay. Not a classic gunfight with two men facing off at high noon, but one that many people would talk about for a good while.

∞

In the coal mining industry, according to the Department of Mines in the State of Kentucky, the total coal production in 1931 decreased by 10,504.41 tons from the previous year, a 20.6 percent loss compared with 1930. In 1931, three hundred and sixty-five mines operated in the state; the officials in Frankfort stated the coal industry was headed backwards unless something extraordinary happened.

∞

The year 1932 could not end without one more gun battle. It was rumored ill feelings had existed between Ben Angel and "Red" Nelson Foster for quite some time. How it got started or what was between the two men, their friends were not willing to reveal, if any knew. According to witnesses, Ben and Lester Angel and Everett Hamlin were hauling wood and met "Red" Nelson Foster and Lester Foster on the road in front of the home of Elmer Duncan. Recognizing each other, both stopped in the middle of the road, only a few feet apart. As Angel and Foster approached within a few feet of each other, Foster is said to have pulled his pistol. According to the best information I could uncover, Angel brushed the gun aside with his left hand saying, "Red, don't do that," at the same time he reached for his own gun with his right hand. Foster fired the first shot and struck Angel in the muscle of his left arm. Another shot severed a finger on Angel's right hand. Foster kept firing, at the same time struggling to keep Angel's gun from pointing in his direction. But Angel got his pistol clear and shot one round, the bullet striking Foster's chin and then his chest. Another bullet struck Foster in the right side of his chest, the bullet on a downward path into the abdomen. Foster had managed to empty his gun before collapsing to the ground, but none of his final bullets hit their mark on Angel.

"Red" Nelson Foster of Stearns died at the age of forty around 4:00 p.m., Friday afternoon, killed by Ben Angel, age thirty. The gunfight happened in Stearns. Sheriff George P. Anderson and Deputy Henry Vanover investigated and arrested Angel. Angel stayed in jail while awaiting a grand jury trial. Foster left behind a wife and five children.

∞

MARRIED THIS YEAR 1932

John (Slim) Wes Nichols married Dessie Gibson. Both grew up in a place called Crackers Neck, not far from Bronston, Kentucky. A few years before her union with Slim, Dessie left the area to marry a Gibson man. They moved to Yamacraw and had a son named Hurstle. The marriage did not last.

Slim was a wild and rowdy teenager. Slim and a friend would walk to Burnside to the Southern Railroad. There, the two men would hobo a train; it didn't matter to them in which direction or how far the train went. The men would jump from box car to box car. Other hobos they encountered they threw off the train. This behavior was before Slim moved to Co-operative to work for Stearns Coal and Lumber Company and before he married Dessie. Slim later in life confessed to Dessie that over the course of a couple summers, he and his friend threw off thirteen men and never knew if those men lived through it or died.

Children in Dessie and Slim's family included Hurstle (from Dessie's first marriage), Geneva, Helen, Ella Mae, and Billy Gene (Buddy).

∞

BORN THIS YEAR 1932

Ralph Thompson
Glen King

Ruby Coffey
Viola Shoopman
Patricia Marcum
Norma Jean Slaven
Vandon Doyle Ball
Clara Stephens
Jewel Dobbs
Christine Freeman

CHAPTER 4

1933

The coal mining communities in the area received a blow in spring 1933. Even if they didn't live in the camp where the disaster happened, all coal miners took pause to catch their breath, knowing it could happen to them.

    The coal mining community of Worley was the second mine Stearns Coal and Lumber Company opened back in 1905. The miners of Worley still had not gotten over the loss of Willis Vanover, a coal loader, who was killed by a slate fall toward the end of 1932. Willis had been working alone in a room when it happened; his body wasn't discovered until hours later by a crew walking through to inspect the roof.

    It was Monday morning when Stobert McGuffey got out of bed, put his work clothes on, and headed off to work as usual. He was born in Williamsburg, Kentucky, in 1901. His father, J. M. McGuffey, was the superintendent of one of the mines owned by Stearns Coal and Lumber Company. For many years the family had made their home in Barthell. Stobert completed the eighth grade in McCreary County, high school in Lexington, and civil engineering school at the University of Kentucky. In 1929, he married Lessie Chitwood, and they had a son, James, now two years old.

In another part of the camp, Hollis Arvine Hembree headed out of his home walking toward the same mine as Stobert. Arvine's father, J. R. Hembree, was one of the oldest employees of Stearns Coal and Lumber Company, and the family had always resided in McCreary County. Arvine's wife, Alma Anderson Hembree, was the daughter of J. M. Murphy. Arvine was educated at Stearns, Kentucky, and had been a member of Stearns Company's engineering crew for the past twelve years.

Three houses from Arvine's house, away from the direction of the mine, Arvine stopped in front of his brother's home, Ralph Dudley Hembree. Arvine stood waiting for Ralph to emerge so they could walk to work together. Ralph and his wife, Etta Strunk Hembree, had a one-month-old daughter named Diane.

The three men met up at the face of the Worley Mine and entered together. Since it was Monday morning, the Worley Mine had not been operating over the weekend; consequently, it had not yet been inspected for gas. The three men had walked a good distance into the mine when the explosion occurred; it was impossible for anyone to survive. The section of the coal mine where the fatal gas ignited was about two miles inside the mine from the entrance. News of the explosion spread and everyone that could went to the mine to help. But it would be several hours before it was safe enough to enter the mine to reach the men inside. Time moved slowly until the okay was given to proceed. Reaching the three men's bodies and the subsequent shock was the hardest blow to hit McCreary County in recent years.

All three men were members of the Stearns Baptist Church and Stobert McGuffey was an active member. Both Hembrees were members of the local junior order at the church. Pallbearers for both Hembrees were Oscar Trammell, George Thomas, Lloyd Crabtree, George Olson, Lawrence Stephens, Curtis Strunk, Clyde Bales, Sylvan Carr, Floyd Murphy, Carl Murphy, Josh Young, and Carl Thomas. Pallbearers for Stobert McGuffey were Ellis Strunk, Jess Strunk, John Holt, Andrew Strunk, Leamon Ross, Estol Sexton, Enos Pryor, and Wilburn Warman.

∞

Less than a month after the explosion at Worley Mine, tragedy struck the community of Yamacraw. Parker Slaven, ten years old, and Cecil, his brother, twelve years old, and another child were playing in the shallow waters of the river when suddenly a strong current carried Parker into deeper water; Parker could not swim. The other two boys went in to rescue young Parker and managed to drag Parker to within thirty feet of shore but were forced to let go of him. Parker's body was found within thirty minutes. Attempts to resuscitate failed. Service for Parker was at the Yamacraw Schoolhouse with Reverend Joe Cox officiating. It's hard to lose the young in the prime of life; the people in all coal mining camps around the area mourned with the Slaven family.

∞

The Southern Railroad announced bargain ticket prices at one cent per mile: round trip fares from Stearns to Asheville, North Carolina, at $4.95; to Cincinnati, Ohio, at $4.00; to Atlanta, Georgia, at $5.70; to Chattanooga, Tennessee, at $2.95; and to New Orleans, Louisiana, at $12.90.

∞

Tommy Roundtree ran for sheriff in the primary election. Mr. Roundtree had made a good showing four years earlier and said he'd do much better this time. Esbon Roundtree, who was running for jailer, had dropped out, but the race for sheriff was shaping up to be interesting.

∞

The 4th of July Celebration was an event many in the county looked forward to from year to year. Always held in Stearns, this year's celebration was more than watermelon stands and plenty of hillsides on which to leave the rinds. This year there were two baseball games during the day: In the morning, the Stearns Ramblers played Barren Fork; in the afternoon, the miners took on the Huntsville, Tennessee, team. In addition, the Stearns Opera House was open all day, showing Zane Grey's famous *The Golden West*, starring George O'Brien and Virginia Chandler.

The K & T Railway ran a special excursion train to accommodate folks from down the line. The first train left Bell Farm at 6:30 a.m. and arrived in

Stearns at 8:00 a.m. The last evening train left Stearns at 5:00 p.m. and arrived back in Stearns at 8:30 p.m.

On Monday, July 3, the celebration began with a dance at the auditorium from 10:00 p.m. to 2:00 a.m. Charlie Ford and His Commanders provided the music. Marjory Lady, bluegrass singer, was featured. The group was a tremendous success throughout Kentucky, where they had been performing. The year's dance committee members were M. S. Marshall and Saul Shipman.

The Stearns Tennis and Golf Course was in excellent condition for the celebration. With the election primary on August 5, the candidates had an opportunity on July 4 to meet the citizens of McCreary County since most everyone was in Stearns on that day. Everyone involved with the planning of this celebration hoped for an old-fashioned shindig, and that's what they got. Since most people from mining camps rarely got to leave their communities, the festivities were a huge success.

The Stearns 4th of July Celebration would never have evolved if not for the founder of Stearns Coal and Lumber Company, Justus S. Stearns. Since Mr. Stearns had died just five months earlier on Valentine's Day, it was a good time to remember the man behind the name. Justus was born in Chautauqua County, New York, April 1845. He did farm boy's chores until his parents moved the family to Erie, Pennsylvania, when he was sixteen years old. Justus's father opened a retail lumber yard, which was the start of Justus's interest in the lumber industry. In 1862, the family moved to Conneaut, Ohio, where his father continued the lumber business. It was there Justus met and married Pauline Lyon in 1869; they had one son born in Conneaut. The young family moved to Ludington, Michigan, in 1876 with his salary of seventy-five dollars a month.

In Ludington, Justus's company prospered, giving employment to thousands, and that helped several more thousands. In the 1880s, when his Ludington mill was producing more lumber than it sold, the foreman told Mr. Stearns the mill would have to shut down because there was no room in the yard for more lumber. Mr. Stearns replied they could find new places and to keep the mill running and the men working. Many years later, several coal mines built in McCreary County were losing money on every ton of coal being sold. Board members were asking Mr. Stearns what should be done. Mr. Stearns asked, "How many men are depending on Stearns Company?" Mr. Stearns was told several thousand. Mr. Stearns asked, "How many tons of coal were produced last year?" He was told one million. Mr. Stearns replied, "Keep the mines open if the company doesn't lose more than forty cents a ton; we cannot let those people go hungry."

Mr. Stearns' reward was the joy of accomplishment in what he did for others. To the needy, he gave opportunity; for willing hands, he furnished work and offered a chance for accomplishment. As Mr. Stearns' coal and lumber business grew, he helped build America through his entrepreneurial abilities and leadership.

With the passing of the founder of Stearns Coal and Lumber Company, only one person was available to step into his shoes and that was Robert, or R. L. as he preferred to be called. R. L., Justus's only child and son, after spending thirty-one years as manager, took over Stearns Coal and Lumber Company.

∞

As the 4th of July Celebration in Stearns came to a close, a serious car wreck happened one mile south of Pine Knot, Kentucky, close to the residence of Arthur Creekmore, involving Mr. Charlie McGuffey, son of J. M. McGuffey of Barthell, and his sister-in-law Mrs. Stobert McGuffey. Mr. McGuffey was returning home from Oneida, Tennessee, with Mrs. McGuffey, who had been visiting relatives, when the accident occurred. Mr. McGuffey's efforts to miss a cow were not successful. The car skidded about twenty feet before overturning down a fifty-foot embankment. From the point of impact where the cow was struck, Mrs. McGuffey was thrown roughly one hundred feet away, indicating Mr. McGuffey was traveling at a high rate of speed. The car, an Oakland Sport Coupe, was found on the railroad tracks close to a local resident's house. The Coupe, made by Pontiac, a division of General Motors of Michigan, had been discontinued in 1931.

Mrs. McGuffey, thrown clear of the car, suffered shock, a cut over the right eye, and a possible fractured right ankle. She was the widow of the late Stobert McGuffey who had been killed in an explosion at the Worley Mine just weeks earlier. Mr. McGuffey was found still in his seat, slumped down, and not expected to live. Riley Musgrove took the couple to Whitley City, where Dr. Acton gave them first aid. The Stearns Coal and Lumber Company took the couple to Somerset General Hospital. Mr. McGuffey suffered several broken ribs and a broken collarbone. X-rays showed his heart had been displaced, straining and partly tearing the arteries to his heart, making breathing difficult. With his chest seriously crushed on his left side, the doctors had little hope he'd make it through the night.

∞

    The baseball team of Fidelity was slugging its way to a perfect season. The home plate at Co-operative was down close to a very small swampy area, so when teams played Co-operative, the batters batted toward the homes of people who lived in Co-operative. Over the years, Othel and Odell Thompson had knocked the windows out of a few houses. Sometimes the fly balls went under the houses and couldn't be found.

    Every time Fidelity played at Stearns, Bob Stearns was there, and he bet on every game. When things didn't quite go to his liking, he'd jump up yelling and cussing. At one game, Arnold Shoopman stepped up to bat. Bob Stearns yelled, "Pitch him a fastball. The little piss queen can't hit it no way." A fastball was just what Arnold liked. The pitcher got ready and threw the ball. Arnold swung the bat and connected; the ball almost went into the Stearns' pond. But when the ball came down, it hit the crosstie on the flat end of the K & T Railway and bounced back toward the field. If not for that, it would have been a home run. Bob Stearns was seen in the bleachers jumping and cussing; he couldn't believe it. At Stearns, Othel and Odell Thompson could hit balls across the highway and up to the other road on the hill; those boys could slug a ball.

∞

MARRIED THIS YEAR 1933

Earl Edison Coffey and Mary Esther Spradlin tied the knot. Their children were Sterling, Forest, Barbara, Albert, Eddie, Gerald, Shirley, Janis, Kenneth, Reba, Charlotta, and Theresa.

Edgar Gregory and Debbie Koger got married.

Elmer Whitehead and Fannie Sellers also got married. Their children were Jimmie, Bobbie, Jewelene, Harold, Jewel Tein, Darrel, Catheryn.

∞

BORN THIS YEAR 1933

Donald Dixon
RL Terry
Bob Shepherd
Joyce Wilson
Ronald Dean Ball
Dester Winchester
Delbert Cooper
Jess Watson
Melvin Dennis Freeman
Elulee Lewis
Lawrence Haynes
Bobbie Duncan
Patsy Dixon

CHAPTER 5

1933 Continued

Up the holler from Jewell Kidd's Grocery, at the end of the narrow wagon road, lived Jack Haynes. After a few years, he moved into Sawmill Camp.

∞

    In the early years at Co-operative, the room used by grades 7–8 in the schoolhouse was also used as the church house. The only church house in Co-operative would later be built on the hill at the east end of the schoolhouse.

∞

    At the July 7, 1933, McCreary County School Board meeting, the Board voted yay to building two new schools and the contracts were released. A two-room school was erected in Hilltop and a one-room school in the area of Rock Creek. The one at Rock Creek could have been the one at Oz, which was later called Paint Cliff, but I can't say definitively. It makes sense, though, because Mines 16 and 17 at St. Mcheil were opened just a short time before.

∞

Mining coal was hazardous work, and when danger was involved, accidents occurred. On Tuesday, July 25, 1933, in Co-operative, tragedy struck. Dave Kidd, twenty-four years old, was working in the Co-operative Mine when he stumbled, lost his balance, and fell onto a trolley wire carrying 250 volts of direct current. Members of the first aid team got to him as quickly as possible, started CPR immediately, and continued working on him for three hours, but Dave died. Dave was the son of Mr. and Mrs. Walter Kidd of Co-operative. He left behind a widow, Mrs. Easter Kidd, his parents, two sisters, and one brother.

∞

It wasn't unusual for each coal mine to have its own first aid team. These teams competed with other teams within Stearns Company to see which team would represent the company at the state competition. Stearns Coal and Lumber Company, represented by the Fidelity First Aid team, left for Hazard one Friday for the state competition. Milford Meadors was the captain of the Fidelity team and George Humble Sr. was the director. The Fidelity team made a strong showing in the state competition with a score of 99% in fifteen total events, good enough for second place.

Saturday, August 25, 1933, the K & T Railway held its second annual picnic at Bell Farm with 409 Railway passengers attending. The train arrived at Bell Farm at 10:00 a.m. After everyone unloaded, they immediately joined together to sing "America." Afterwards, folks found the horseshoe grounds crowded the rest of the day.

The first event of the day was the fat men's race in which the previous year's winner, Ledford Rowe, failed to defend his title. The entrants in this event were Bill Redmond, Denham King, Josh Young, and Oscar ("Big Boy") Boyd. Conductor Bill Redmond danced across the finish line as if he were all alone. The rest, resembling a young tornado, were bunched up panting and snorting in a struggle to cross the finish line.

Next on the program was the tug of war event between teams representing Stearns, White Oak Junction, and Exotus. White Oak Junction eliminated Stearns. Exotus, the defending champs, and White Oak Junction battled for the championship; White Oak Junction pulled Exotus across the line with little effort. To make sure the winner was truly the winner, the two teams battled a second time with the same results. The captain of the White Oak Junction boys attributed the win to eating lots of beans and bacon.

The morning baseball game was next and the two captains, Ed Winchester of the Wild Cats and Jess Young of the Bears, chose their teams. When it was over, the Winchester team won, seemingly easy, by a score of 13–2. The Winchester team pitcher, Oda Stephens, had everyone on Young's team baffled except Carl Simpson. Another player, Jimmy Foxx, hit a long drive across the Wayne County line. With Simpson on third base, the hit went for a home run because the outfielders were afraid to cross the county line without permission. Oscar ("Big Boy") Boyd, playing right field for Young's team, in the second inning made a spectacular barehanded catch, without question the best play of the day. At the time, the bases were loaded. Jess Young said, "I'm so proud of my players, but the umpiring wasn't that good. But what can you expect from Doc. Meese and Doc. Smith?"

Jess Young, Manager	AB	R	H	Ed Winchester, Manager	AB	R	H
Jess Young, P	3	0	0	Bayne Smith, C	3	2	1
Jerome Marcum, 1B	3	0	0	Sherril Smith, 3B	3	2	2
Oscar Boyd, RF	3	1	2	? Sexton, 3B	1	0	1
Carl Simpson, C	2	1	1	Edgar Jones, RF	4	1	1
Claud Murphy, 3B	2	0	0	Ray Human, 1B	4	1	1
Clyde Bales, SS	2	0	0	Joe Dupree, SS	4	1	1
John McCarthy, 2B	1	0	0	Bill Bass, CF	1	1	0
Alec Vickery, 3B	1	0	1	Floyd Murphy, 2B	2	1	1
John Romanger, CF	2	0	0	Conley Bell, CF	1	1	0
Josh Young, 1F	2	0	0	Bill Redmond, 2B	1	1	0
				Oda Stephens, P	2	1	1
				Francis Vickery	3	1	1
TOTALS	21	2	4		29	13	10

F. R. Lear and the Music Masters (C. M. Scott, H. J. Alcorn, Oda Stephens, W. S. Schick, and W. H.

Gresham) entertained from 11:00 a.m. to noon. Everyone then took a break and enjoyed a great "dinner on the ground." The food was more than enough to go around.

Another group of musicians, The Stearns String Band, played the rest of the afternoon; the members were John Hall, Miss Norma Hall, Mr. and Mrs. Bill Gresham, the Ball Brothers, Bob Foster, and Buford White.

In the next event, the married men took on the single men in a ball game; it was a slow start but ended in a 17–17 tie.

Then came a race of the hefty women. The contestants were Mrs. Bill Redmond, Mrs. Clyde Bale, Mrs. Joan Gronwald, Mrs. M. W. Alston, and "Tom Boy" Taylor from Davenport, Iowa. They lined up and were given instructions. Mrs. Joan Gronwald took the ribbon.

The watermelon eating contest was fun to watch. Carl Roysdon needed to patent his style of eating. He ate on one side of his mouth and spat the seeds out of the other corner of his mouth. He won the men's division easily, and Mark Ball won the boy's division.

In the sack race, old man Jess Young hobbled across the finish line ahead of the rest of the old timers. Old Papa McCarthy's sack came off and he was disqualified. For the boys' group, Eugene Vickery won with a hop, skip, and a jump.

The day passed quickly, and everyone enjoyed a day of games and old-fashioned camaraderie. It was a day similar to a family reunion with forty-one people getting bumps and bruises in the friendly competitions. Before anyone boarded the train, the crowd sang the hymn "God Be with You" to close out the joyous occasion. The old steam engine pulled into

Stearns at 5:30 p.m. The traffic manager for the K & T Railway, L. C. Bruce, said he believed every single person told him they enjoyed the day.

∞

A month later, the Southern Railway System advertised roundtrip fares to the Chicago World's Fair at $6.50. The train left Stearns at 10:14 a.m. and arrived back at Stearns around 7:00 p.m. The residents of Co-operative who made the trip were A. S. Logan and daughters Betty Jo and Jacqueline, Mr. Robert White, and Mr. C. D. Rose and son Junior.

∞

The last Saturday night of October, a pie supper was held at the Co-operative School to raise money for the school. The event was a success with standing room only, and as the evening closed, Miss Dorothy Lewis was awarded the pretty girl cake contest.

∞

In the middle of the following week, Deputy Sherman Corder came to Co-operative and arrested Elisha Spradlin on the charge of stealing chickens and took him to jail. The case could not be proven and Mr. Spradlin was later released.

∞

In Co-operative, the following Saturday night, Hubert Kidd was arrested and charged with drunk and disorderly behavior; he was fined and released.

The following Monday night, a call went out that Hubert Kidd was shooting up Co-operative. Deputies drove to Co-operative and arrested Hubert, and this time, Hubert stayed in jail.

∞

At Christmas time in Co-operative, before the students were dismissed for the holidays, most of the community came out to watch the Christmas play performed by the students. Stanley Parks, who had to be taken to the doctor for medical attention with an abscessed tooth, missed the evening entirely. In addition to others attending, Miss Opal McGuffey from Worley, who was visiting Mrs. Morris Blevins, Kenneth Larmee, and Mr. and Mrs. Lee Phillips attended. A few business leaders of Co-operative also attended: C. D. Rose, A. S. Logan, Morris Blevins, Grant Roberts, and J. C. Slaven.

CHAPTER 6

1934

Tommy Roundtree took over as the new sheriff in 1934, and he didn't waste any time getting acclimated. He and his deputies hit the road running. They captured a moonshine still (often referred to as *still*) and destroyed seventy gallons of mash near Yamacraw on his first official day in office.

∞

    While the McCreary County Sheriff's Department was taking care of business enforcing the law, the Fidelity Cagers team was taking care of business on the basketball court, taking on Burnside. The Burnside team was highly favored since the season began even though their last outing ended in a one-point loss to the Ferguson Netters. The first half of the game looked like anybody's game. But when the second half got under way, the Cagers' Ivan Edwards took charge of the ball game. Ivan hit shots from all over the court and seemed unstoppable. Fidelity took the lead and never relinquished it, beating Burnside by a score of 36–18.

∞

Just weeks later, the weather turned bad, and a hailstorm swooped down into Co-operative and wreaked havoc on several roofs of the homes by the creek; in front of the Co-operative schoolhouse was hit the worst. The hail beat shingles off the roofs so bad it wouldn't have been any worse if someone had taken a shotgun and blasted them off. Four families spent the night in the schoolhouse. The next day they found shelter with family or friends until their homes were repaired.

∞

While Co-operative was reeling from the storm, a notorious crime gang had its sights set on McCreary County, likely because of the many trips through our county. Neal and Howard Bowman led a gang that started in the Southern Ohio hills and moved into Kentucky and Virginia. They were bad men not afraid to go where they wanted and did go into various parts of the country. They were similar to a modern-day Wild West gang. After several years of terrorizing folks and robbing banks, the gang faced a nationwide manhunt for its capture.

When Neal and Howard Bowman were captured, the gang broke up. The Bowmans were each sentenced to life terms for bank robbery and incarcerated in the Ohio Penitentiary.

Neal Bowman was sent to the Ohio State Hospital for observation and was to be transferred to Kentucky State Penitentiary, but he escaped. While Neal was on the loose, his brother and seven other convicts came up with a daring plan to escape by dynamiting a wall of the penitentiary, which would allow many convicts to escape. However, a note Howard Bowman wrote addressed to Neal was intercepted by Warden Thomas. The note never reached its destination. The note told how and where Neal was to place the dynamite and suggested a raid on a National Guard Armory to secure weapons. It also stated they would need two fast cars for the getaway; the cars were to be stolen. The note was given to experts to decipher, and when the plot was revealed, extra guards were placed at the prison.

While Neal Bowman was loose, he was credited with holding up a wholesale grocery truck near Somerset, Kentucky, bank robberies committed in Ohio, and several other attempted robberies. Neal also allegedly had a part in hijacking a whiskey truck near Louisville, Kentucky.

Neal befriended a young man by the name of Stanley Mercer of Wayne County. Mercer had friends and contacts in McCreary County, which he and Neal traveled through extensively. On one of those trips, the two pulled into a gas station on the south side of Somerset to fuel up. The gas station attendant had just started pumping gas when a police car pulled in and parked. The two policemen, Chief of Police J. B. Jasper and Captain George Blaydes, stepped out of the car and started walking toward the Bowman car. Bowman pulled his .44-caliber revolver and opened fire behind his steering wheel, shooting through the windshield. The gas station attendant dropped to the ground after the first shot. In all, five shots were fired at the officers, and Jasper's hat was shot off his head before they ducked behind their car. Bowman, age thirty, was shot in the right arm and another bullet, believed to be a ricochet, grazed the back of his head, rendering him unconscious. Mercer, age twenty, was wounded in the left cheek.

In less than two minutes, the gun battle was over. The Ohio gangster, an escaped convict, was in custody along with his companion. Their wounds were treated at Somerset General Hospital. Bowman admitted to everything and exonerated Mercer from any connection with any crime. Bowman described Mercer as a dumb kid who didn't know him from Dillinger. Bowman would not disclose any names of any of his other accomplices. A life sentence awaited him in Ohio, and he would most likely have another one when Kentucky got through with him.

∞

Back at White Oak Junction, Imogene Logan, daughter of Vern and Eli, store manager, died in surgery on a brain tumor at Louisville Kentucky Hospital. The community was saddened by the news and mourned with the Logans.

∞

One half mile west up the road from White Oak Junction on the way to Co-operative at the coal mine, Dewey Gibson was close to having his workday completed when the unthinkable happened. Dewey got caught in the motor cable and there was no escape. The high voltage threw his body off the motor cable; his body was badly battered by the roll it took. Death was instant. The accident happened at 2:00 p.m. Mr. Gibson left behind a wife and five children. The White Oak Junction community mourned his untimely death.

∞

MARRIED THIS YEAR 1934

Willard Bell married Bernette Chitwood. They had ten children: Conley, Earl, Anita, Wanda, Donald, Larry, Georgia, Brenda, Tim, and Danny.

Sylvester Shook married Goldie Gregory. They also had ten children: Edward, Shelby, Iva Sue, Bill, Hazel, Bruce, Jim, Wayne, Ellen, and Dale.

∞

BORN THIS YEAR 1934

Geneva Nichols
Espy Haynes
Willie Thompson
Vella King
Sherry Dobbs
Claudette Marcum
Regal Gregory
Clara Hall
Lois Stephens

CHAPTER 7

1935

Prohibition ended in 1933. Through those trying years and beyond, moonshine was the popular drink, especially in the mountainous regions of McCreary County, Kentucky. In the heart of the coal mining communities of Co-operative and White Oak Junction, moonshine sales continued to be profitable, although illegal. Out of sight, out of mind, or so some thought.

∞

April 2, 1935, was a holiday with the miners celebrating contract day. The drinking and celebrating started early. Edward S. King, age twenty-four, the son of Columbus and Permelia King of Fidelity, and Corbett Cooper, of Co-operative, were friends and both worked in the same mine. It is alleged both men were well inebriated and short tempered. They began to argue, which escalated into a wrestling match; off the front porch they rolled into the gravel road at Copin Camp. Corbett discovered Edward's pistol. When the pistol became visible, it turned into a fight for the gun. Edward had bought the pistol just days before. In the struggle, the gun discharged, and the bullet entered the back of Edward's head and lodged in his brain.

Edward was a brother to Fred King who had drowned in the Big South Fork at Yamacraw almost three weeks earlier. Deputies Esbon Roundtree and Sherman Corder arrested Corbett near his home.

Edward survived the trip to St. Joseph Hospital in Lexington but died soon after. Edward S. King was survived by his parents, five brothers (Logan, Walter, Everett, Jess, and Joel), and two sisters (Mattie and Alice).

∞

The following month on Saturday, May 25, according to the *McCreary County Record*, a gunfight broke out in Co-operative. Patrolman Marion King and Deputy Constable Claude Frady, both of Fidelity, died, and Constable Omer Hall, also of Fidelity, was wounded as a result of the gun battle. Coroner C. S. Dunesmore, who held an inquest of the bodies, said King was shot seven times in the back and once in the face. Frady had five bullet wounds in his back.

Sheriff Tommy Roundtree and Deputy Esbon Roundtree were called immediately after the trouble started and Sheriff Roundtree reported he found King and Frady dead on the floor of the poolroom owned by Lee Phillips of Co-operative. Beside the bodies lay four guns: two Colt .45s and two .38 Specials. A Smith and Wesson .45 Special was taken from Hall. Also on the floor was a half pint of moonshine whiskey and a pair of handcuffs. I do not know why the *McCreary County Record* reported Lee Phillips as the owner of the poolroom unless he leased it because the building was owned by Neil Kidd.

Witnesses told Sheriff Roundtree the shooting started when Frady and King engaged in a scuffle. Both men drew pistols, each trying to keep the other from pointing his gun at them, and one of the guns discharged into the floor. Frady then managed to point his pistol at King and King knocked the gun out of Frady's hand and up toward the ceiling; the shot went wild. This shot is supposed to have hit Hall. King and Frady fell to the floor, still locked together, wrestling. It was at this time when Hall and his son started firing at the two men on the floor. Everyone else fled the poolroom leaving the four men alone. As a result, there were no eyewitnesses to the crime, except those involved in the crime.

Claude Frady was survived by his wife, four children, and one brother, Bill Frady, also of Fidelity. The body of Frady was taken to Rockwood, Tennessee, for burial services. The Stearns undertaker was in charge of Claude Frady and Marion King.

According to a descendant of one of the families, the happening on May 25 drove a wedge between the families that remained until recently; family members have now, at least, begun to talk to each other.

According to the descendant, the story went like this: In the saloon, Claude Frady and Marion King were drinking and they were trying to force Omer Hall to drink; also, the three men were allegedly rivals in the moonshine business. Frady and King wanted to get Hall drunk because possibly he had money on him from moonshine sales earlier in the day, but Hall didn't want to get drunk.

One of the men pulled out his pistol—which one is unknown—but that man either intended to shoot Hall or the gun discharged accidentally and struck Hall in the leg. When that shot rang out, people scrambled and ran outside. Somebody ran down to Copin Camp and got Vester Hall (Omer's son) who was either visiting friends or lived there. When Vester, his friends called him Vess, got to the pool room, Hall was unconscious, bleeding excessively, and Vess first thought that Hall was dead. Because there was so much blood, it wasn't clear where Hall was shot. Vess then grabbed Hall's gun and shot both King and Frady. Allegedly, other people had shot also, but no witnesses ever came forward to verify this account. It was never determined which man shot Hall in the leg.

Vess (Vester) went to prison for a long time. It's debatable whether his dad, Omer Hall, went to prison at all. But a family member thinks he did based on census records that listed him as being a resident of Lagrange Prison.

The gun battle at Co-operative split the family. The Halls had married into the Frady family. Omer Hall talked about the incident all through the years. His wife and Ruth Frady were close friends and may have been childhood friends. Allegedly, when Vess and Omer Hall were incarcerated, there was no one to put food on the table, and the family was starving. Omer's daughter, Emma Hall, married Darius Watson. The two of them—Emma and Darius—stole a hog and Cecil, Emma's brother, took the blame because Cecil didn't want his sister to go to prison. In the courtroom that day, another relative heard the proceedings with Cecil. People kept telling Cecil, "You don't have to go to prison; you didn't do this." But Cecil kept saying he did.

The judge finally concluded, "Well, Cecil, you'll get three meals a day and a roof over your head."

Cecil said, "I'm not worrying about me. I'm just worried about my family. That's why I'm here." Cecil didn't come right out and say it, but it was evident he was taking the blame.

A couple of years passed and Hazel Ann Hall married Dewey Pennington. Thelma Hall married Thed Winchester. Emma and Darius, and likely others, moved to Fort Mountain, Tennessee. So there ended up being a whole group of people working in the coal mines that were related: the Halls, Penningtons, Watsons, and Winchesters.

Allegedly, while living at Fort Mountain, Darius Watson and Thed Winchester got into a disagreement that became very heated. Darius got his shotgun, walked into Thed's house, and blew his head off. The widow, Thelma, Hazel Hall's sister, moved to Salt Lake City, Utah, and never returned. This information was discovered when one of Thelma's daughters came back to visit family several years later. So they had to deal with their dad being shot by a relative. Those wild times all led back to a Saturday night in the saloon just past Jewell Kidd's Grocery.

During those days, Ezekiel Hall left wife Carolyn Brown and remarried a woman the son of Ezekiel and Carolyn allegedly didn't get along with. The son came to McCreary County from Tennessee after allegedly stabbing his stepmother.

It took some time before the gun battle of that Saturday night on May 25 was laid to rest. Back when it happened, there was only a mountain separating the two coal communities of Fidelity and Co-operative.

∞

Four days after that Saturday night gunfight, the high school in Fidelity celebrated seven graduates who received diplomas:
- Alma Jo Bell
- Espy Bell
- Helen Trebelo Cooper
- Osborne Gregory
- Estil Jones
- Hershel Koger
- Eva New

Professor of Social Science at Richmond, Kentucky, Dr. Charles E. Keith delivered the commencement message to the graduates.

∞

Meanwhile, on the marquee at the Stearns Opera House for the coming weekend was a new movie called *Mississippi*, starring Bing Crosby, W. C. Fields, and Joan Bennett.

∞

MARRIED THIS YEAR 1935

Ruby Opal Coffey's dad, Albert Coffey, worked for a company that drilled and pumped oil in Oil Valley, Wayne County. Stearns Coal and Lumber Company hired Albert to look after their oil interests in White Oak Junction.

Also, Albert was to take care of the oil wells located not far from the railroad tracks in Logan Holler in Co-operative. Ruby was twelve years old when the family moved to White Oak Junction in 1928. She was one of thirteen siblings; three of the siblings died young. Ruby's oldest brother, Earl, worked at Co-operative Mine.

Jess Fulton Chitwood followed his uncle Dewey to Co-operative. Dewey and Kizzie Chitwood and their two daughters, Deloris and Francis, lived beside Jim Lewis. As soon as Jess got old enough, he got a job working for Guy Kidd. While working for Guy Kidd, Jess met Ruby Coffey. Delivering groceries took Jess all over the different coal mining communities and into many homes.

At the age of nineteen, Jess got a job with Stearns Coal and Lumber Company. A few months later, Jesse (Jess) Fulton Chitwood and Ruby Opal Coffey got married and started their life together. Children born in Jess and Ruby's marriage were Robert Earl, Mildred, Roger, Joan, Wallace, and Patricia.

Artie Winchester was born in Robbins, Tennessee. When she was young, her dad moved the family many times. Many a time, Artie's dad would come home from work and say, "Pack your stuff; we're moving." So, it went like this for years until finally they ended up in White Oak Junction.

George Troxell's dad and mom were Garfield and Barbara Troxell. They lived in White Oak Junction. George was born there and at the age of fourteen went to work to help his mom and dad with living expenses.

As time moved on, there was an event at the Co-operative schoolhouse. Artie went to the event with her sister and her sister's two kids. Inside the schoolhouse, the two kids became restless, so Artie took the kids outside. It was a hot day and the kids were getting hungry. George had also walked outside and saw Artie having a bit of difficulty with the kids. George walked over to where Artie was sitting on the big rock between the two school buildings and said to Artie, "You wait right here. I'll be back."

George walked to Stearns Company Store and bought a nickel's worth of bologna. When George got back to the schoolhouse, Artie was waiting and he gave her the bologna. She fed the kids, and they walked to the water pump and drank some cool water. That was enough to satisfy the kids, and George and Artie talked a long while, and from this encounter, they began seeing each other and walking together to church. They got married a few months later.

George worked at Co-operative Mine, then at Mine 16, and for a short time at Mine 18. After George and Artie married, they lived several years in White Oak Junction. They also lived for a while in Trace Branch and Bald Knob. Their children were Luther, Denzil, Arlena, Ernest, and Mary.

∞

BORN THIS YEAR 1935

Anita Bell
Bob Coffey
Lora Shepherd

Donald Allen Slaven
Thurston Wilson
Vonda Shoopman
Luke Watson
Ella Mae Lewis
Lecil Hall
Vonnie Cooper
Espy Haynes
Edward Shook
Fred Clark

CHAPTER 8

1936

In 1936, the price of a Chevy car started at $495.

∞

This year, the director of the Civilian Conservation Corps (CCC) program issued a report that since its inception on April 5, 1933, to the end of 1935, 1.5 million young men had been provided work. The report also stated for the fiscal year that ended June 1935 a total of $212,000,000 had been sent back home by the young men in the CCC program.

∞

Winter was still hanging around in Co-operative. The first day of spring was a month away when

Harley Worley became ill at the home of his brother-in-law Marvin Jones of Co-operative. Relatives were preparing to take Harley to the hospital when he suddenly died. Harley Worley, age thirty-two, of Jones Hollow, was the first victim of spinal meningitis in McCreary County, diagnosed by local physicians. The Kentucky State Board of Health was notified, and they requested the body be taken to Louisville for an autopsy to verify diagnosis.

Following the autopsy, which proved local physicians were right in their diagnosis that Mr. Worley had died of meningitis, Dr. R. M. Smith, Chairman of McCreary County Medical Association, received a command to place a strict quarantine on the home of Mr. Worley, on the church and school, and on all public gatherings. In the event no other case of the disease occurred, the quarantine could be lifted in two weeks.

Within seven days, a second victim, Estle Elmore, in the Pine Knot area, was put under strict quarantine and all those that had been in contact with Elmore. Sadly, Estle later died.

The following day, another victim, Othel Thompson, a known Fidelity athlete, was stricken at the home of his father-in-law, Auston Koger, in Co-operative. Thompson's critical condition stabilized after receiving a serum rushed from Cincinnati, Ohio. The Kentucky State Board of Health sent Dr. Fred Candille to McCreary County. Dr. Candille traveled to Co-operative and placed a strict quarantine on the camp. A guard was placed on the outskirts of Co-operative with strict instructions that no one could enter or leave. Physicians continued to keep a close watch on Co-operative because cases had originated there.

The CCC camp at Bell Farm was also placed under quarantine as a preventive measure. The New Haven Baptist Church did not hold Sunday services and would not during quarantine. Also basketball games were called off and the Stearns Opera House was closed.

Just days later, nineteen-year-old Tommy Haynes became the fourth victim of spinal meningitis at the home of his father, Jack Haynes, in Co-operative. Young Haynes was a muscular youth and a member of the Co-operative basketball team. Young Haynes had recovered from influenza when he suddenly became ill and within a few minutes died.

All three young men who had died from the disease worked at Co-operative Mine. Othel Thompson recovered. All four victims of the disease originated in the same mining community, yet doctors couldn't find any connection that they had contracted the disease from each other. The quarantine in Co-operative continued under strict enforcement; violators would do jail time.

At Pine Knot, the quarantine where Estle Elmore died was lifted. After two weeks, no new cases had been reported.

After several weeks, the Stearns Opera House resumed its regular schedule and churches and Sunday school services got back to regular meetings. Health authorities were hopeful the epidemic had been stopped since the spread had not been countywide.

∞

Russell Strunk of Co-operative had a terrible thing happen to his ten-year-old son who seriously injured his eye when the bottle he threw against a rock broke into pieces, the smaller pieces bouncing off the rock and one of them back into his eye. The boy was taken to Lexington, Kentucky, for treatment. He needed one follow-up visit. His young friends in Co-operative visited him at his home to wish him well.

∞

Then without warning, a new case of spinal meningitis was reported. Roy Coffey, twenty-six, son of Jay Coffey of Co-operative, was stricken with the deadly disease. Roy responded favorably to the new serum and doctors were hopeful he would recover completely.

The meningitis cases to date that originated in Co-operative were all men over eighteen years old, the oldest thirty-two years old. Doctors were encouraged that a countywide epidemic had been averted, although the deadly disease gripped a good portion of Tennessee and Kentucky. The largest number of deaths (thirty-five deaths) were reported in Harlan County, Kentucky.

Co-operative continued under quarantine with no new cases reported. Mr. Othel Thompson continued to improve and the newest case, Mr. Roy Coffey, was still improving.

∞

Time seemed to move slowly as the epidemic threatened to take over the community, but no new cases were reported in Co-operative for six weeks. Then suddenly two children in the same family of Charlie King, a fourteen-month-old baby and a seven-year-old, came down with the dreaded disease.

Mr. King and family lived in Trace Branch about five miles from Shoopman. Mr. King worked in Co-operative, where the epidemic started. The serum that was used on the two men who survived was administered to the seven-year-old King boy.

Doctors waited two weeks and when no new cases were reported, they felt confident lifting the quarantine in Co-operative. As they continued to monitor that community very closely, the two King children were improving, and full recovery was expected.

∞

From Co-operative, over the mountain, tragedy struck suddenly at almost quitting time at Fidelity Mine. Lemmie Austin Wright, age eighteen, had gotten off the mine car to adjust the trolley wire when he encountered 260 volts. Mr. Wright's companion standing nearby came to him immediately, but nothing in his power could be done. Lemmie was gone instantly at about 3:00 p.m. The young man's father, also Lemmie Wright, was in charge of the mine where the accident occurred. The young Lemmie had four sisters (Odessa, Desdia, Nola, and Margaret) and three brothers (Bob, Winfred, and Alonzo). The young man was well liked by everyone, and the community of Fidelity was deeply saddened by this loss.

∞

The new high school south of Whitley City was inspected by officials on December 1, making sure everything was ready for the school to open the following year. Fidelity, Stearns, and Pine Knot also had a high school; Co-operative included ninth and tenth grades. Fidelity High School would be closed the following year in 1937 and Co-operative's ninth and tenth grade not long after.

∞

The community of Worley won first place in the Red Cross drive with a total of 181 memberships, with Stearns coming in second place with 169. The McCreary County goal of 400 was surpassed with a total of 665 memberships. However, the good feeling from this amazing accomplishment was short lived.

∞

Only days later following the Red Cross drive on the east side and deep within the Worley Mine, a slate fall occurred. Slate (the shiny, fine-grained, foliated rock that accompanies coal) forms in particular ways; one of the ways is known as "horseback" formation. When this happens, the slate will fall no matter how well the timbers are placed. Tom Gibson, age forty-nine, lived in Worley and worked at Worley Mine and was beneath the slate when it fell. He had no chance of surviving. Mr. Gibson left behind two brothers (J. T. Gibson and Jimmy Gibson), two sisters (Mrs. Joe Hickman and Mrs. Henry Smith), and his mother, Mrs. Jane Gibson.

∞

Just prior to Christmas break, at the Fidelity School Auditorium, parents and teachers and 225 youngsters enjoyed an afternoon of fun, music, and gifts for the kids. It was all made possible by the working men in the community and teacher cooperation.

Mr. Holmes addressed the gathering and expressed how well behaved the Fidelity kids were and how they were a credit to the community. Holmes, also coach of the Fidelity basketball team, commented on the slow start his team had so far but was confident they would improve as they learned to play with each other. The musical group came together for the first time for this special occasion. The group played two selections: "Silent Night" and the school song "Fidelity." The individual members of the group were Miss Evelyn Bell on piano, Mr. Conley Bell on saxophone, Miss Ruth Bowden on clarinet, Miss Alma Crisp on trombone, Miss Charlene Vahle on trumpet, and Mr. C. C. Shepherd on drums.

∞

MARRIED THIS YEAR 1936

Charlie Childers, age 26, of Co-operative, married Velma Gibson, age 18, also of Co-operative.

In the northern section of McCreary County, Jake Haynes grew up in the Greenwood area and Elsie Spradlin grew up in Bell Farm. Little is known how they met. I do know Jake was already working for Stearns Company at the Co-operative Mine. Possibly Elsie may have visited friends in Co-operative or maybe Jake went to Bell Farm and stopped in at Oren Spradlin's store and ran into her there. One thing's for sure, as beautiful as Elsie was, if Jake got one look at her, he wouldn't have forgotten her.

Soon in their relationship, they began to discuss marriage. But Jake wasn't in a hurry to take the final step. Elsie figured she would have to nudge Jake; she talked to Grant Roberts and Grant was more than happy to marry them. Grant agreed to walk to the mine entrance with Elsie. On that day when Jake's shift was over and he walked out of the mine, there stood the beautiful Elsie next to Grant Roberts, and Jake knew full well what was going to happen.

Jake talked about this moment later in life and said, "When I walked out of the mine that day, I had two choices: marry this girl or go back into the mine. Well, I might as well go ahead and marry her." And so they were married. They had seven children: Carroll, Jane, Nina, Gay, Joe, Bruce, and Boris.

Another marriage this year was Oscar Jones to Pearly May Worley. Oscar and Pearl had eight children: James, Glen, Arnold, Rose, Ernie, Ella, Tom, and Lisa.

∞

BORN THIS YEAR 1936

Robert Chitwood
Luther Troxell
Fayrene Terry
Darrell Thompson
Wanda Bell
Carroll Haynes
Mary Jo King
Jimmy Whitehead
Clifford Gregory

Varcila Kay Ball
Lawrence Stephens
Norman Freeman
Willie Gibson

CHAPTER 9

1937

In 1937 in the coal camp of Fidelity with no mine operation on a Saturday, Arnold Shoopman walked on a path by Harvey Terry's home on his way down the hill to the track. Arnold was all dressed up in a suit and tie.

Making a lot of noise down on the tracks was the old cog engine pulling several flat cars loaded with logs headed to Stearns. The old engine moved slowly but was very loud.

Arnold reached the tracks with perfect timing, hoboed the train, and sat down on the edge of one of the loaded flat cars. When the train reached Guy Kidd's Grocery, Arnold jumped off; the cog engine never slowed and kept moving along. Arnold was at Guy's for a long time talking with some of the boys at the feed house. The feed house was a building off to the west side of Guy's store. There, I've been told by two people, is where Guy kept his personal bottle of moonshine. When Arnold got ready to leave, he bought a couple dozen eggs to take home and staggered up the railroad tracks. Arnold hadn't gotten far when he heard the old cog engine coming back, headed to Bell Farm. Arnold managed somehow to hobo the train. This time he had both flat cars all to himself.

Reaching close to home, Arnold jumped off the flat car and waddled up the path toward his house. Arnold was doing okay until he got in front of the Terry home where he staggered and fell face down on top of the brown paper bag that held his eggs. Slowly raising himself up, some of the wet from the broken eggs mixed with dirt was all over the front of his suit. When Arnold finally got to his feet, there was no cleaning or knocking anything off with his wet slimy hands. He reached down, picked up what he could of the brown bag, and walked on home.

∞

On the other side of the mountain from Fidelity, Co-operative was beginning to see some relief from winter.

∞

A few of the men who worked at the Co-operative Mine and a few of the women, in particular, Miss Virgie Troxell and Mrs. Herbert Colyer who worked for the Red Cross, were generous givers to the community of Co-operative, donating three hundred dollars for flood relief.

∞

A new council formed in Co-operative: the Junior Order of the United American Mechanics installed a new unit known as the Co-operative Council No. 58. New officers and several visitors were called on to speak before the group. Among the visitors who spoke were Leamon Cooper, councilor of Whitley City Council No. 218; Dr. M. Thomas, deputy state councilor; J. R. Hayes, councilor of Cal Hill No. 10; Lester Cooper, secretary of No. 218; and J. H. Marcum and G. W. Redmond of Council No. 218. The Hickman quartet entertained at the event, singing several musical selections.

During the inaugural ceremony, brothers G. W. Redmond, Jesse Young, and Jerome Marcum oversaw the floor team; these three sat in the councilor chairs. The following officers were elected and inducted into office: Isham Duncan, councilor; C. D. Rose, vice councilor; Lee Baker, junior past councilor; Grant Roberts, chaplain; Carson Whited, conductor; Joe Winchester, warden; Bradford Duncan and Jimmy Dodson, sentinels; Fred Kidd, Lloyd Lewis, and Robert Duncan, trustees; Robert B. White, recording secretary; Elmer Barrier, financial secretary; and James Lewis, treasurer.

The new lodge, together with the team of Whitley City Council No. 218, was set to work with forty-nine members by degree. With the help of state deputy councilor, Dr. M. Thomas installed the new members, sharing important instructions to the new council. The new council agreed to meet the first and third Saturday nights each month in the school building. The new lodge closed the meeting, and the K & T Railway, which made the trip especially for this occasion, returned all Stearns' visitors back home.

∞

The following week, White Oak Junction scored another oil well. The Pigeon Rock Oil Company, with their lease from Stearns Coal and Lumber Company, drilled. After drilling through several feet of dirt and sand, oil gushed thirty feet into the air with such force it was necessary to cap it. They estimated that using pumps to fill tanks would yield 600 barrels per hour. However, nothing more could be determined until the oil was pumped later. The Pigeon Oil Company had been shipping its oil to the Stall Oil Company in Louisville. But because of recent rains, Louisville experienced flooding, so the Stall Oil Company was temporarily out of business.

Spirits ran high in McCreary and Wayne counties as the citizens pondered sharing in an oil boom; from all indications, the well would be the best struck in McCreary County. The Pigeon Rock Oil Company called representatives from several oil companies to investigate the well. While that was going on, the company busied itself installing pumps they already had, knowing the pumps would be inadequate to keep up with the flow if the well was as good a producer as they thought it would be, but the company was unable to get better equipment from Louisville because of the flooding the city was experiencing. Several tank cars were filled and the men pumping said there were no signs the well was weakening.

The representatives were well pleased with production even though the pumps were pumping only sixty barrels a day. They did say after testing the quality of the oil, it was slightly better than the well at Beaver Sand. Also, the well was the best the Pigeon Rock Oil Company had drilled in recent years.

∞

The community of Worley recorded the first fatality of the year for Stearns Coal and Lumber Company. Mr. Carl Hansford, age twenty-five, was employed by Stearns Company as a motorman. He was pulling a string of loaded coal cars out of the mine when the motor derailed. When that happened, Carl jumped on the tracks in front of the six-ton motor. The motor ran over him, pinning his body between the wheels. Carl's fellow workmen had to use a jack to rescue Mr. Hansford. He was immediately taken to Stearns and then taken by ambulance to Somerset Hospital where he died from his injuries shortly afterwards. Carl was the son of Mr. and Mrs. J. H. Hansford, also of Worley, and was a native of McCreary County. Carl was highly regarded in the Worley community. Survivors included his widow, Ethel Daugherty Hansford, their two small children, and four brothers (Bert, Tate, John, and Eugene). The community mourned Carl's death.

∞

Almost a month later, the man after whom the coal mining community of Barthell was named, Mr. E. E. Barthell, died on May 8 in Chicago. Mr. Barthell was vice president, director, and general counsel of Stearns Coal and Lumber Company. Although Mr. Barthell had been ill for several months, a heart attack was the immediate cause of death. Mr. Barthell was the brother-in-law of Mrs. R. L. Stearns of Ludington, Michigan.

∞

The community of Fidelity was beginning a transition that left people wondering what was next. The post office continued to be called Shoopman. With the high school recently closed, the graduating seniors would receive their diplomas with the seniors at Whitley City High School. The graduation ceremony of the two schools was held May 1 at 7:30 p.m. Graduating seniors included the following:

- *Fidelity High School*: Evelyn Bell, Paul Waters, and Oren Spradlin.
- *Whitley City High School*: Frank D. Howard, Robert Cundiff Morris, Edward Spradlin, Donald Holloway, Leamon Perry, Everett T. Mason, Thomas M. Knight, Arless Dewey Webb, Theophilies McDonald, Glen D. Cooper, Elmer Haynes, Dorothy Virginia Price, Maxine Roder, Mildred L. Perkins, Carrie May King, Mary Ann Bryant, Mary Virginia Alcorn, Mildred Josephine Henry, Agiler Johnson, Katheryn Bryant, Avil Allen, Fay Wilson, and Cloda Lewis.

Miss Nextel May arranged the musical program. The quartet was composed of Mr. J. S. Wright, Mr. A. W. Holmes, Mr. W. S. Schick, and Mr. James Wilson.

∞

Stearns High School graduated fifteen seniors: Augusta Wright, Mary Jo Brattom, Iona Hickman, Leone Hickman, Mary Helen Storie, Ruth Winchester, Mildred Redmon, Gladys Ball, Pauline Spencer, Ruth

Anderson, Marion Privett, Charles Hamm, Jarvis Bell, John Ed Larmee, and Vernon McCartt.

∞

Pine Knot High School graduated seven students: Marjorie Hays, Anna Manning, Mabel Stephens, Lena Kidd, Houston Chitwood, Berdell Corneilus, and Viola Moore.

∞

The following week after graduation ceremonies, on Monday, Fred Clark, age thirty-seven, left his home and wife in Co-operative and walked to Co-operative Mine. He had worked for Stearns Coal and Lumber Company for several years. He hadn't been married long, and the talk was his stepson, Russell West, and Fred had never gotten along. The ill feeling had escalated in recent days. It was alleged Fred drove to Paunch Creek to Russell's home. Fred got out of his vehicle, drew two guns, and said he was going to kill Russell. Russell was on the porch feeding his dog next to the doorway. Russell reached above the inside doorway, retrieving his shotgun and fired. The shot hit Fred between the eyes, killing him instantly. When Russell shot, Fred was only about ten feet away. Russell was arrested and taken to jail and was released the next day on bond.

∞

The following weekend after the shooting, Mr. and Mrs. John Risden of Stearns lost their daughter to pneumonia. John worked for Stearns Coal and Lumber Company on the carpenter crew. Shirley Louise

Risden, eight months old, died at the home of her parents. The child was buried in Oneida, Tennessee.

∞

On Monday of the following week, Tom Bell received painful injuries to his face and hands when slate fell on him inside the Co-operative Mine. Mr. Bell was rushed to Boyle County Hospital in Danville, Kentucky. After treatment, his condition was said to be stable and he would later be released.

∞

The community of Co-operative welcomed the Dester West and Charlie Winchester families, both of Fidelity. Dester and Charlie were transferred to Co-operative Mine when the Fidelity Mine closed and had been waiting on a vacant home to move into.

∞

In the community of Worley on a Thursday night, Steve Haynes and Everett Lyons both received burns on their face and hands when gas exploded inside Mine 4. The men were taken to Boyle County hospital for treatment, where they were reported to be in stable condition. Mr. Haynes had received similar injuries a month earlier and had recovered, but now he would be out of work for several more weeks.

∞

News spread about a man claiming to be Jesse James, the story a bit extraordinary. The man claiming to be the noted stagecoach, train, and bank robber had appeared in several southern towns, giving performances and making an offer of $5,000 to anyone proving he wasn't the famous outlaw. In Columbia, Kentucky, this same man showed up claiming to be the notorious outlaw. The show was scheduled not more than fifty feet from the site of the old bank of Columbia in Adair County. On record, the bandit Jesse James, his brother Frank, and three other outlaws stole several hundred dollars and killed R. A. C. Martin in a robbery in 1872. When questioned about his whereabouts during the fifty-one years on the run as a fugitive of bank robbery and murder, he said he'd been hiding out in Colorado.

Old timers reminisced, as many had for years, about the time the famous outlaw came through their town. Fifteen minutes before the eighty-year-old man claiming to be the outlaw Jesse James was to perform, Deputy Marshall Evan Akin stopped by to engage in a brief conversation. At the octogenarian Jesse's trailer truck, Deputy Akin produced his U.S. Marshall's badge and informed him that if he was Jesse the government still wanted him. Also, there was a law against obtaining money under false pretenses. Less than five minutes after Deputy Marshall Akin left, the showman Jesse, his manager, and his trailer truck left town. To my knowledge, he never was seen performing again.

∞

In the month of July, cases of typhoid fever were all traced to contaminated water supplies. Throughout southern Kentucky, the numerous cases had a direct link to contaminated springs and wells. The Kentucky Health Department urged everyone to get inoculated against the disease and use only boiled water for cooking and drinking. Anyone having a well that was found to be contaminated was urged to chlorinate their wells before using the water. Anyone planning on camping trips or swimming in the river or creeks should seriously consider getting the shot for safety.

∞

On August 21, the fifth annual picnic of the K & T Railway employees was held in Bell Farm. At 6:30 a.m., the K & T Special train left Stearns and arrived at 8:00 a.m. with 450 men, women, and children, all ready for a day of picnicking and fun. The first picnic held for the employees by K & T Railway was back in 1932, and it was such a success it had become an annual event. The purpose of these events was to give the employees and their families a chance to get better acquainted and to enjoy a day of recreation and fun.

Among the many games was the usual baseball game played between the married men and the single men. The single men prevailed by a close score of 43–37. The game posted some spectacular plays, like the clever base running of Claude Murphy, the Silerville merchant. The third base crash by Elisha Spradlin's attempted steal inspired the players to play hard. Jess Young and Dr. Thomas provided several thrilling plays. Dr. Thomas delivered a two-base hit with the bases loaded and the score tied, which contributed to the good showing of the married men. L. C. Bruce, on second base, and Jess Young carried out sensational infield plays.

While members of the two baseball teams rested, they were able to watch some of the other events. The hog calling contest was up next, and Arch Angel won. He was given the first-place prize, a large ear of corn. Angel won over hog callers Elisha Stephens, Henry Burk, and John McCarthy. During the event, the hogs made a lot of noise. It was speculated this event might be dropped the following year unless there was a lot of interest shown by those planning the events.

Another event of special interest was the woman with the largest feet. The contest was won by Mrs. Tom Monroe. Her closest rivals, Mrs. John McCarthy and Mrs. Joe Taylor were teased about wearing shoes for comfort, not style.

Probably the most popular contest was held for the fat women; these hefty women deserved praise for the way they handled their tonnage in such graceful style.

The section men (railroad track workers) finally, for the first time, won over the carpenter crew in the tug of war. Floyd Kidd, Luther Jones, Ledford Roe, the Vanovers, the Kings, and the Blevins boys were powerhouses and more than the carpenters could withstand. A huge watermelon was the prize and the section men carried it off.

And finally was the watermelon eating contest; the champ, George Hudson, disposed of the seeds through the space left by a missing tooth, which was just plain mesmerizing for the onlookers to watch. The other contestants were Tom Monroe and John McCarthy, who were on George Hudson's flanks.

Everyone enjoyed themselves, and on the train ride home, many were already talking about the next year's event. This picnic was one of the best things the K & T Railway had done for its employees and no one wanted it to end.

∞

Also this week, Kenneth Larmee left Co-operative for Louisville, where he had accepted a position with Louisville Refining Co. Co-operative would surely miss Mr. Larmee and wanted him to come back to visit as often as he could.

∞

In the fall of 1937, twelve groups met to compete in the Southern Appalachian First Aid Team contest. The contest was managed by the State Department. John F. Daniel, Chief of the State Department of Mines and Minerals, oversaw the contest.

Of all the teams who competed, Stearns Coal and Lumber Company won first, second, and third prizes.
- $50 first prize was awarded to Mine 4, west side, captained by Frank Strunk
- $45 second prize was won by Mine 4, east side, captained by Ned Duncan
- $40 third prize was awarded to Mine A team, captained by Claude Marcum
- $35 fourth prize was won by Prudent Coal and Coke Company, Prudent, Tennessee
- $25 fifth prize was awarded to Blue Diamond Coal Company, Westbourne, Tennessee

Other contestants were Blue Diamond Coal Company, Eagon, Tennessee; Stearns Coal and Lumber Company, Co-operative Mine; Prudent Coal and Coke team, No. 2; Pioneer Coal Company, Kettle Island; Straight Creek Coal Company, Straight Creek, Kentucky; Black Diamond Coal Company, Marion, Tennessee; and Stearns Coal and Lumber Company, Mine 15. Each team finishing below fifth place was presented twelve dollars in cash. All awards were presented by Stearns Coal and Lumber Company and its employees.

The contest was held in the Stearns school gymnasium instead of the ballfield because of rain; several mine rescue contests had to be eliminated. Members of the Women's Club served lunch to 157 folks.

A special prize given away to the first aid teams was a new Plymouth Sedan, won by Clarence King of Bald Knob, an employee of Mine A. Presented to the winning team by the National Coal Association, Washington, D.C., was a silver loving cup. Also, each member of the winning team was given a Red Cross medal and a pocketknife. Second place winners were given flashlights by their contributors. Mr. George Humble, Chief Engineer of Stearns Coal and Lumber Company, was director of equipment and grounds, making sure everything ran smoothly.

∞

Earl Coffey worked at Co-operative Mine and got in trouble with Stearns Company either because of a picket line or because he was working to try to organize a union. I don't know which. But I know Stearns Company fired him for ninety-nine years and six months. Mr. Coffey moved his family to Eagon, Tennessee, where he worked for Eagon Coal Company until retiring.

∞

Della Winchester, wife of Pete Winchester of Co-operative, gave birth to twin girls, named Faye and Kaye, at Somerset General Hospital.

∞

McCreary County citizens voted to go wet by a margin of 234 votes.

∞

MARRIED THIS YEAR 1937

Carl Phillips, age 22, son of Shelve Phillips of Co-operative, and Clara Young, age 21, daughter of Millard Young also of Co-operative, got married.

The following month, Vola Dixon, age 21, of Co-operative, and Flonnie Taylor, age 15, of Co-operative, tied the knot.

Another Co-operative couple tied the knot: Shelly Dixon, age 25, and Klas Sellers, age 21, got married.

The weekend following the gas explosion in Mine 4, Corbet Gregory, age 22, son of Jake Gregory of Co-operative, married Gladys Bell, age 18, daughter of Laura Bell of Bell Farm.

William Maples, age 27, son of Harrison Maples of Shoopman, married Edna Gregory, age 25, daughter of Willie Gregory also of Shoopman. From this union, these children were born: Joyce, Buck, Bobby, Ray, Jim, Clifford, Bonnie, Clinton, Glen, Gene, Geraldine, Judy, Ruby, and Shirley.

Two weeks later in the community of White Oak Junction, Crit Waters, age 28, son of Noah Waters, wed Cardie Meadows, age 21, the daughter of Jim Meadows. Both were residents of White Oak Junction.

One week later, R. W. Winchester, age 22, son of Bill Winchester, married Ella Mae Burnette, age 21, the daughter of Walter Burnette, both of White Oak Junction.

Robert Jones, son of Ephraim and Ollie Mae Jones of Slavens, married Ethel Worley, daughter of Reverend William and Rebecca Worley. Ethel gave birth to Carl, Viola, Opal, Lonnie, Irma, Zadie, and Russell.

The week following the K & T Annual Picnic, Everett Anderson, age 22, of Co-operative, son of Mr. and Mrs. Ulysses Anderson, married Vera Gaw, age 21, of Co-operative.

John Sidney Waters married Altie Mae Gregory; Sid had recently transferred to Co-operative from Fidelity. Altie gave birth to Ella Mae, Kenneth, Janice, Chester, Fayrene, Shirley, Paul, and Mary.

Another marriage this week was Clyde Gregory to Della (last name unknown), both of Co-operative.

Andy Cox and Louise Strunk also got married. Louise gave birth to Kenneth, Geraldine, Barbara, Fayrene, Brenda, and Stan.

BORN THIS YEAR 1937

Clara Dixon
Mildred Chitwood
Faye Winchester
Kaye Winchester
Joyce Kidd
James Gregory
Coy Worley
Eugene (Beaver) Wilson
Ella Mae Waters
Joyce Lewis
Ruby Hall
Denver Haynes
Thurman Cooper
Charlene Gibson
Jewelene Haynes
Ella Mae Dixon

CHAPTER 10

1938

In 1938, George Walker, after being elected Sheriff, hired Bill Freeman and Sherman Corder as deputies.

∞

Jeff Kidd of Gregory, Neil Kidd's dad, hurt at his logging operation near Bell Farm, was rushed to Good Samaritan Hospital in Lexington, Kentucky, in serious condition. All of Jeff's friends and neighbors wished him a speedy recovery.

∞

When Fidelity Mine closed in 1937, Bill and Nettie Bell and their youngest daughter, Betty Lois, moved into the little house next door to Jewell Kidd's

Grocery as you started up the holler. Bill, Jewell's father, had been transferred to Co-operative Mine. He welcomed the shorter distance to walk to work. Bill became an ordained Baptist Minister and pastored at Oak Grove Baptist Church in Bell Farm. Betty Lois later married Gib Carson.

On up the holler from the store and across the creek, Neil Kidd built a small house with two rooms, intending to develop it into a small rental house. Putting that idea on hold, he decided instead to move the pool table there and use the building to sell beer.

∞

On a Saturday night, Ome Coffey was going home to Co-operative. Coffey attempted to pass a truck, which moved over to his side of the road, forcing him off the road. His car turned over into a ditch. Allegedly, the truck driver did not stop after the accident, and the identity of the man was undetermined even though the Sheriff's Department searched diligently for the truck and driver. Noble Roberts, a passenger with Mr. Coffey, also of Co-operative, was taken unconscious to Stearns for treatment. From there, he was sent to Boyle County Hospital in Danville, Kentucky. Examination revealed severe chest and head injuries with a possible skull fracture. The accident occurred on Smithtown Road. Mr. Coffey, age twenty-one, died. His survivors included his father (Captain Coffey, also of Co-operative), two brothers (Othel Coffey of Co-operative and John Coffey of Oneida, Tennessee), and two sisters (Mrs. Abe Lewis of Eagon, Tennessee, and Mrs. Maude Davis, of Oneida, Tennessee).

The following week on Friday morning, Glen Winchester, son of Bill Winchester of Co-operative, had been hauling logs to the Stearns Mill. Officers were waiting and arrested Glen when he showed up. The Sheriff's Department had been informed that Glen was the man driving the truck which forced Ome Coffey's car off the road that led to his death the previous Saturday night. Winchester denied any involvement. He was taken to jail and later released on bond. The case against Glen was never proven.

∞

Stearns Coal and Lumber Company had been pondering a serious question for some time, which had filtered down through the ranks: Is coal mining profitable in McCreary County only in rare boom periods? The coal mines in McCreary County were not making money for the company. The company furnished wages for its employees that turned into purchasing power which often benefited other businesses. The company also provided a market for goods and services of professionals, such as doctors, dentists, lawyers, and schoolteachers. For the company to make a profit, it would have to branch out into other areas of the local economy. So in those early years, Stearns Coal and Lumber Company also sold groceries, clothing, and furniture and provided undertaking services. The company even paid its employees with its own money in the form of scrip.

The 1934 government reports obtained by NRA—a National Reposting Agency—showed that there were several reasons why coal mining in McCreary County was unprofitable, but only the top three I'll mention.

First, the consuming markets were too far away from McCreary coal mines. Stearns Company sometimes had to ship through or into other coal fields, so with their hauls being longer, Stearns Company had to absorb the high cost of freight. So the number one cause was that profits were being eaten up by the high freight rate.

The second leading cause of no profits in coal mining in McCreary County was the irregular coal deposits. It was no secret that coal seams could be thin, and a difference of thickness led to uncertain continuity. Although excellent in quality, Stearns coal required cleaning before consumers would accept the coal, which was expensive to do. High mining costs were the result of these factors. The government reports obtained by the NRA showed that Harlan County, Kentucky; Hazard County, Kentucky; Virginia; and West Virginia produced coal from fifteen cents to forty-five cents per ton less than the cost that Stearns Company could produce it at but with the same wage scale in Southern Appalachian of which Stearns Company was the largest single producer. With that in mind, the difference of one cent per ton could make or break a sale. The high cost of coal mining kept Stearns Coal out of a lot of markets.

Third was the cut-throat competition of some mine owners and truckers. The truckers would secure coal from the so-called snowbird mines and deliver to the bins of consumers at any price that resulted in a sale. As the name implies, as cold weather broke and spring began, some mines chiseled on the miners by paying any wage that distressed men would work for. The truckers chiseled on the railroads, hauling for rates barely enough to pay for the truck expense. Both chiseled on the producer, forcing the legitimate mining business to lay off miners as well as railroad workers, increasing unemployment that added to the social burden of communities; cutthroat competitors did not consider or care about these outcomes. These pirates of the trade could and often would eventually close markets to a legitimate business. These scoundrels distributed coal that was often the worst in quality, but when so-called bargains were offered, consumers closed their eyes to quality and ethics.

Legitimate mining in McCreary County faced these problems and others every day. How could they continue in business and overcome the obstacles? To survive, Stearns Coal and Lumber Company employees and the rest of the citizens of the county had to form an alliance and work together to overcome these obstacles because one was dependent on the other for self-preservation, in the grand scheme of things. So the struggle to survive continued.

∞

McCreary County High School graduated twenty-five seniors this year; no high school graduates were listed for Fidelity High School. My research indicated the Fidelity High School closed at the end of the previous school year in 1937.

Eleven finished the eighth grade in *Co-operative*: Bill Gregory Jr., Fred Lee Slaven, Lillian Colyer, Denzil Wilson, Noble Davis, Doris Byrd, Don Bowden, Jeweline Winchester, Geneva Monroe, Irene Duncan, and Christine Winchester.

The other Stearns Company mining communities saw significantly fewer students finishing eighth grade:
- *Fidelity*: Ottis Walters
- *Worley*: Imogene Kidd and Eugene Vahles
- *Yamacraw*: Angie Hamby
- *Barthell*: Howard Cecil Human and Imogene Vahles

∞

The month of June saw Dr. and Mrs. Vinson Pierce of Worley coal mining community leaving for Louisville, where they would make their home. During their residence at Worley, Dr. and Mrs. Pierce made many friends who regretted seeing them leave.

In turn, Dr. and Mrs. Zwickel left Louisville and arrived in McCreary County to take Dr. Pierce's place. Stearns Coal and Lumber Company made sure a doctor was available for the miners and their families.

∞

Estel Thompson, formerly of Co-operative, had the misfortune of breaking his leg while playing ball on the Eagan, Tennessee, baseball team. Everyone wished Estel a speedy recovery and his friends in Co-operative hoped Estel would come back for a visit.

∞

In June at the New Haven Baptist Church, Bible school for the young people was held by Miss Connell and Miss Mayer; these two women, along with the citizens of Co-operative, reorganized a B.Y.P.U. (Baptist Young People's Union) and a Woman's Missionary Union. Both certainly benefited the community of Co-operative.

∞

Two weeks later, Southern Railroad promoted excursions to Cincinnati: Each Sunday during July–

October, a round trip from Somerset would cost only $1.75.

∞

MARRIED THIS YEAR 1938

In White Oak Junction early in the year, Clyde Meadows, age 25, son of Jim Meadows of White Oak Junction, married Rachel Tucker, age 21, daughter of Henry Tucker of Yamacraw.

Roy Jones, age 19, son of R. C. Jones of Yamacraw, married Elsie New, age 16, the daughter of J. B. New.

Lloyd Dolen, age 31, son of T. B. Dolen of Bell Farm, married Erma Coffey, age 18, daughter of Milford Coffey also of Bell Farm.

Maynard Smith, age 31, son of Alford Smith of Bell Farm, married Euva Louise Jennings, age 18, daughter of Andy Jennings of Gregory.

James William (Bill) Shoopman, age 40, of Shoopman, married Lela Gregory, age 22, daughter of Mr. and Mrs. Will Gregory also of Shoopman. Children with first wife Amanda Mills: Williard, Glen, Ruby, Irene, Ivory, Betty, Vernon, and Gladys. Children with Lela: Bobby, Wendell, and Sue.

On May 14, J. H. Dobbs, age 45, of Shoopman, married Neva Watters, age 38, also of Shoopman.

In June, on the west end of McCreary County, John Worley (my dad), age 22, son of Reverend William and Rebecca Worley, married Lexie Mae Jones (my mom), age 16, the daughter of Ephraim and Ollie Belle Jones of Slavens. In this marriage, seven children were born: LD, Carroll, Sherdina, Wanda, Charles Danny, Sheila, and Gloria. John got a job with Stearns Coal and Lumber Company, working at Co-operative Mine. When the mine closed, John found work in Ohio, while Lexie raised the children in Co-operative.

In White Oak Junction, Edwin Kidd, age 18, son of Floyd Kidd, married Geneva King, age 14, the daughter of W. C. King of White Oak Junction.

Herman Winchester, age 22, son of Charlie Winchester of Co-operative, married Jean Koger, age 21, daughter of Auston Koger also of Co-operative. In an unusual circumstance, the marriage license was issued, but the ceremony was not performed. What happened is unknown.

Sometime around June, Daveson E. King, age 21, son of C. C. King of Co-operative, married Carrie Corder, age 16, the daughter of Mr. and Mrs. Alfred Corder of Slavens, Kentucky.

Four weeks later, Noble Roberts, age 22, son of Grant Roberts of Co-operative, married Christine Winchester, age 21, the daughter of Harve Winchester of Co-operative.

Three weeks afterwards, in Fidelity, Doyle Watson, age 19, son of Bert Watson, married Evelyn Dobbs, age 21, the daughter of Hence Dobbs of Shoopman.

Six weeks later, John Cooper, age 65, of Shoopman, married Dorothy New, age 55, of Shoopman.

The following weekend, G. B. Tucker, age 23, of Shoopman, married Christine Jones, age 18, the daughter of Nelson Jones of Shoopman.

In Co-operative, Melvin (Buck) Anderson married Jean Kidd. In this marriage, five children were born: Norman, Deena, Margie, Danny, and Joan.

Also in Co-operative, Roy Orvin Black married Martha Ellen Loudermilk. Roy and Martha had two children: Wanda Faye and Roy David.

That same week in Co-operative, Roy Jones married Elsie (last name unknown).

∞

BORN THIS YEAR 1938

Helen Nichols
James Lonnie Dixon
Denzil Troxell
JT Terry
Charles William Davis
James Roy Jones
Bobby Thompson

Jane Haynes
Jimmy King
Neil Coffey
Roger Shepherd
Bobby Gene Thompson
Bobby Whitehead
Ed Shoopman
Della Gregory
Donald Lee Hall
Erma Jeanette Ball
Bobby Stephens
Evelyn Gregory
Shelby Jean Shook
Oma Freeman
Joyce Maples
Ruth Ann Keith
Kenneth Cox

CHAPTER 11

1939

In 1939, Mary Chitwood resigned as manager of the Co-operative boardinghouse after eighteen years of service. Mary lived in Co-operative from the time it was developed in 1920–1922. Ms. Oma Freeman took over as manager of the boardinghouse the day after Ms. Chitwood left.

∞

Cack Slaven returned home in January after getting hurt in the Co-operative Mine from a slate fall the last week of December 1938. Cack spent a month in Lexington Hospital; his wife, Betty, spent the last week with him before they returned home. Mr. and Mrs. Estel Thompson took care of the Slaven's home while Mrs. Slaven was away.

CO-OPERATIVE, KENTUCKY
STEARNS COMPANY BOARDINGHOUSE.
PHOTO COURTESY OF ROGER CHITWOOD.

∞

Usually, it was a Saturday night when tempers flared and fights took place, but for the town of Barthell, it was a Sunday night when a gunfight happened. One of the participants in the duel was Tom Vahles, born in Tennessee, the son of Mr. and Mrs. Henry Vahles. For several years, Tom had been employed by Stearns Coal and Lumber Company and was a mine foreman; he was also a McCreary County Deputy Constable. The other participant, Ellis Strunk, was the son of Mr. and Mrs. Willie Strunk.

Ellis and his wife, Anna May Downs, at the time of the incident, were walking home from visiting her parents, Mr. and Mrs. Tobe Downs. Ellis had been employed at Barthell Mine for a number of years.

According to witnesses, Vahles was attending church at Barthell and had gone out to investigate what sounded like firecrackers with maybe a few pistol shots mixed in. The loud sounds were disturbing church service. Vahles was walking across the railroad tracks when he came upon Strunk and his wife. Apparently, the disturbing noises had been going on long enough for Vahles to work up a good mad.

We will never know the words spoken between them or if Vahles attempted to arrest Strunk who was not about to be arrested if he were innocent. What we do know is that four shots were exchanged. Vahles was hit in the left leg—the bullet severing the main artery—and within minutes died where he fell. Strunk was hit in the abdomen and lived long enough to make it to Boyle County Hospital in Danville where he was pronounced dead. Strunk left behind a widow. Vahles was survived by his wife and nine children. The community of Barthell mourned the loss of these two men. In these coal communities, everyone knew everyone, so this was devastating to the Barthell community, which would take a long time to heal.

∞

The Stearns Coal and Lumber Company revealed some interesting facts about itself. From 1903 when the first coal was mined at Barthell through 1938, a steady stream of coal had been flowing into markets. The tonnage amounted to 18,357,107. At fifty tons per coal car, that was a total of 367,143 cars of coal from all its coal communities that Stearns Company exchanged with the Southern Railway. If, for example, all this coal could be loaded into one train, the train would extend approximately 3,234 miles. That would reach across the country, as the crow flies, and go on into the Pacific Ocean a few hundred miles. From a standstill, an engine pulling such a train would travel forty-six miles before the last car would move. Between each car there was a slack of eight inches. If the train started at Stearns, the engine would pass Science Hill as the last car would start to move, according to the *McCreary County Record*. Amazing.

∞

In the town of Stearns, Mr. and Mrs. Thomas Jefferies got off the Southern Railway No. 3 to spend the day with the President of Stearns Coal and Lumber Company. Mr. Jefferies was a manager with the Hickman Williams Company that shipped the coal from Stearns and made sure it got to its destination.

During the day, the Jefferies, along with R. L. Stearns, Jack H. Price, and Gloria Bradley, visited Mines 4, 11, and 18. The year before, due to coal orders by Mr. Jefferies, Mines 4 and 11 were extremely busy. Stearns Company was hoping the relationship between the two companies would grow even stronger. For Stearns Company to have a summer outlet meant coal production would continue to be strong.

∞

L. L. Craig, Co-operative Company Store manager, and his wife became the proud parents of a baby boy.

∞

The following week in the community of Worley, Robert Waters was working Wednesday night inside Worley Mine when powder prematurely ignited. Robert received burns to his face and body and was rushed to Boyle County Hospital in Danville.

∞

Following the accident at Worley Mine, the next morning in the Blue Heron community inside Mine 18, Fred Spradlin, who currently lived in Bald Knob, received severe injuries from a slate fall. Fred suffered a fractured arm and leg and internal injuries and was also rushed to Boyle County Hospital in Danville.

∞

The following Friday, Millard Crabtree of Co-operative received injuries while working inside Co-operative Mine; a piece of slate fell on him. He was also taken to Boyle County Hospital in Danville, where his condition was said to be stable.

∞

On June 1, Burman Slaven was seriously injured when a Coca Cola truck ran over him. Details of this accident can be found in my book *CO-OP: Coal, Community, & House 52*, published in 2020.

∞

Dr. Simpson, the resident doctor at Co-operative, had to be out of the community for three days and Dr. Floyd filled in for him. Stearns Coal and Lumber Company made sure the coal camps had a doctor available as long as the mines were operating.

∞

Once upon a time when automobiles were still in the future, for many, hayrides were at the top of the list for excitement on a Saturday afternoon. Some would say a car ride couldn't match the thrill of a hayride; the simplicity of it, I think, may have added to the thrill of the experience.

All you needed was a wagon, hay frame, some hay, and a tarpaulin (in case you were caught in the rain). There was nothing much more fun than sitting on the edge of the wagon with your legs dangling off the wagon. It was a slow, easy ride. Having a particular place to ride to was best and stopping for a picnic

CO-OPERATIVE, KENTUCKY
CO-OPERATIVE'S RESIDENT DOCTOR—
DR. SIMPSON—
STANDING BY THE
CO-OPERATIVE COMPANY STORE.
PHOTO COURTESY OF BURMAN SLAVEN.

lunch added to the pleasure. Oh, can't you just taste fried chicken and blackberry dumplings. People in those days didn't need a reason; all somebody had to say was "I'd like to go on a hayride."

Many young people today can't imagine their ancestors had any fun back then. Some think all they did was walk to church on Sunday and work the fields all week. Truth is that they did have fun, just in a different way. Besides, praise singing or a church service could be accomplished on a hayride with a merry group that loved old-fashioned fellowship.

Back then, it was customary for the guys to furnish the wagon and horses and the gals to furnish the grub. That way everyone felt a part of the fun. The horse-drawn cart or wagon may have faded from some memories, but a good thing such as the excited feeling of an old-fashioned hayride should not be forgotten.

∞

At company headquarters in Stearns, the Board of Directors of Stearns Coal and Lumber Company called a special meeting. Mr. R. L. Stearns, well known in the coal business and art circles throughout the Midwest, was head of numerous other corporations besides Stearns Coal and Lumber Company, but because of health issues, he was forced to retire this year. Mr. Stearns stepped down as President of Stearns Coal and Lumber Company but remained Chairman of the Board. John E. Butler was installed as President and General Manager, Robert L. Stearns Jr. as Vice President, Roger W. Henderson as Treasurer, and Harry C. Trent as Secretary. Their terms were effective July 31, 1939.

Except for the Chairman, all the officers were located at Stearns Company Headquarters in Stearns, Kentucky. It was quite unusual for a company the size of Stearns Coal and Lumber Company to have its executives located so close to the operating coal mines. Management always kept a close relationship with its employees. When decisions were made, results happened faster at the base of operations because of this close physical proximity.

∞

The annual picnic of the Kentucky and Tennessee (K & T) Railway employees and their families was held August 13 at Mine 18. The special train left Stearns with over four hundred picnickers. Along the banks of the South Fork of the Cumberland in a beautiful grove, everyone enjoyed a delicious dinner—in these parts of the U.S., when I was growing up, we called the meal eaten in the middle of the day 'dinner' and the meal eaten at the end of the day 'supper.'

For those who had not seen Mine 18, the gathering gave them an opportunity to see one of the most modern coal tipples in Kentucky.

The baseball game between the fat guys and the lean guys got under way about forty-five minutes after dinner. When the game was over, there were many sore arms and sprained ligaments, which wasn't much fun for the players but expected since many of the players played only once a year.

Up next, the section crew and carpenters battled in a tug of war, with the section crew winning. Members of the section crew were Ledford Rowe, Luke Perry, George Hudson, Leamon Stephens, Earl Neeley, and Elisha Stephens. Members of the carpenters' team were Ben Ball, Sassal Davidson, Jim Ball, Arch Angel, Tim Godsey, and Bill Gresham.

The art of hog calling was next. Those who entered were Bill Powell, Dr. Thomas, Carl Neeley, Arch Angel, and Elisha Stephens. The judges awarded the grand prize to Bill Powell, the Best Hog Caller.

In the pie eating contest between Reverend Miller of Comargo and Elisha Stephens of Stearns, it took Reverend Miller only one minute and forty-seven seconds to eat a whole pie. He was named the winner.

In the foot race and sack race, Doris Webb won the girls' team race, and Earl Neeley won the men's team race.

So ended another successful picnic. Everyone enjoyed singing and fellowship on the train ride back to Stearns. These picnics were so much fun that folks started looking forward to the next one as the current one ended.

∞

Sunday, September 3, sadly, World War II began as British and Nazi ships clashed. An estimated one hundred men died.

∞

Past Guy Kidd's store and up the tracks at Trace Branch, there was a baptism that Obie Winchester and Virgil Young attended. Later in the day, Obie and Virgil obtained a bottle of liquor and began celebrating. The good time turned violent. It was not known what the two men began arguing about, but Virgil pulled his knife and stabbed Obie in the shoulder close to his neck. Guy Kidd took Obie to the hospital.

∞

Alfred Kidd applied for a liquor license to sell by the package in a building at White Oak Junction. I'm not sure if the license was approved or not or how long Alfred remained in White Oak Junction. I do know he entered the car business and began selling new and used cars.

∞

In several (maybe all) of the Stearns Coal and Lumber Company mining camps, a Christmas tree was put up in an outside central location, and on Christmas morning, all the children of the community that came out to see Santa received a candy treat. For many of the poorer families, this event was the highlight of the year. This particular year in Co-operative, fireworks were added to the festivities.

∞

MARRIED THIS YEAR 1939

During Mary Chitwood's time working at the boardinghouse, her daughter Myrtle helped out at times, and it was there that Myrtle met Marion Wilson. After a brief courtship, Myrtle and Marion were wed and raised their family in Co-operative.

In January, Arnold Winchester, age 22, the son of Pete and Della Winchester, married May Foster, age 21, the daughter of Bill and Fanny Foster. The children born in this marriage were Jerry, Sue, Kay, and Eddie. Jerry became a lawyer and was elected Circuit Judge. Sue married Bob Kidd, prominent businessman. Eddie became a pilot in the U.S. Armed Forces, and in civilian life, continued his craft, spending many years working for private airlines flying the rich and famous around the world.

A young Cordus Keith joined the CCC program in Bell Farm. A young, beautiful Laura Stephens worked with a staff of women doing the laundry. Laura's dad, Abraham, worked for the CCC program as a carpenter and was influential, helping Laura get the job. Laura spent her early years at Marsh Creek and went to school at Otter Creek. Cordus grew up in the Parkers Lake area.

When the young couple met, it was love at first sight, and they were married before the end of the year. The children born in this marriage were Jim, Estle, Ronnie, Beverly, Sheila, Thelma, Doyle, and Sandra.

While living in Paint Cliff, young Cordus, working at the tipple at Mine 16, got trapped between two coal gons and died. The young Laura was left alone to raise her children, which she did well, despite the profound grief the entire family experienced. All the children grew up to be responsible, model citizens in the communities they lived. (Gon is short for gondola and means an open railroad freight car.)

Harley Hardwick came to Fidelity, moving in with his older brother Deck. While there, Harley joined the CCC in Bell Farm. Imogene Reed who grew up in Knoxville, Tennessee, came to Co-operative and stayed with her older sister Myrtle who was married to Deck Hardwick. At the time Imogene came to stay with her sister Myrtle, Deck had already moved his family to Co-operative.

Imogene and Harley met and began their courtship. Harley's dad and mom were J. D. and Rowena Hardwick and Imogene's dad and mom were KT and Jenny Reed. Harley, age 23, and Imogene, age 19, were married this year.

Harley knew when he and Imogene decided to get married, he would have to leave the CCC program. He landed a job with Stearns Coal and Lumber Company at Co-operative Mine. Harley's favorite pastime was hunting and fishing, which he did every chance he got. These children were born in this marriage: Joyce, Jimmy, Judy, Terry, and Diane.

Jim Springfield, age 49, of Sunbright, Tennessee, married Mary Gibson, age 24, daughter of Mattle Gibson of Co-operative.

In the community of Worley, Hurstle Boyd, age 24, son of George Boyd, married Della McDonald, age 24, the daughter of Phil McDonald.

In Yamacraw, Coy Keith, age 18, son of Mart Keith, married Linda Morrow, age 18, the daughter of George Morrow of Wolf Creek.

Luther Bertram, age 24, son of Austin Bertram of Yamacraw, married Eualine Shepherd, age 18, the daughter of Elmer Shepherd of Barthell.

In Co-operative, Virgie Dodson, age 21, son of Bud Dodson, married Edith Welch, age 21, daughter of James Welch.

White Oak Junction lost another of its single girls to marriage. Aretha Duncan, age 21, the daughter of Joel Duncan of White Oak Junction, married William Sizemore, age 21, son of Dock Sizemore of Stearns.

Two weeks after Aretha and William married, Arlie McCoy, age 27, the son of Mr. and Mrs. George McCoy of Co-operative, married Dovie Phillips, age 19, the daughter of Mr. and Mrs. Shelby Phillips of White Oak Junction.

The next week in May, Oscar Worley, age 21, son of E. Z. Worley of Marshes Siding, married Beulah Cassada, age 16, daughter of Lewis Cassada of Greenwood. Oscar became a preacher of the gospel. He also had a long and successful career as a contractor and builder. Oscar and Beulah had six children: Dorman, Betty, Boyce, Kathy Ann, Wanda, and David.

In the community of Barthell, William Meadors, age 31, married Edna Watters, age 21, of Shoopman.

Eight days after William and Edna married, in the community of Worley, James Rosydon, age 21, son of Jake Rosydon of Worley, married

Dien Watters, the daughter of Henry Watters of Barthell.

The community of Co-operative lost one of its single daughters to marriage: Maude Bowman, age 23, married Louis Thomas, age 24, from Baltimore, Maryland.

Also, in the same week, Carson Whited, age 31, of Co-operative, married Eva New, daughter of John New of Co-operative.

A couple of days later in the Bell Farm community, Margaret Jane Stephens, daughter of Mr. and Mrs. Hobart Stephens, married Bill Ball also of Bell Farm. The couple traveled to Huntsville, Tennessee, to tie the knot.

As August began, the community of Barthell lost one of its eligible females to marriage: Altha Waters, age 21, daughter of Mr. and Mrs. Pete Waters, married Guy Gregory, age 21, the son of Mr. and Mrs. Bob Gregory of White Oak Junction.

Three days following the K & T Railway Annual Picnic on August 16, William Thurston Whitehead, age 19, son of John Whitehead of White Oak Junction, married Zora Waters, age 23, the daughter of Pete Waters of Shoopman.

On Saturday, September 2, Roy Dobbs, age 25, son of Sherman and Ada Dobbs of Dobbs Town, married Greedle Jones, age 18, the daughter of Ephraim and Ollie Jones of Slavens. Children born in this marriage were Lindell, Jean, and Clifford.

Also this year, Stanley Parks married Opal Christine Bell, sister to Jewell Bell Kidd and the daughter of Bill and Nettie Bell of Co-operative. Stanley and Christine had four children: Rankin, Jerry, Stanley Jr., and Debbie.

∞

BORN THIS YEAR 1939

Carl Jones
Donald (Buster) Bell
Ethel Gregory
Doyle Wilson
Barbara Coffey
Kenneth Ray Waters
Edward Lewis
Betty Lou Hall
Norman Ray Anderson
Warren Jones
Willard Gibson
Harold Haynes
Buck Maples

CHAPTER 12

1940

In 1940, RL Terry was seven years old. He was out in the front yard playing. The Terrys lived in the Lower Camp of Co-operative. RL happened to look toward the railroad tracks that ran directly in front of their home and noticed a man walking the tracks heading west toward the Co-operative Company Store. RL kept watching the man, trying to make out who he might be, or if he knew the man at all. To RL's surprise, when the man got in front of their house, he turned and headed toward RL. The Terrys had a fence around their house. RL's dad had installed the fence a couple of years earlier to keep the family dog from straying off. The man stopped at the gate and asked RL, "Your mom or dad home?"

"My mom is," RL said. "Come on. I'll get her." RL ran ahead and up the steps leading to the front porch. The door was standing open, it being a summer day. Hattie, RL's mom, hearing the voices, came to the door within seconds.

The man asked, "Ma'am, I've walked a long way. Would you have a piece of bread and some water you could spare?"

Hattie said, "Sure I do. You come in and sit down at the table."

Hattie served the man a plate full of food and the man ate it all. He said he'd been walking long before daylight and he was going to try to get a job with Stearns Coal and Lumber Company here in Co-operative, that he'd heard the company needed men. He went on to thank Hattie for the food and for her kindness, and as he left, he said, "My name is John Bolen Clark, but everyone calls me Bo." RL watched Bo walk on toward the coal tipple.

∞

Harrison and Rose Dixon moved their young family to White Oak Junction from Paint Cliff. By now, there were four sons and one daughter: Cecil, Hobert, Donald, Clara, and James Lonnie. Rose was pregnant with Roy Gene. Eventually, there would be three more children: Betty Imogene, Hershel Lee, and Junior.

On those hot summer days, the three oldest boys loved to slip off and go swimming at Rock Creek. Don was seven years old; Hobert, nine; and Cecil, twelve. If they stayed too long, their mom, Rose, would start yelling. The boys knew they'd better be home or very close before Rose yelled the third time. Because if she got to the third yell, the boys knew they'd get a whipping.

On one particularly hot day, the boys took off to Rock Creek for a few hours of fun. At the creek bank, pulling off their overalls and throwing them over a limb, they had to get into the water as quickly as possible because without their overalls they were naked as jaybirds.

Now, Robert Whitehead—everyone called him Rob—lived nearby and saw the boys on their way to the creek. Rob was a few years older than the Dixon boys and was a prankster. While the Dixon boys were distracted splashing water on each other, Rob snuck down and took the Dixon boys' overalls and threw them in a briar patch. Later when Rose began yelling for them, the Dixon boys got out of the water and finding their clothes in the nearby briar patch, they had no recourse but to get back in the water. "Maybe somebody might happen by and help us out," Cecil said.

At that moment, Rose yelled the second time. No one came by to help them out of the tight spot they were in. The next few minutes that passed seemed like time stood still. When Rose yelled the third time, she came walking up the creek bank with a handful of switches—a switch was a small branch of a tree used to spank a child.

All three boys at the same time began explaining to their mom, "We couldn't walk home naked. While we were swimming, someone took our clothes and threw them in the briar patch. Look."

Rose got their overalls out of the briars. But as soon as the boys were back in their overalls, all three got their bottoms tanned.

∞

Harrison Dixon, the boys' dad, could be cantankerous, whether he'd been drinking or not. One evening he was particularly so when he got home from work. The Dixons, like so many others in Co-operative, didn't have a refrigerator. Rose had sent one of the boys to a neighbor's house and was able to get a half gallon of fresh milk. The milk was in a small bucket with a towel over it to keep the flies out. Rose hung it up high on the back porch. It would be fine there, Rose thought, until supper was ready.

Harrison, getting home from work, stepped up on the back porch and, seeing the bucket hanging there (he had no idea if the small bucket was empty or not), took a swing with his fist, hitting the bucket. No one knew why but it was obvious he was in a mood. The bucket went sailing out in the yard, spilling all the milk. Rose ignored the incident as if it never happened and continued fixing supper.

After a hard five days of work shoveling coal in the mine, Harrison usually left on Saturday afternoon to go somewhere to drink moonshine. Most Saturday nights, the Dixon house was not a place you wanted to be, even by accident, but Rose and the kids had little choice. Rose was a woman that could hold her own with another woman, but she was scared to death of Harrison when he was drunk.

On Saturday evenings, Rose and the older kids that wanted to would listen to the Grand Ole Opry. When the radio program was over, she'd get the kids all bedded down. Then she'd go to bed. There was no need for her to lose sleep waiting up for Harrison. There had been times Harrison would pass out somewhere and not come home until Sunday morning. Rose thought on those things and had just drifted off to sleep when a voice woke her. It sounded like Harrison singing. Rose got up and heard it again. She was sure this time it was Harrison. Then Harrison yelled as loud as he could, "You better grab your children because your daddy's coming home."

Rose knew Harrison was drunk. She hurried and got the kids out of bed, and just as she and the kids went out the back door, Harrison came in the front. Rose took the kids to a neighbor's house where they stayed the rest of the night. She and the kids returned home late Sunday morning. Generally, Harrison would be on the couch still sleeping off his hangover when they got home, which is where he was this time. When he did wake up grumpy, grouchy, and mean, if Harrison told any of the kids to do something, he meant they were to do it now, and if what he said wasn't done immediately, Harrison would grab a piece of wood and hit the kid over the head with it. Don remembers getting several head bumps growing up.

∞

The women that lived in White Oak Junction had their own particular day of the week to go to Rock Creek and do their laundry in the creek. The women who had lived there the longest had their choice of what day and time they'd do laundry. Those families who had recently moved into the area had better not try and crowd in. A few had tried, which had led to cuss fights. A few of the women, including Rose Dixon, started carrying a knife in their aprons. When word of this circulated through White Oak Junction, cooler heads prevailed and there was no more arguing.

∞

A few weeks after Joel King and Eula Roberts got married, Austin Slaven of Co-operative was arrested by Deputies Mitt Tucker and Bill Freeman on the charge of bootlegging. Slaven had in his possession one quart of moonshine at the time of the arrest. The next day, he was fined $150 and spent thirty days in jail.

∞

In high school basketball, McCreary County High School played the Co-operative team. The Co-operative School, in the early years, included the first two years of high school, and at the time, Conley Bell coached the Co-operative team. Co-operative lost by a score of 37–19.

∞

Before the school year was over, the *Courier Journal* sponsored a spelling bee in all McCreary County schools. Those who wanted to participate had to first pass a fifty-word written contest with a score of eighty-five percent or better. The ten best scores earned the privilege to be in the oral contest. A Parkers Lake student Pauline Johnson scored ninety-six percent, the highest score on the written contest.

The oral contest was held on a Saturday afternoon at the McCreary County Courthouse in Whitley City under the direction of W. O. Gilreath, McCreary County School Superintendent. An eighth-grade student from the White Oak Junction school Thelma King was the winner of the countywide contest. Thelma, the smallest in size, was the daughter of Mr. and

Mrs. W. C. King of White Oak Junction. Thelma was coached by her teacher, Adriane Stephens of Whitley City.

Thelma King's competitors who participated in the countywide contest, their schools, and the words they misspelled were as follows:
- Pauline Johnson, Parkers Lake: "Carriage"
- Ale Spradlin, Westapple Tree: "Manufacturing"
- Marge Neal, North Mill Creek: "Height"
- Velma Duncan, Pine Knot: "Laboratory"
- Mildred Terry, Whitley City: "Indefinitely"

The pronouncer of the contest words was Mrs. Rankin Powell; judges were Hobson Stephens, Edd Ball, and Attorney George Stephens.

Two years earlier, Mildred Terry, eighth-grade student of Whitley City, won the countywide spelling match and came in second place this year.

This year's winner, Thelma King, would represent McCreary County in the statewide spelling contest to be held in Louisville in April 1941.

∞

Geneva Wright, age fifteen, got a job at Fidelity working for the "Wives of Coal Miners Who Became Ill." While the husbands worked, Geneva helped take care of the wife who didn't feel like doing the rigorous work that was required of a housewife. Geneva was born in Winfield, Tennessee, where they lived until her dad, R. D. Wright, got a job with Stearns Coal and Lumber Company.

Arnold Shoopman was born on a forty-acre farm in Forbus Pall Mall, Tennessee, on the Wolf River, the same area where Alvin York grew up. At the age of nineteen, Arnold went to work for Stearns

Coal and Lumber Company at Fidelity Mine. Arnold loved the game of baseball and joined the Fidelity team not long after moving to Fidelity. Arnold was a member of the 1933 undefeated baseball team.

During the summer, on a Saturday afternoon, Geneva began seeing people walk by her house in the direction of the ballfield. Geneva had her work all caught up and had not been to any of the ball games. Today she decided she'd walk over to see what the excitement was about. The ballfield was across the creek and up to the left from where she lived. The ballfield was complete with bleachers. At this game, she would meet Arnold Shoopman.

The baseball game got under way, and it was a close game. The Fidelity team was on the field. A player on the opposing team hit a ball in Arnold's direction, who was playing outfield. To have a chance to catch the ball, Arnold began running hard to the edge of the field. However, the field went all the way to the creek. Arnold, still running hard, knew he was fast running out of dry land. At the last moment, Arnold jumped in the air with his arm stretched up as far as he could reach. Arnold caught the ball as his feet came down in the middle of the creek.

The umpire had been running toward Arnold and stopped at the edge of the bank and saw what appeared to be a catch before Arnold hit the water. The umpire yelled loud enough for everyone to hear; everyone watching was deathly quiet. All the crowd could see was that Arnold had gone out of sight. The umpire yelled, "If the ball comes out dry, it's an out; if it comes out wet, it's a home run." Arnold waded the creek and climbed up the bank; the umpire reached for the ball, took it out of Arnold's glove, and held it up high. Everyone was waiting for the decision, including all the players. The umpire yelled, "The ball is dry; it's an OUT."

The Fidelity spectators stood cheering. The opposing player who batted the ball, still standing at home plate, struck the ground hard with his bat—it broke. He threw the remaining piece to the ground and walked off the field. The Fidelity team won the game that day.

Arnold and Geneva met at the refreshment stand and Arnold walked Geneva home. They began seeing each other regularly and got married before year's end. It was fairly easy to find an empty house since the Fidelity coal mine closed in 1937, so Arnold rented a house that they lived in for one year.

Families had been slowly migrating out of Fidelity as the miners found work elsewhere or were transferred to other Stearns Company coal camps; some men had to leave the state altogether. As it was with Fidelity and other coal communities with closed coal mines, it would take several years before the community would disappear; houses were torn down one at a time as people moved away.

∞

While Arnold and Geneva were starting their life together, in another coal camp in another part of the county, an incident was about to happen between two residents of Yamacraw. Allegedly, Dan Caddell and Virgil Craft did not like each other; my research did not uncover why. It was a Saturday and Craft began drinking early and people heard him say that when he saw Caddell again he would kill him and cut his head off. Word got to Caddell that afternoon, but it didn't change Caddell's behavior. Late in the day, Caddell met up with some friends, and like most Saturday evenings, they walked the tracks and ended up close to the train bridge. They enjoyed each other's company and hung out talking way into the night when a couple of the boys decided to go get their guitars. They built a fire close to the tracks and had a good time, singing and listening to some good ole down-home music.

Caddell had been standing close to the fire, listening to the boys play and to an occasional song somebody would sing. Then Caddell went over and sat down on one of the crossties. Without warning, Craft came up behind Caddell from the dark and swung down with his knife. Caddell heard something or someone step on the gravel behind him and by instinct dodged to protect himself. As Caddell attempted to escape the assault, Craft's knife caught Caddell near his eye and cut a deep wound on his face toward his ear. Caddell rolled and was able to see Craft slashing with his knife in hand and managed to stay out of range of any more cuts.

Everyone else, upon seeing Craft, jumped back out of the way except a couple of the boys who jumped between Caddell and Craft. Craft didn't advance, figuring he'd done all the damage he was going to do, and walked off into the dark. Josh Keith immediately took Caddell to Stearns for treatment where he was sent on to the hospital in Danville. The Sheriff's office was notified of the incident and Deputies Mitt Tucker and Bill Freeman arrested Virgil Craft in Yamacraw and held him in jail.

∞

Two weeks later, on Monday morning, Hobert Burk stepped into Anderson Store at Kidd's Crossing. Anderson Store was on the left corner at the intersection of Clark Holler Road and Slaven School Road on Highway 92 just before crossing into Wayne County. The Bell Brothers store was on the right side of the corner. Everett Anderson, son of Zeke Anderson, was the manager of Anderson Store and postmaster of the U.S. Post Office inside the store.

Burk asked Anderson for a nickel's worth of salt. Soon after, their conversation turned into an argument. It is unclear why or what may have happened between the two men to cause the argument. Maybe Anderson told Burk not to come back to his store or maybe Anderson told Burk that he'd give him no more credit; we'll never know exactly what caused the argument. It was alleged that Burk pulled a knife on Anderson. Anderson was standing behind the counter with only his head and chest exposed. Burk could not see Anderson's hands. While staring straight ahead at Burk, Anderson felt around for his pistol. When Anderson got hold of it, in one motion, he swung his pistol up and shot Burk in the chest. Lying on the floor bleeding, Hobert Burk died over a nickel's worth of salt.

∞

MARRIED THIS YEAR 1940

Grant Roberts' first wife died giving birth to their fourth child. Before her death, the Roberts had three daughters—Eula, Helen, and Betty. By the time Eula was eighteen, her dad, Grant, was with his fifth wife. The Roberts were living in White Oak Junction. The stepmothers had generally put most of the workload on the three oldest girls. One of Eula's jobs was doing the laundry, and on one of her trips carrying clothes down to Rock Creek, Joel King came by. Joel, seeing Eula, walked to where she was, and they talked while Eula did laundry in the creek. Before leaving, Joel asked Eula what day she would be doing laundry again. She told him and Joel asked if he could come by and talk with her. She said he could.

After the next meeting, they began taking evening walks together and walking to and from church. This was the beginning of a long, successful union. Joel King, age 17, and Eula Roberts, age 18, married and had six children: Janice, Noel, Judy, Gayle, Tommy, and Donna. Years later in Joel's life, he would be the pastor at the New Haven Baptist Church in Co-operative.

Geneva Wright and Arnold Shoopman also got married. They had eleven children: Lucille, Archie, Delois, Roger, Faye, Lena, Roy, Robert (Robbie), Jerry, Paul, and Katherine.

∞

BORN THIS YEAR 1940

LD Worley (my brother)
Ella Mae Nichols
Roy Gene Dixon
Arlena Troxell
Jerry Winchester
Glen Lee Jones
Patsy Thompson
Lindell Dobbs
Donald Shepherd
Wanda Faye Black
Alma Jo Hall

Glen Gregory
Edna Irene Hall
Janice Slaven
Shirley Stephens
Leroy (Greg) Gregory
Christine Haynes
Mary Jo Cooper
Iva Sue Shook
Bobby Maples

YAMACRAW, KENTUCKY
YAMACRAW TRAIN BRIDGE
PHOTO COURTESY OF BURMAN SLAVEN.

CHAPTER 13

1941

As 1941 began, the Stearns community heard the surprising news that the State Bank of Stearns would be closing. After twenty years of faithful service, the doors would close for good at the close of business on January 15, 1941. A notice was mailed to all depositors, pursuant to a resolution passed by the Board of Directors of the State Bank of Stearns: Cashier Shelby Martin and board members H. C. Trent, W. A. Kinne, and R. W. Henderson. Depositors were urged to withdraw or transfer their balances before close of business January 15 because after close of business, checks would be mailed to the last known address for the customer.

∞

Two weeks following the news of the State Bank's closing, the Boy Scouts of America held its first pack meeting of the recently organized club in Co-operative. Mr. William Gregory, club master, asked parents to attend with their sons to hear about the many plans for the coming year and to receive information that would benefit the program.

∞

On the same night as the Boy Scouts of America had its meeting, on the road to Co-operative, Mitt Tucker arrested Virgil Conatser of Yamacraw and Lonnie Winchester of Co-operative for drunk driving. They were taken to jail.

∞

Two days later, a moonshine still was captured by deputies. The still owners, Johnny Green and Johnny Cordell, were arrested in Silerville.

∞

The next day, not far from Co-operative in the community of Bell Farm, Huey P. Smith was arrested when he was caught at the site of his twenty-five-gallon moonshine still.

∞

It was recess at the Co-operative School and the school kids were outside playing. A crew of men from the CCC camp came into view of the school playground. The crew was working on the road, some with picks, some with shovels and steel rakes, and

CO-OPERATIVE, KENTUCKY
CO-OPERATIVE SCHOOL
THE BUILDING IN THE FOREGROUND HOUSED GRADES 5–8. IN THE EARLY DAYS, NINTH AND TENTH GRADES WERE ALSO IN THIS BUILDING. THE BIG ROCK WE PLAYED ON SEPARATED THE TWO BUILDINGS. WE LOVED THAT ROCK AND SPENT MANY HOURS JUMPING OFF THE BACK OF IT. THE BUILDING THAT IS BARELY VISIBLE HOUSED GRADES 1–4 AND A CAFETERIA AT ONE POINT IN ITS HISTORY.
PHOTO COURTESY OF SAMUEL PERRY.

some with wheelbarrows. The men with the wheelbarrows walked back and forth to get the gravel to put on the road. Other men with steel rakes leveled the gravel as it fell from the wheelbarrows.

RL Terry was one of several boys who walked through the playground to the edge of White Oak Creek and watched the work in progress. The crew appeared to be following the dirt road where vehicles now traveled—and before them, horse-drawn wagons. It was fascinating to young boys like RL to watch these men work, turning the dirt road into a gravel road. Besides, RL figured he could play marbles or a ball game any ole time.

Before the school year was over, the crew had worked its way out of the main view of the playground. But they were still close enough that the schoolboys could hear them working. Down the railroad track leading back to Co-operative and on the curve with the schoolhouse buildings still in view, on the left side were some large rocks running parallel with the railroad tracks. Some of the older boys climbed the huge rock that was shaped like a box. It was a good spot to watch the progress of the crew building the road. But it wouldn't be long till the crew would be out of sight even from the rock's vantage point.

∞

In White Oak Junction, a half of a mile east of Co-operative traveling by the gravel road, three men were working at the sub-station for Stearns Coal and Lumber Company: Mr. Andy Sutton, a carpenter; Mr. Noel Shorter; and Mr. Barclay Bass, chief electrician and father-in-law to Shorter.

Mr. Shorter, age twenty-seven, came to Stearns Company approximately four years earlier following his marriage to Myrtle Bass the previous year. Mr. Shorter first worked with the carpenter crew. He was then moved to the painter's crew, but lately he had been working with the electrical crew. Noel Shorter had studied at the University of Kentucky and, before coming to Stearns Company, was a lieutenant in the CCC camp at Cadiz. He was respectful to everyone and respected by everyone he met. Faithful to his job and family and strong willed to succeed, it was evident he was willing to work wherever he was placed.

The three men had been moving some transformers Tuesday morning. Mr. Shorter needed to position himself higher than he could reach by standing on the ground, so he moved the metal drum close to him into position. He climbed on top of the drum and stood up, and as he did, the barrel shifted beneath him. Bringing his arms down to catch his balance, he fell backwards. His ear touched the high-tension wire carrying 13,000 volts before he hit the ground. Mr. Bass and Mr. Sutton ran to Mr. Shorter within seconds; their attempt to resuscitate was futile. Death came quickly to Mr. Shorter.

His untimely death was felt throughout Stearns Coal and Lumber Company. Mr. Noel Shorter was survived by his wife, a four-year-old son (Billy Barclay), and a sixteen-month-old daughter (Mary Lynette). Mr. Shorter, a member of the Christian Church of Middlesboro, was laid to rest in the Stearns Cemetery. Pallbearers were James Wright, Lem Hatfield, Mack Crabtree, Clarence Cook, Luther Swain, and Chester Williamson.

∞

After Mr. Shorter's death and for the next three subsequent months, Stearns Coal and Lumber Company suffered a series of accidents in its mines—two of which happened on the same day of the month and each accident in a different mine:
- In Co-operative Mine, while working, Homer Crabtree, son of Gar Crabtree, suffered a fractured pelvis when slate fell on him. He was immediately taken to the hospital in Danville, where his condition was reported satisfactory, a much better report than expected when the accident first happened.
- A month to the day following, in Yamacraw Mine, Luther Cooper died as a result of 400 pounds of coal falling on his chest.
- The next month in the community of Worley, Mr. Corbett Whalen, age forty-three, who had been employed by Stearns Coal and Lumber Company for more than six years, died. It was Friday night and he was working the night shift. Men near him thought he was disconnecting the trolley wire when he lost his balance and fell from the motor. The motor then rolled over him. The men at Worley Mine No. 4 would deeply miss him. He was highly respected and a member of the Second Baptist Church at Whitley City. Mr. Whalen was survived by his widow, Dortha Neal Whalen, three sons (James, Finley, and Donald), and two brothers (Kawood and Tom).

∞

The next Saturday evening in the community of Co-operative, some of the boys got together as usual to play cards and drink moonshine. The sheriff's office was called after the men began fighting. Deputy Sheriff Mitt Tucker came to the scene and questioned the men. When these men broke out into another fight, they were arrested for drunkenness: Walter Dixon, Slim Nichols, Cleve Gregory, and Corbett Gregory.

∞

  On June 14 in the local election with a total of 3,424 votes, the McCreary County voted to be dry by a margin of 418 votes. The wet votes carried twelve precincts, while the dry votes carried twenty-three precincts. Two years earlier, the north end of the county voted dry, and now it would be dry. Liquor stores had sixty days to close their businesses. The election had no fights, other than verbal; both sides had worked very hard to get the results they wanted.
  An unfortunate incident occurred at Greenwood where all ballots disappeared between Friday afternoon and Saturday morning. On Saturday morning, election officers opened the ballot sack to find a railroad tariff book, but no ballots. Monday morning County Attorney James A. Inman, along with other officials, including County Court Clerk, Mrs. Lola King, opened an investigation to determine what happened to the ballots. On Saturday, June 21, Greenwood allowed its citizens to vote again; polls opened at 9:30 a.m. The clerk for the precincts, Mrs. Arthur Clark, signed for the ballots when she received them. The investigation into why the Greenwood ballots were lost placed Mrs. Arthur Clark and Mr. Rube Green in jail under a $500 bond each and the case was held for the Grand Jury.

∞

Friday afternoon, August 1, Dr. Dewitt Stockton Floyd was riding a motor car with Ed Jones, who was operating the car. In a rare occurrence, just east of the river curve, the motor car collided with coal cars being pushed by an engine of Stearns Coal and Lumber Company. Walter Thomas was engineer and Robert Foster, the conductor—both from Stearns. Ed Jones escaped with minor injuries to his leg when he jumped from the motor car. Dr. Floyd received grave injuries and was given medical aid at the scene, then rushed to Boyle County Hospital in Danville, where he later died.

Dr. Floyd was sixty-nine years old and at the time on his way to Blue Heron (Mine 18) to see one of his patients Elmer Bryant. Dr. Floyd met his death as he had lived his life, devoted to his patients. He not only treated his patients' ailments, but he counseled them, helping them iron out many problems. He was a man with a high degree of love for his fellow man and a willingness to help with his patients' difficulties. It was often said about Dr. Floyd that no hour of night was too late nor home too humble or inaccessible for him to reach. He gave of himself freely. His name stayed long in the hearts of his fellow men and women.

It is safe to say Dr. Floyd was one of the most beloved doctors ever to live in McCreary County. His sense of humor and wittiness in telling stories was legendary; he was delightful to be around. Dr. Floyd had practiced medicine for twelve years in the mining camps of Stearns Coal and Lumber Company. He resided for ten years in Fidelity, but when the mine closed, he transferred to Barthell. Dr. Floyd was laid to rest in Danville, where he lived prior to coming to McCreary County.

∞

Back in Co-operative, Mr. Herbie Lee Jones, thirty-four years old, of Slavens, while working inside Co-operative Mine, received serious injuries when three coal cars ran over him. Rushed by ambulance to the hospital in Danville, he died enroute north of Somerset.

∞

In Dixie, south of Whitley City, Edward King, who had been operating King Edward Café, left the Café to work on the Wolf Creek Dam project. Mrs. Elsie Litton took over management of the Café.

∞

In the northwest portion of McCreary County, the dedication of the Nature Arch with a picnic lunch was well attended. Editor of the *Louisville Times*, Tom Wallace, was the principal speaker. The Kentucky Federation of Women's Clubs planted 30,000 pine and poplar trees in honor of one of the state's unique landforms. An intermittent light rain didn't stop approximately one hundred people from attending from all over the state. The dedication was the first of its kind in Kentucky. (The Natural Arch Scenic Area in Parkers Lake is currently part of the Stearns District of the Daniel Boone National Forest.)

∞

In Co-operative early Saturday morning about 4:00 a.m. on October 4, Tom Dunegon, who lived in a house owned by Jess Cox, only about 150 feet from where Cox lived, yelled for Cox to come out. Unconfirmed reports stated Cox came out with his gun and fired a shot. It was also reported Cox had borrowed a gun from a neighbor, telling the neighbor he was going squirrel hunting. That same neighbor told Dunegon he would sell the same gun for three dollars. Tom Dunegon shot Jess Cox, killing him instantly.

After the shooting, Dunegon paid the neighbor the three dollars for the gun and then hid out on a hill above Co-operative. Officers came Saturday afternoon and apprehended Dunegon who didn't resist. He was placed in jail under a $5,000 bond, awaiting trial. Liquor stores in McCreary County closed the following Saturday morning; the case had been sent to the Court of Appeals. A week later, the liquor stores reopened after Judge Samson ruled on the case.

∞

Mr. John L. Shepherd died suddenly, creating a vacancy at Co-operative School. The first of November, Mr. E. B. Farley was transferred to Co-operative as the principal. Mr. Farley came to McCreary County originally from West Virginia and, at the time of his transfer to Co-operative as principal, had recently been teaching at Pine Knot High School.

∞

Near Co-operative, Bethel Smith was digging up potatoes on the Berton Owens farm. After considerable time, he stopped to smoke a cigarette. After lighting up, without thought, he threw the match into dried grass. During the day, the wind picked up, carrying the fire to heavy growth of dried grass. It didn't take long for the fire to spread out of control. A crew from the CCC camp rushed to the scene and was able to contain the fire, but the fire burned three acres of prime natural forest timber. The U.S. Forest Service pressed charges and Ledford Perry took Bethel Smith into custody. Mr. Smith pleaded guilty before Judge J. E. Stephens and County Attorney James A. Inman. Mr. Smith was fined ten dollars and court costs which was the minimum since this was Mr. Smith's first violation. Judge Stephens went on to say Mr. Smith's carelessness could have caused the loss of Owens' home. This case was one example where carelessness caused a forest fire.

∞

On December 7, disaster struck the United States Navy at Pearl Harbor. The Japanese dealt our Navy the severest blow in its history and by some accounts elevated the Japanese fleet to a temporary superiority in the Pacific. The attack cost the U.S. Navy a destroyer, a battleship, and a number of smaller ships. It wounded approximately 1,000 people and killed approximately 2,400 Americans.

On December 8, the United States declared war on Japan with the Senate voting 82–0 for the declaration, and in the House, the vote was 388–1. The one negative ballot in the house was Jeanette Rankin (R-Montana). President Roosevelt signed the declaration of war. The Japanese had representatives in Washington at the time of the attack. Supposedly the representatives were there to discuss peace, when, in fact, they were there to disguise their treacherous attack.

Eight days before Christmas, Sheridan (Sherd) Dobbs, the oldest resident of McCreary County, died at his home. Sherd Dobbs, age ninety-seven, lived in Dobbs Hollow for many years. Mr. Dobbs was the son of George Washington Dobbs and Mrs. Leuratney Strunk Dobbs. He lived his life devoted to his family and God. Few men attain the age and wisdom of Mr. Dobbs. He lived through the Civil War, the Spanish American War, and World War I. Mr. Dobbs' wife, Sally (Coffey) Dobbs, had died January 23, 1910. They had four children: Frank, deceased; Tom of White Oak Junction; El of Jacksonville, Florida; and Angeline of Yamacraw. Mr. Dobbs was buried on the property he had donated, which to this day still bears his name.

MARRIED THIS YEAR 1941

Homer Coffey and Ada Clark married this year. The children born in this marriage were Joyce, George, Lenna, Larry, Donald, Brenda, Gary, Cindy, Anita, and Mike.

BORN THIS YEAR 1941

Carroll Worley (my brother)
Roger Chitwood
Bob Kidd
Norma Davis

Viola Jones
Lucille Shoopman
Jim Keith
Larry Bell
Randall Coffey
Gerald Wilson
Jewelene Whitehead
Albert Coffey
Rankin Parks
Eston Lewis
Patricia Carol Ball
Deena Anderson Swafford
Nina Haynes
Evelyn Jones
Lois Gibson
Harold Gibson
Helen Whitehead
Ray Maples

CHAPTER 14

1942

Starting January 5, 1942, the local Rationing Board announced tire rationing to take effect until further notice: one truck tire and tube by most retailers with some limited to two. The government's new rubber rationing program included traveling salesmen and taxi drivers. Residents of isolated rural areas were prohibited from buying new automobile tires.

∞

The Local Board announced plans to register men ages twenty to forty-four for the U.S. Armed Services per proclamation of the President of the United States of America and the Government of the Commonwealth of Kentucky. Monday, February 16, was set for all males residing within the United States to

CO-OPERATIVE, KENTUCKY
PHOTO OF THE UPPER CAMP SHOWING PART OF
THE BALLFIELD AND A FEW OF THE HOUSES,
INCLUDING THE MINE SUPERINTENDENT'S HOUSE
AND THE RESIDENT DOCTOR'S HOUSE.
PHOTO COURTESY OF
THE *MCCREARY COUNTY RECORD*.

be registered if they hadn't reached their forty-fifth birthday on February 16, and had reached their twentieth birthday by December 31, and were not exempt by law.

The Local Board No. 111 prepared for registration in McCreary County. Each community needed people to serve as chief registerers. Superintendent W. O. Gilreath and Superintendent C. W. Hume offered school buildings as places for registration and asked teachers to assist in the registration process.

Registration locations were open from 7:00 a.m. to 9:00 p.m. Here are only a few of the locations used for registration:
- Bell Farm—Bell Farm schoolhouse
- Barthell—Barthell schoolhouse
- Blue Heron—Blue Heron schoolhouse
- Co-operative—Co-operative schoolhouse
- Slavens—Mr. G. A. Bell's store
- White Oak Junction—White Oak Junction schoolhouse
- Wolf Creek—Wolf Creek schoolhouse
- Worley—Worley schoolhouse

"Those required to register must do so at places convenient to them. It's necessary to say that this is one of the efforts in our victory campaign. The collaboration of all citizens is most necessary," said R. L. Stearns Jr., Chairman, Local Board No. 111.

∞

G. Lee McClain, supervisor of Kentucky Salvage Community, announced a new program called Salvage for Victory Drive. Its purpose was to ensure that no communities in the Commonwealth had one piece of scrap metal material lying around that could be used in the making of tanks, planes, ships, guns, or any other war supplies. This effort made sure Kentucky did its part in the war effort.

∞

In Co-operative, on Tuesday, February 3, Harry and Hazel Nichols, in honor of their son Harry Jr.'s twelfth birthday, gave him a birthday party and let him invite all his friends. The kids who attended were Pauline Carson, Aldie Lewis, Wilma Lewis, Wilma Dee Spradlin, Katherine Koger, Billy Jean Dolen, Dona Abbott, Yuonne Lovett, Lois Tucker, Wilma Duncan, Chloetine Chitwood, Francis Craig, Peggy Dixon, Marcella Grego, Luther Newport, Junior Craig, Bobby Winchester, Roland Bray, Eugene Wilson, Thurston Wilson, Debolin Gregory, Harold Koger, Harold Winchester, Earl Bell, Cleatus Slaven, Burman Slaven, Gerald Barrier, Shannon Cook, and Tony Max Nichols. The two ladies who helped Mrs. Nichols were Mrs. Joe Winchester and Mrs. Elmer Barrier.

∞

In the summer of 1942, Cack Slaven was promoted to Co-operative Mine Superintendent and his family moved into the big house reserved only for mine superintendents in Co-operative.

Prior to his promotion, Cack bought a late 1930s model car and decided to take the family from Oneida, Tennessee, to Grave Hill, where he grew up. In those days crossing the Big South Fork River at Yamacraw was an adventure, especially after a rain. The CCC built the raised ford of arched tunnels with a concrete slab over the top, the top being close but above the surface of the water not more than a couple feet. Often heavy rains would cause the river to crest above the ford. When that happened, no vehicles could cross. That wasn't the case when Cack and family reached the ford, but it was wet after the recent rain shower. As the Slaven's car started across, the rear wheels began spinning and Cack stopped the car and backed up to get another run at it.

Betty, Cack's wife, asked, "Are you really going to try again?"

Cack said, "Yeah."

"I want out," Betty said.

Cack said, "Just sit back and hold on."

"Now, Casalow," Betty said, "You're holding me against my will."

That time the car made it across, and it was a good thing cause if it hadn't, Betty would have walked across the ford. Betty settled down and they continued on and enjoyed the rest of the trip. On the way back home, Cack stopped at Tobe's Motel on the northside of Oneida, Tennessee, and got the family ice cream. Their son Don always remembered that stop as clearly as if it was yesterday. He would say "Stopping at a restaurant in those days was a big deal."

∞

At Co-operative, Don and Cleatus Slaven were playing around the Company Store. Cleatus was underneath the store, climbing on the beams that went from bank to bank supporting the store above the creek. Boys regularly played on those beams, but Cleatus didn't see what rolled up and parked close to the store—a pop truck. Don, on the other hand, saw the pop truck and wasn't about to leave the porch of the store, seeing the driver carry in those different colored pops. Don saw orange, strawberry, and grape; he didn't think he could live if he didn't get one of those pops.

Don broke into a run as fast as he could toward home. Cleatus, seeing him running, yelled, "Where are you going?" Don didn't answer nor was he going to waste time to slow down. What was on his mind was getting home. For Don to get home, he had to run across the ballfield and up a small hill to the mine superintendent's house. Going through the front doorway—his mom had the door open—he scanned the front room as he continued walking into the kitchen. There she was at the cookstove. Don walked up close to his mom and asked, "Mom, you got a nickel?" He explained why he needed the nickel. Betty, his mom, reached out and patted him on the head and said, "Honey, I don't have a nickel."

Don didn't want to hear that cause he had his heart set on one of those colored pops, which he had never seen before. Don walked out of the kitchen and off the back porch; he thought he would die if he didn't get one of those pops. With no choice, Don dealt with the fact he wouldn't get a pop today and probably wouldn't tomorrow. It would be several days later when Don finally got the money to buy a grape pop; he thought he'd died and gone to heaven.

∞

Summer break ended and the new school year began. Co-operative teachers announced that the students would help our soldiers win the war by collecting anything made of metal. The students got a couple of afternoons off from school each month to do just that. The metal they found, they brought back to the playground and put it in a single pile. When the kids gathered enough for a load, a truck came and picked it up.

∞

Going across the creek in front of Co-operative School and up the mountain, E. B. Farley, principal, often took fifteen to twenty boys with him to look for fallen trees. Any tree already on the ground, the school could use for firewood. Two buildings each housing two large rooms meant starting a fire in four stoves each day through fall and winter, which took a lot of wood. Upon finding a fallen tree, the boys paired up and took turns cutting the tree into manageable lengths to drag back to the school. By taking turns cutting, no two boys did all the work.

After the tree was cut, they tied ropes around each section and three or four boys dragged each section of the wood down the mountain, across the creek, and up close to the school wood/coal shed. There, they sawed the sections into shorter chunks, and then the boys would pair off and use a wedge and an axe to split the chunks into manageable pieces for burning. In those days, using a wedge about twelve inches long, one end pointed and the other flat for hitting, to drive into the wood was common practice. The single blade axe did double duty; opposite the sharp edge was a flat side for hammering the wedge.

After the wood was split by the wedge, some pieces were split again into smaller pieces for kindling, which made a good fire starter. The storage shed was out in front of the schoolhouses. Half of the little building was used to store coal, the other half, wood that needed to be dry for starting a fire. Gathering in wood from over on the mountain was done two to three times a month until the principal felt there was enough to get them through the winter months.

Through the years Co-operative Mine operated, the railroad track went right by the front of the schoolhouse. In the fall, the Stearns Coal and Lumber Company would drop coal off close to the shed. The principal would let a few of the older boys leave the classroom to throw the coal in the shed. The boys that got picked to do the job felt they were the lucky ones; getting out of the classroom sometimes was fun even if the work was hard.

∞

Another rationing order was handed down—food commodity. Starting in early March, sugar was limited to one pound a week per person. According to Leon Henderson, price administrator, the order would recover some excess from persons who had hoarded supplies. So hoarding was the reason behind taking action against the first food item of the war. Mr. Henderson also stated the most important reason for rationing sugar was to ensure all customers were treated fairly. There would be enough sugar to go around if people did their part by restricting their purchases of sugar to the minimum allowed amount. Retailers were expected to adhere to the rationing order and to restrict the amount of sugar an individual family could purchase.

Gas rationing went into effect November 22. Application forms were placed at gas stations, garages, and other convenient locations. Anyone owning a car or motorcycle was required to pick up an application form if they wanted to purchase gas, said Chairman of McCreary County War Price and Rationing Board, R. G. Powell. The completed application forms along with vehicle registration cards were taken to one of the authorized locations, where folks were issued a rationing book for 240 miles of driving a month. The authorized locations included schools in Co-operative, Parkers Lake, Whitley City, and Pine Knot, and the Local Rationing Board. Motorcycle owners were issued rationing books good for similar mileage. No supplemental rations would be issued, period.

∞

The daughter of Mr. and Mrs. Bill Bell of Gregory, Dorthea Bell, fifteen-years-old, died at home. Dorthea was survived by her parents, two sisters (Mrs. Christine Parks and Mrs. Jewell Kidd), and one brother (Estill Bell, U.S. Army).

∞

Our nation's capital issued this statement because of the war effort: We request businessmen, every elected official, and the general public to not use outdoor Christmas lighting this year. This request doesn't apply to indoor Christmas decorations.

In Co-operative, even though there would be no outdoor Christmas lighting, some of the boys got together and set up a Christmas tree in the middle of the ballfield to continue the tradition.

∞

(In my book *CO-OP: Coal, Community, & House 52*, in Chapter 2, I told the story about Frank Gregory and the gunfight outside of Neil Kidd's beer store in Co-operative. After the book was published, I learned more details.) Frank Gregory and Charlie Burks stepped out into the night and off the porch of the beer store. Charlie, who remembered he'd carried his rifle with him earlier that evening and propped it on the porch, within a few steps had his rifle in hand. Not waiting to find out if Frank had a weapon, Charlie took aim and fired his .22 rifle, the bullet hitting Frank beneath the heart.

Could it have been the boys had too much to drink and argued over a billiard game? Could Frank have been arguing with Hubert Burks, Charlie's dad? We'll never know the answer.

Charlie left the scene and ended up at a friend's house at Kidd's Crossing. Frank Gregory, age twenty-six, was taken to McDowell Hospital in Danville, where he died Sunday morning at 9:00 a.m. Frank was employed by Stearns Coal and Lumber Company at Co-operative Mine. Frank's family, his parents, brothers, and sisters, lived in Co-operative.

After Frank died, the charge against Charlie Burks, fourteen years old, was changed to murder. Another warrant was sworn out for Guy Smith, Estil Smith, Lincoln Burks, and Hubert Burks, father of Charlie. They were charged with "banding and considering." Newly elected Sheriff Sam Thomas arrested Charlie Burks.

∞

MARRIED THIS YEAR 1942

In the community of Barthell, Robert Vaughn, age 19, son of Henry Vaughn, and Truie Waters, age 19, the daughter of Henry Waters, tied the knot.

Also, in Barthell, Alfred Douglas and Emma Daugherty got married.

In Co-operative, Ted Foster, age 28, the son of George Foster, married Ocle Roberts, age 26, the daughter of George Roberts.

∞

BORN THIS YEAR 1942

Billy Gene (Buddy) Nichols
Archie Shoopman
Elmer Shoopman
Joyce Hardwick
Sue Winchester
Lucille Troxell
Opal Thompson
Johnny Gregory
Jean Dobbs
Barbara Shepherd
Janice Pauline Waters
John Simpson Hall
Grace Gregory
Eugene Hall
Brenda Gregory
Bobby Haynes
Judy Freeman
William Clark
Sue Blevins

CHAPTER 15

1943

Arnold and Geneva Shoopman moved to Hickory Knob from Fidelity so Arnold could be closer to his work at Co-operative Mine. Co-operative Mine had a mine on top of the incline and one at the bottom of the incline. This move to Hickory Knob got Arnold very close to the mine on top of the incline, where he worked.

They moved into the house Frank King had built years before. The house was to the right of where the Hickory Knob Church would later be built. When Frank and his wife lived there, the house had a five-acre field on the backside. But they found water on the frontside, so they dug the well there, a good walk from the house. Frank got tired of hearing Mrs. King complain about how far she had to go to get water. One day Frank took a team of horses, cut logs, and laid them down to give the house something to ride on when moved. Frank and his horses pulled the house across the field close to the well.

So when Arnold and Geneva moved into the house, it was sitting close to the well. The house didn't have a porch but the house they'd moved from did. And they wanted a porch. Arnold talked to Stearns Company officials. Stearns gave him permission to take the porch off the house in Fidelity, the house they had moved from. The Stearns officials said the house in Fidelity would be torn down eventually anyway. Arnold and Geneva walked to Fidelity to their old house and disassembled the porch and carried it home to Hickory Knob. It took Arnold and Geneva several trips. Arnold then reassembled the porch to their new house.

While the Shoopmans lived in Hickory Knob those couple of years, their milk cow died, so Arnold decided to bury the cow in the cellar on the backside of the field where the house used to be located. Arnold thought it was the perfect place since the hole was already dug.

Where Arnold worked, the incline was almost perpendicular with the cliff face, and Stearns Company built a double track on the incline that was operated and winched by steel cables. As the empty cars went up the incline on one track, the two-ton cars loaded with coal from the mine came down the incline on the other track. Reaching the bottom, the coal cars moved on to the tipple. There the cars were emptied and the coal separated into the different sizes.

The mine on top of the incline closed this year and Arnold was transferred to the mine at the bottom of the incline. The mine at the bottom had eight-foot coal, and in some places, nine-foot coal. Knowing he would soon be working at the bottom of the incline, just before the mine on top of the incline closed completely, Arnold and Geneva moved. At the bottom of the incline, there were five houses that lined the tram track going around a curve before reaching the tipple. They moved into the first house just down from the pond to the right of the incline track.

The system of getting the coal off the top of the incline had its share of danger and mishaps. But at the time, it was the best Stearns Company could come up with.

No one knew how or why the loaded car got loose that day, and it was lucky no kids were in the yard playing. It may have been a school day, but when the loaded car got loose, it was going too fast to stay on the track. It came off the track hitting the small embankment in front of the Shoopman home, then went airborne, and came to rest on the porch. One corner of the car was just inches away from the front door. If it had made contact, it would have torn the door off its hinges and sent it somewhere inside, but thank goodness that didn't happen. But there was coal all over the porch and front yard. The derailed coal car scattered and flung coal all down the right side of the Shoopman home and into the backyard. That year, Arnold didn't have to worry about getting coal in for the winter.

∞

That summer, Neil Kidd asked his oldest son, Bob, to round up three or four of his friends for a job Neil had for them. RL Terry and the boys walked to Jewell Kidd's Grocery store the next morning. Neil asked the boys if they would wash some cars in the creek for him. "Sure," they all said.

Bob, RL, and three other boys walked up the holler past Grant Roberts's place. Sitting there in a row were eight beautiful cars, especially beautiful to these boys since they rarely saw a beautiful car. The best that can be figured out, Neil had connections with a big dealership, either in Somerset or Danville. RL remembered hearing Louisville tossed around a couple times. But the boys had no way of knowing for sure where exactly the dealership was. At the time, those boys didn't care where the dealership was and since the factories were converted to support the war effort, 1941 models would be the last cars made for a while, at least till the end of the war, maybe longer.

Neil would bring out one of the cars at a time; when it sold, he'd bring out another one. Neil kept a watchful eye on those cars. When they got dusty, Bob would round up the boys and they'd spend a Saturday afternoon cleaning the cars. It wasn't widely known where Neil kept the cars; the cars were completely hidden from any passersby. The boys didn't gossip about their job of washing the cars, even though Neil hadn't told them not to. They just knew it was the right thing to do. Neil paid the boys well for their work: Each boy got a quarter, a bologna sandwich, and a bottle of pop. That was good money for a boy in those days and they felt lucky to get it.

∞

In White Oak Junction, Sergeant Woodrow Winchester came home on furlough to visit his parents, Mr. and Mrs. Charlie Winchester. At the time, Sergeant Winchester was stationed at Fort Hood, Texas. Winchester had been in the army for four years and was home only four days when he had to be taken to the Darrell Government Hospital in Danville. He and

Dewey Pennington and others were playing cards on a hill up from the White Oak Junction Church. Suddenly Pennington jumped on him. He had no idea why Pennington cut him. Pennington had his knife ready and began slashing when he attacked. Sergeant Winchester had wounds on both hands, both legs, one arm, and one severe cut to the back of the neck. It took fifty-two stitches to close up all of Sergeant Winchester's wounds.

Dewey Pennington fled the scene, and it wasn't until two weeks later he was arrested by Scott County Sheriff Butler in Huntsville, Tennessee. Pennington was arrested on two charges: one for selling moonshine and the other for maliciously cutting and wounding Sergeant Winchester while the Sergeant was on furlough.

∞

A few weeks later in another part of McCreary County, four Yamacraw boys climbed into a Model A Ford and drove to Marshes Siding, between two and three miles north of Whitley City. The boys no doubt had preplanned the excursion. They pulled up and stopped in front of Anderson Barnett's business, got out, and left the car running. Mr. Barnett, a former coal miner, was now a merchant, owning a store and gas station next to his home. It was 2:00 a.m. Mr. Barnett and his wife were likely sound asleep, but he had the reputation of getting up any hour of the night to accommodate the public.

The boys woke Mr. Barnett. He got up, walked out of his home, and opened up his store. One of the boys followed Mr. Barnett into the store. After Mr. Barnett turned on the lights, the boy said he needed a quart of oil, a pack of cigarettes, and four bars of candy. Shortly after Mr. Barnett had placed the boy's items on the counter, one of the other boys came in with a handkerchief over his face holding a pistol. Mr. Barnett refused the demands for money. He likely told them if they couldn't pay for the items to get out of his place, that he was going home and back to bed. He must have turned his back to them to turn off the lights because the boy holding the gun fired three times, two shots hitting Mr. Barnett in the back, one through the heart.

Mrs. Barnett testified that she became suspicious after her husband got up and went out. She got up to investigate. When she reached the door of their home and looked in the direction of the store, she saw the Model A Ford with the engine running. Then she saw a boy come out of the store and hurriedly get in the car; it left heading north. Mrs. Barnett had not heard gunshots, probably because the engine of the car made so much noise. When she reached the store door, she looked in and saw her husband lying on the floor. From the way the store looked, it appeared there had been a struggle. Mrs. Barnett immediately called the sheriff's office and then summoned relatives.

It was apparent the boys got scared and ran because the quart of oil, cigarettes, and candy were still on the counter. Sheriff Sam Thomas and Highway Patrolman Lane Bertram drove off in the direction Mrs. Barnett said the car went and before morning rounded up two cars fitting the description: one group of boys on Day Ridge Road, another group of boys at Hill Top. Not long after their arrest, the four boys at Hill Top confessed to the murder. The other group found on Day Ridge Road was released Sunday morning.

The four boys who confessed to Sheriff Thomas and Highway Patrolman Bertram were Ray Nelson, Pascal Foust (sixteen years old), Louis New (eighteen years old), and Chester Inman who had received a medical discharge from the army only two months earlier.

Within three weeks, Ray Nelson was tried, found guilty, and sentenced; he was given the death penalty for the murder of Anderson Barnett.

The following week, Attorney Crit Bird filed affidavits for Ray Nelson to the Court of Appeals; the defense argued that not enough time had passed between indictment and trial. It took over four months for the high court to decide; the court gave Nelson a new trial, which took place later in 1942.

∞

Away from the courtroom, what was on people's minds was the war. Rationing books were issued and local newspapers published instructions on how to use them. People were being asked to save everything from grease to tin cans. Salvage Chairman for McCreary County, Lucien Bryant, asked all mothers to save all excess grease from their kitchens. School children were asked to collect cans and any scrap metal in their neighborhoods. In Co-operative, the drop-off place continued to be the school playground in the far area next to the creek. Also, across the country people were asked not to save their pennies; the army needed the copper.

∞

Those days, a pie supper was a pleasant distraction, and one was planned and held at Co-operative School. The young women of the community brought their home-baked pies in colorfully decorated boxes or wrappings, which usually meant a pretty display for folks to admire. Mrs. Luther Newport made a "guess cake"; to win the cake, you had to guess what kind of cake it was. Your only clue was a wrapped, small piece of onion blade that went with the cake. The one who finally guessed it was Debloise Gregory.

The winner of the prettiest girl contest was Miss Anna Belle Winchester. The title of the ugliest man was won by William Spradlin. Prizes were awarded for each of these events. The teachers of the Co-operative School were in charge of planning and preparing for the event. L. C. Bruce, Chairman of the Local USO Drive, helped in the planning. The Kentucky Ramblers furnished the music for the evening. All proceeds of $82.80 went to the USO Drive. The night was a complete success, and for the community of Co-operative, it was a night of entertainment and fun. For a brief couple hours, those who attended had a chance to forget the rationing and the hardships they were enduring.

∞

Moonshine continued to be the preferred drink for many. One thing was for sure, you didn't want to be caught with it or be under suspicion of making it, as it was for Dick Slaven and Austin Slaven who were arrested on moonshine charges on the same day. Just days apart from that, Charles Anderson of Yamacraw was arrested in Hill Top with a gallon of moonshine. Just hours later, Bill Dulin Slaven of Co-operative, riding his mule down the road from Exotus, had two gallons of White Lightning in grass sacks (grass sacks were burlap bags that potatoes and other items came in when purchased from the store) slung across his mule. He was stopped and arrested on the spot: the charge, transporting an illegal drink.

∞

Before the year ended, Ray Nelson, facing death by electric chair, was brought back to trial. When the new trial was over, Nelson was given a life sentence. Ray took the stand and testified he was drunk at the time and was not responsible for his actions. The other three accomplices, already beginning to serve their life sentences, stated Nelson had drunk a pint of liquor just thirty minutes before stopping at Anderson Barnett's business.

∞

MARRIED THIS YEAR 1943

Raymond Clark, the son of Arthur and Nancy Clark, grew up in the Wolf Creek area. In those days, Wolf Creek had a one-room school which also served as a church house on Sundays. The one-room school accommodated grades 1–8. Arthur, Raymond's dad, was transferred to Mine 16 in Paint Cliff, and when a house became available, he moved his family there. Paint Cliff also had a one-room school and it was there Raymond got acquainted with the beautiful Darkie Coffey.

Darkie was the daughter of William and Laura Coffey. Raymond's sister Nellie and Darkie were best friends in school and their friendship continued throughout their lives. I assume Raymond and Darkie were childhood sweethearts since not long after Raymond secured a job with Stearns Coal and Lumber Company, at the age of seventeen, Raymond and Darkie were married. Hobert Perry performed the ceremony. Born in this marriage were Linville, Glenna, Wanda, Rayma Dean, Reba, Kay, Faron, and Ila.

Another couple started their journey together also: Andrew (Andy) Herbert Watson and Bonnie Clark. Andrew Herbert Watson, whose parents were Frank Kelly Watson and Sarah Watson, was born in Elna, Tennessee. As a boy, Andy grew up in the Bald Knob area. At the age of twenty-two, Andy went to work with K & T Railway under the umbrella of Stearns Coal and Lumber Company. Andy's first day of work was the day after Christmas 1939.

Bonnie Clark was born in 1927 to Bo and Louvada Clark. Bo also worked for K & T Railway, and the Clarks lived in White Oak Junction. As a young girl growing up, Bonnie learned from her mother, and as she grew older, she eased the burden of her mother's work by carrying drinking water and washing their clothes in Rock Creek as other ladies did in those days. During those early days, Andy's means of getting around was his horse. When he was not working, he rode his horse everywhere he went.

One day, Bonnie was at the pump getting water when she saw a horse go by and the guy riding was good looking. Bonnie began noticing that the horse went by about the same time every day, so Bonnie made sure she was at the pump around that time. The pump was close to the White Oak Junction schoolhouse, and in those days, the road crossed the creek and curved around under the train bridge. But before going under the train bridge, the road ran close to the school playground. One day Andy saw Bonnie and he rode over close to her. They began talking. They made a point of seeing each other at the same time for several days. The courtship flourished and they got married before year's end on the railroad tracks in White Oak Junction. Born in this marriage were Louise, Clora, Novella, Jack, Dovie, Betty, Wanda, Jerry, Barbie, Andy Jr., Stanley, and Robert (Duke).

(Bonnie Clark is the only woman I know in those days who met her man riding a horse. I don't know if the horse was white or not, but Bonnie got her knight in shining armor.)

In Co-operative, Okley H. Bowden and Ruth Aleen (last name unknown) got married.

Also in Co-operative, Reverend Henry Cox and Vern New got married.

∞

BORN THIS YEAR 1943

Joan Chitwood
Betty Imogene Dixon
Gene M. Davis
Delois Shoopman
Janice King
Georgia Bell
Lou Wilson
Harold Whitehead

Joyce Coffey
Virgil Leon Lewis
George Slaven
Margie Anderson
Wilma Douglas
Sharon Jones
Virgie Gibson
Dallas Whitehead
Jim Maples
Joyce Moore
Barbara Cox

CHAPTER 16

1944

In 1944 and even at the start of the war, the administration in Washington, D.C., felt the men who went inside the earth to dig for coal were essential to our nation's victory in the war.

Deputy Solid Fuel Coordinator for the war, Howard A. Gray said the coal miner was as essential as the soldier: We can't win a war without an adequate coal supply. The man who swings a pick and shovel in the mines and stays on the job is making a contribution that is as patriotic as the man who joins a branch of the military. Furthermore, the man who stays on the job and works every day without fail getting out the nation's fighting fuel has a devotion of duty just like the soldier marching off to the battlefield.

Sadly, this positive attitude toward the coal miner was not popularized with the general public sufficiently to stay the test of time. Instead, I fear the coal miner has become a mere footnote in history. I hope as you read this book you gain a deeper understanding and appreciation for the men who risked their lives daily to dig the fuel our nation ran on and the war depended on. With this enormous responsibility on their shoulders, they still found themselves barely able to provide food and clothing for their families.

These same people had a giving heart; even with so little, they were willing to give to others in need and, in this case, a nation in need. The war bond drive for the month of February in McCreary County exceeded its goal of $150,000. Rallies were held three different nights throughout the month in the schoolhouse in Co-operative. The Kentucky Ramblers provided music for those on hand. The total for the Co-operative School was $5,600 and Miss Marcella Gregory worked independently and raised an additional $1,675. White Oak Junction posted a total of $7,300.

∞

Only days following the war bond drive, Jewell Kidd's Grocery in Co-operative was burglarized, the thieves stealing $300.00 in cash and scrip. The next day, a Whitley City merchant reported to the sheriff's office that three teenage boys wanted him to trade a large amount of scrip for cash; since these three young boys did not work, the merchant wondered where they had gotten the scrip. The three boys were Stacy Spradlin, Conley Bell, and Rufus Kidd; all were arrested by Deputy Sheriff Ottis Clark on charges of breaking into Jewell Kidd's Grocery. More scrip was found on the ground behind the store. Did the youths take only what they thought they needed or could carry, or did they accidentally drop the scrip in their haste to get away?

∞

The following Saturday, a group of young boys went to the picture show in Whitley City. Returning home, they cut across a field where they noticed two sagging electric wires. Curiosity got the best of one of the boys, and Orville Perry, age twelve, the son of Mr. and Mrs. Ernest Perry of Whitley City, grabbed a wire in each hand. Orville collapsed to the ground the very instant he touched the wires; his companions carried him a quarter of a mile to the home of John Strunk where he was given first aid. Orville received severe burns on both hands, arms, and chest. The boy was saved from electrocution by an automatic cut-off switch breaker that cut power as soon as he made contact.

After Orville Perry was given first aid, he was rushed to the hospital in Danville, where it was first believed he might lose his fingers, but according to medical staff, that action would be the last resort. He remained in the hospital.

The superintendent of South Kentucky Rural Electric, Sam Hoard, released a statement that the line was a primary extension wire carrying 6,000 volts. He also stated the heavy rains in recent weeks had soaked the ground so much that the anchor to the pole had pulled loose, causing the pole to lean and the wires to sag. According to Hoard's statement, Rural Electric had not been notified of the condition of the pole and electric wires.

∞

In White Oak Junction, Rose Dixon had not seen her Uncle John and Aunt Mollie Flynn since she was pregnant with Betty, and Betty was now a little over a year old. Saturday morning, Rose told Harrison, her husband, she wanted to visit them. Harrison said, "Go on. I have things to do." Rose knew what that meant: playing cards and drinking moonshine with the guys. Rose was determined not to let what Harrison might do stop her. The older kids knew their mom's intentions and couldn't wait to get started; they promised they'd help with young Betty.

From White Oak Junction to Wolf Creek where the Flynns lived, in those days, Rose took the shortcut as everyone would have. She walked the road by the White Oak Junction Church, went up the holler, and walked about a half a mile past several family homes. Then the road turned into no more than a wagon trail. Following the wagon trail to the top of the mountain, Rose and the kids ended up on Rattlesnake Ridge. They then walked the gravel road west about three quarters of a mile, turned north (or right), and walked down the other side of the mountain. The Wolf Creek area included most of that side of the mountain. But Rose's Uncle John and Aunt Mollie's place was where the road leveled out.

Mollie and John were happy to see Rose and the kids, and they were them. It was close to lunch time. Mollie had everything ready—a kettle of pinto beans on the stove and a pone of corn bread in the oven, ready to come out. John took the boys to the back porch where they washed their hands in a pan of water, there for that purpose.

They all ate, and after the meal, the boys said they wanted to go out and play. The Dixon boys walked a ways down the gravel road and found some neighborhood boys. It didn't take long to get a ball game going. It also didn't take long before two of the neighbor boys and Don Dixon started arguing. Well, Don argued, but when he got mad, the fight was on. Don whipped every boy there, and they all ran home not to be seen the rest of the day. Don's brothers knew better than to say anything when Don was mad, so they all watched. Paul Walters, a neighbor of John's, had walked over to visit about the time the ball game started, and Paul and John were sitting on the front porch talking. The two men saw everything that happened. Paul looked at John and said, "There's a dynamite fist," speaking of Don Dixon. Old man Paul Walters perfectly named Don that day, because along life's journey, several men would taste and feel the wrath of Dynamite Fist.

∞

The twelve-year-old Orville Perry who was hospitalized from taking hold of two electric wires a few weeks earlier got more bad news. The hospital informed the family that Orville's left arm had to be amputated below the elbow and the right arm might have to be done the same on a different day. Such devastating news.

∞

On Friday at Co-operative Mine, Walter Watson had been working outside most of the day, but in the afternoon he went inside the mine for something. In the process of doing that, he sat down, not realizing he was close to the lead wire. With his clothes wet with sweat, there was no escaping electrocution. Men close to him ran immediately and tried for over an hour to resuscitate him, but their friend was gone. Walter, age thirty-four, was the son of Ransom and Rose Emerine Watson of Barthell. Walter was survived by his wife and four sons (Luther, Lester, Chester, and Jesse). They lived on the mountain in front of Guy Kidd's Grocery.

∞

On Sunday, September 10, a revival started at New Haven Baptist Church in Co-operative. The revival was held at the schoolhouse because the church house was not yet built. In the upper room where seventh and eighth grades were taught, also dubbed as a church house on Sundays, Reverend Leland Thomas from Oneida, Tennessee, took charge of the revival.

∞

Summer break for school kids in Co-operative was over. The new school year began September 12, which was a Tuesday, because a teachers' meeting was called on Monday, September 11.

∞

The following month, in October, a pie supper was held at the schoolhouse also in the seventh and eighth grade room. The ladies who organized it were Miss Chloetine Chitwood, Miss Ruby Gregory, and Miss Pauline Simpson. The Kentucky Ramblers played music, and at the end of the evening, $143 had been raised, all given to the war fund drive.

CO-OPERATIVE, KENTUCKY
CO-OPERATIVE COAL TIPPLE
PHOTO COURTESY OF
THE *MCCREARY COUNTY RECORD*.

∞

Three men in suits got off the train in Stearns and walked up the street to the Stearns Company Office Headquarters. Mr. Butler had been notified ten days earlier the men were coming. Mr. Butler had arranged for Mr. Thomas Arthur Creekmore to drive the men to Co-operative. Mr. Creekmore owned and operated a taxi service and Mr. Butler hired the taxi service from time to time when Stearns Company visitors needed to go to a particular location. There had been many times when coal buyers visited Stearns, and Stearns Company officials would take them to show off their operation in a particular coal camp. Today was much the same except these three men were from the War Department in Washington, D.C.

In those days the gravel road to Co-operative went around Rattlesnake Ridge and connected to Dobbs Mountain. It then went through and down Dobbs Mountain hill into Co-operative. From Jewell Kidd's Grocery to Stearns Company Store in Co-operative was a mile east. Mr. Creekmore pulled his taxi close to Stearns Company Store, and the three men got out and went into the store. Inside the store, the men were directed to the coal tipple where Cack Slaven's office was, the man they needed to see.

From the Company Store, the three men walked up the hill close to the hotel to the tram tracks. The men walked the tram tracks to the top of the tipple, quite a jaunt, and as they started walking out on the tipple, as long and as high as the Co-operative tipple was, it must have given those men an exhilarating rush. For anyone afraid of heights, this wasn't the place to be. From the top of the tipple, it was roughly eighty feet to the ground, farther in some places. The tipple stretched from cliff to cliff. At the time it was built in 1920–1922, it was one of the largest, if not the largest, tipple Stearns Company had built. The offices of the mine superintendent, tipple foreman, and tonnage keeper were at the center of the tipple. The center was also where coal was emptied out of the coal cars into a conveyor that separated the coal by size and loaded it into coal gons on the railroad tracks below. (Gon is short for gondola and means an open railroad freight car.)

Each loaded car the tipple received had a brass tag attached to it that the coal loader put on it when he loaded the car inside the mine. Each miner had a unique number stamped on brass tags which told the tonnage keeper which coal miner loaded the car, the system for keeping track of each miner's coal production each day.

The following is part conjecture on my part. Cack would have been alerted by the tipple foreman that the men were on their way to his office and Cack would have come outside to greet the men. Cack would have let the men look around the tipple before taking them into his office. Cack's office wasn't directly over the conveyors and shakers. The three offices extended out from the side of the tipple, so when Cack closed his door, you could still hear noise, but the noise was muffled and business could be conducted.

One of the men handed Cack a single-page document explaining who and why they were there, and the man said, "It's our understanding that one of your mines has candle coal."

"Yes, that's correct," Cack said.

The man said, "We want the candle coal to help in developing a bomb. Starting next week, we want you to run nothing but candle coal every day, including the night shift, for five days. We'll have it picked up at Stearns."

Cack would not have questioned the request. Everyone did what they could to support the war effort. The three men in suits left and were not seen in Co-operative again. Cack ran nothing but candle coal for one week. The coal gons were left together on the sidetrack in Stearns. Just as the men had promised, at the end of the week, an engine came, hooked to the loaded cars, and took them away.

∞

MARRIED THIS YEAR 1944

John Calvin Williams, age 40, of White Oak Junction, and Barjilla Adeline Watson, age 22, daughter of Ransom Watson of Barthell, got married. Reverend J. B. Dabney of Whitley City performed the ceremony.

The same day Rose Dixon and her kids went to Wolf Creek to visit relatives, in Co-operative, John Cox, age 48, and Fronia Phillips, age 44, both of Co-operative, got married.

∞

BORN THIS YEAR 1944

Sherdina Worley (my sister)
Jimmy Hardwick
Lindell Kidd
Linville Clark
Opal Jones
Kay Winchester

Estle Keith
Helen Gregory
Eddie Coffey
Eugene Shoopman
Roy David Black
Nelson Hall
Linville Lloyd Hall
Alma Ruth Haynes
JB Cooper
Bill Shook
Goman Clark
Clifford Maples
Sue Cox
Guy Sherman Blevins
James Murphy

CHAPTER 17

Uncle Roy

Roy Dobbs became my uncle when he and Mom's sister Greedle married back in 1939. Roy, the son of Sherman and Ada Dobbs, grew up on Dobbs Mountain along with his brother, Dewey, and sister, Lela. By 1945, Roy and Greedle's first son, Lindell, and only daughter, Jean, were born. Son Clifford was born the following year.

∞

Uncle Roy's brother, Dewey, was in the army and the last known place he was stationed was Pearl Harbor. In those days, very little news of the war trickled in over the radio. Parents with sons halfway around the globe, hearing almost no news about the war, I'm sure, had a very difficult time coping. Es-

UNCLE ROY DOBBS
FAMILY PHOTO

pecially if they'd received no letter from the son in several weeks.

Ada, Roy and Dewey's mother, wrote to Dewey regularly. Ada had written a letter but had no envelope to mail it in. Uncle Roy and Aunt Greedle lived in Copin Camp in Co-operative and Uncle Roy would go see his mom and dad every weekend. Ada gave the letter she'd written Dewey to Uncle Roy to mail. She had the address on a separate piece of paper and told Uncle Roy to ask Mr. Craig, postmaster, to address the envelope. Ada folded it all up together and gave it to Uncle Roy, and he said he'd take care of it.

Uncle Roy walked into the Company Store in Co-operative and asked Mr. L. L. Craig to address an envelope for him. The U.S. Post Office section sat on a part of the counter space and took up about six feet of the overall length of the counter and stood about four feet high on the counter. The mail slots were tilted slightly downward and inward so any mail placed in the boxes would stay in as it was inserted. The side customers faced had glass doors and the number of the mailbox was the same number as the house they lived in. So each customer could glance in their box and could clearly see if they had mail. In the center of the mailboxes on the counter was an open space. The space was used to pass mail to the postmaster to be mailed or for the postmaster to give the customer mail if they had mail in their mailbox.

Mr. Craig walked behind the post office counter and reached down and got an envelope. He then asked, "Okay, Roy, where's it going?"

Roy pulled the piece of paper out of his pocket his mom had written the address on, and said, "Put, put Dewey Dobbs, Hala Woola, Hala Walla."

"What?" Mr. Craig asked, hiding laughter behind his voice.

Roy said, "Here. This is what Mom writ."

Mr. Craig looked at the address. "Oh," Mr. Craig said, "It goes to Private Dewey Dobbs, Honolulu, Hawaii." It took a good long time before Mr. Craig let Ole Roy live this one down. At least once a week, Mr. Craig broke out in laughter and told somebody. Uncle Roy didn't go around the Company Store often because if he did Mr. Craig was sure to ask him about Hala Woola, Hala Walla.

∞

My cousin Carl Jones, son of Robert and Ethel Jones, spent a lot of time at Uncle Roy and Aunt Greedle's house. Carl's dad was a brother to Greedle and my mother, Lexie Mae. Uncle Roy's older son, Lindell, and Carl were not only cousins but also good friends.

Uncle Roy came home one day and said he had stopped twice on the way home to put the fan belt back on the car. After supper, Uncle Roy said he was going out to see if he could figure out what was wrong with his car.

Carl said he'd go, too, so Carl followed Uncle Roy. As Carl got to the door, Lindell said he was going to wait a while before bringing in the coal and wood so he'd just hang in the house.

Through the front yard of about twenty-five feet, then about three steps down, on across the main gravel road going through Dobbs Mountain is where Roy parked his car. Getting to the car, Uncle Roy raised the hood and walked around and started the engine. Uncle Roy got out of the car and walked around to the front of the car to watch the engine idle.

Cousin Carl was there watching also. Then it happened.

The fan belt started trying to come off the generator pulley. The belt was no doubt old and worn, maybe even stretched some. With the engine still running, Uncle Roy reached down, grabbed a hold of the belt to try to push it back in place. Almost at the same instant, he jerked his hand back and the tips of three fingers were burned and cut where the rotating belt peeled the skin back. Uncle Roy clasped his fingers with his right hand and told Carl to turn off the car and bring the battery inside because it was going to be very cold that night.

Carl did as Uncle Roy asked. When Carl came in with the battery, Uncle Roy was sitting at the kitchen table and Aunt Greedle was bandaging his hand. Uncle Roy said, "Just put the battery in the corner behind the heating stove."

By now Lindell said he was going out to bring in the coal and wood. Carl went back out with Lindell. Lindell said, "I need to bust up some kindling for Mom's cookstove for the morning fire." When Lindell figured he had enough kindling, he loaded it in his arms and picked up several sticks of bigger wood. Carl grabbed the two buckets of coal. By now Carl had been outside altogether quite a while and he had gotten cold after the sun went down.

Carl placed the two buckets of coal close to the heating stove in the front room and sat down on the floor behind the stove to warm up. After Carl had sat there long enough to get the front of him warm, he stood up, thinking he might warm his back side. But as he got up, he couldn't help but think something didn't feel right on his behind. Carl reached around to his back side and could feel his long handles were damp with something, but he had no idea what. He also had no idea why he could feel his long handles since he should have felt his pants. Carl jerked his pants around as far as he could and saw the whole seat of his pants was gone. When Carl looked at the floor behind him, he saw the seat of his pants on the floor and noticed the floor was wet. Carl figured the wetness had to come from the battery and that meant battery acid. The battery must have gotten too hot making the battery acid seep out and run to the very spot Carl had been sitting.

Carl quickly went into a bedroom and pulled his clothes off. Lucky for him the acid had not reached his skin. Greedle said his pants and long handles would have to be discarded; they had soaked up too much acid, but that was what saved his skin. Uncle Roy let Carl borrow a pair of his pants but said he would need to bring them back when he next visited. Carl had no problem with bringing those pants back. Uncle Roy was heavy, and those pants went around Carl a lot more than he needed. Carl would most definitely bring them back.

Several days later, a friend of the family stopped by after hearing Roy had hurt his hand. At this time, I can't remember the gentleman's name. But that's not as important as what happened next. Uncle Roy's hand had almost healed, so Uncle Roy was explaining what the car was doing and everything that happened.

The man said, "I still can't figure out how you hurt your hand, Roy."

Uncle Roy said, "Well, just come out here and I'll show you."

They both walked outside across the road to the car, and Uncle Roy raised the hood. Uncle Roy secured the cable to the hot (positive) post and went around and started the car. Uncle Roy came back to the front of the car, and when the fan belt started trying to roll off the generator pulley, he reached down, grabbed a hold of the belt, pushing it at the same time, and jerked his hand back in one motion. He injured the same tips of his fingers on the same hand, but this time he lost a little more blood. Anyone standing close by could hear Ole Roy say "Yeah, yeah, yeah" as he hurried back inside to be bandaged—again.

∞

Uncle Roy, Aunt Greedle, Mary Smith, and Grace Davis sang together in church. Mary Smith was Veto Smith's wife and Grace Davis was Earl Davis's wife. The four became rather popular in the area and various churches invited them to sing, especially during revivals when they were featured singers. At the time, they were quite good and revered by all who heard them.

One day, Ole Roy found a good deal on a pair of imitation leather gloves with pretty white fur lining. He was forever the consummate bargain finder. It was late fall or early winter and cold, and that same evening the group was scheduled to sing at a church.

In church as the service got underway, Uncle Roy kept his gloves on until it was time for the group to get up and sing. He was proud of those gloves, and he had been complimented several times before church started. When it was time to get up and sing, Uncle Roy pulled his gloves off, laid them on the seat where he was sitting, picked up his song book, and walked to the front of the church. When his hand brushed across his nose, he had not noticed his hands were almost completely white with fur, a little fur stuck to the tip of his nose, which was now causing a tickle on his lip. He brushed his lip and left a lot of fur on his lip and then he rubbed his mouth with his whole hand and more stuck to his lips and mouth. Then he noticed his hands.

By now people were snickering and a few were laughing. Uncle Roy stopped, walked to where he had been sitting, sat down, took out his handkerchief, wiped his nose and mouth, cleaned his hands, and got back up. Those close by could hear him softly say, "Yeah, yeah, yeah," as he walked back to the front of the church to join the ladies.

∞

When Uncle Roy and Aunt Greedle got on in years, they sold their property on Dobbs Mountain and bought a place in Stearns, Kentucky, to be closer to a doctor and amenities older people typically needed.

After the move, they had just enough time to get settled in, when Arlin and Stella Winchester decided to pay Uncle Roy and Aunt Greedle a visit. They were old friends from the Co-operative days and Arlin and Stella wanted to see the Dobbs' new place.

It was a hot summer day and the sun was at its hottest when Arlin and Stella arrived that afternoon. Uncle Roy greeted them at the door; he was surprised and pleased to see their ole friends. It was common practice down home to drop by to see friends and family without prior notice or invitation. You were always welcomed, no matter the time of day. Aunt Greedle came into the living room shortly afterward. When the initial greetings were over, Aunt Greedle invited Arlin and Stella to sit for a spell. When the four of them found a place and sat down, Uncle Roy wiped sweat from his face and neck.

Then Uncle Roy said, "Arlin, I believe this is the hottest summer I've ever seen. We've got the doors open, all the windows up, and the air conditioner running full blast, and we're still about to burn up."

∞

There was never a dull moment around Uncle Roy. I loved him dearly.

CHAPTER 18

The Co-operative Prince

Born in Owenton, Tennessee, in 1918, James Prince Richards, a small boy, moved with his family to the newly opened coal community called Co-operative, Kentucky. Mr. Richards worked in the Co-operative Mine. The Richards family would have been one of the first families to live in Co-operative. It was at Co-operative that young Prince received his education, finishing under Hobson Stephens around 1933.

∞

At twenty-one, Prince Richards joined the United States Army on November 21, 1939. After receiving his training, he was assigned to an artillery battery on the Island of Corregidor in the Pacific Ocean. This little-known island may have seemed to the rank and file as a place to be put to be forgotten by the army. But when World War II started, the little-known island became a strategic battleground; the Japanese wanted it and the U.S. wanted to keep it. After five months of fierce fighting, the Japanese overran Corregidor, forcing an end to the fighting. The soldiers pleaded with their commanding officers to continue fighting, but the order to surrender came down from General Wainwright. The Japanese captured every soldier on the Island of Corregidor as POWs (Prisoners of War).

It was May 6, 1942, at 12:00 p.m. when the American flag came down. Many of the troops wept. Eight thousand troops marched off to a gorge the Japanese had made ready, and it was here the real battle began, the battle to survive. The prisoners suddenly were living like animals. With not enough to eat, starvation always at the door, and contaminated water, their strength was depleted. Many did not survive the first few weeks. They were made to do tasks they were not always able to do with their depleted strength and the brutal treatment.

In those beginning weeks, four American soldiers escaped, but they were soon caught. Everyone was required to watch what the Japanese did to these four men. Early morning, they were tied to stakes in the hot sun. Commanding Officer Breacher pleaded for their lives, but he was ignored. That same evening before the sun went down, those four men were untied and taken to four freshly dug graves. One by one each soldier was shot standing beside his own grave. The last man shot was from Prince Richards' Artillery Battery; he did not fall. A Japanese Officer walked close to him and emptied his pistol into Corporal Lee.

Time moved on slowly for the POWs. The Japanese began building an airfield; they expected long hard hours of manual labor each day from the POWs. One of the jobs Prince did was carry as big a rock as he could to the site and bust it into smaller pieces. Toward the end of one day, he was tired and weak. The sledgehammer the Japanese made him use was heavy and ricocheted off a rock and hit the inside of his ankle, cutting a gash in the skin.

Infection soon developed without any medicines and with no way to clean and bathe the wound. Prince knew he had to find a way to get rid of the infection before he lost the use of his ankle. Any man that could not work was shot. One evening while looking around the camp, he found what he thought was the answer, maggots. Prince scooped up several in his hand and put them on the wound and wrapped his whole ankle. The maggots ate out the bad infection, which no doubt saved his life.

Most always their food was made into soup. That way by boiling the water, at least they made sure it was clean. When the soup was ready, it was rationed to every man. Any food left over was distributed on a rotational basis, making it as fair as they could for everyone.

One day the Japanese figured out food was missing and unaccounted for. They determined the prisoners somehow took it. The next morning all prisoners were made to stand out in the open and had to remain there until those responsible confessed. All day they stood there without food and water. When night came, four men stepped forward. The Japanese took the four men and confined them for three weeks. One morning everyone was ordered outside. The Japanese marched the four men to a place all could see; they were skin and bones. One by one, they were beaten and dragged away. Prince never saw them alive again.

Prince said, "Burying the dead was the worst detail. Digging the graves wasn't as bad as taking their clothes and blankets. We had to. They were needed since there was never enough for the men. Throwing dirt on a man's face, I could not do, so I would put an old rag over his face before covering him with freshly dug earth. Then the chaplain would say a prayer over them."

One day all the remaining prisoners were marched to a dock where an old freighter waited. It was December 1943.

Prince said, "We were packed into the ship like sardines, until the ship couldn't hold anymore. Don't know if there were any men who couldn't get on the ship. We were never told. Nor were we told where the ship was headed. It was a living hell for the next thirty-eight days with only one bowl of soup and if we were real lucky a canteen of water. Several men died on the ship; two were British soldiers who were next to me."

Finally, when the prisoners got off the ship, they found themselves docked at a port in Japan. Their treatment was better, no more public beatings, but the food was still scarce and rationing continued. They were still required to do hard laborious work, but they were all so weak, they could hardly do any work at all in the beginning.

One morning without warning the first prisoners got up and discovered all the guards were gone.

"No one could figure what happened; many of the men wanted to leave, but the commanding officer said everyone needed to stay where they were," Prince said. "It was September 10, 1945, and no one yet knew the war was over. No one tried running; everyone was too weak to try anyway. We sat around, talking mostly in small groups. Everyone wondered if the guards were testing us to see if we would run. That way, the Japanese would have another excuse to kill more prisoners."

By late afternoon, an airplane got everyone's attention; everyone was laser focused on it.

Prince said, "A thought crossed my mind. They're going to kill us all and be done with it. Suddenly, the sound of the engine changed and it came in awfully low. It was going to try and land. At that point we saw it was one of ours. Some of the men struggled to get to their feet and began waving their arms and yelling, and I was among them. Many of us were holding on to each other."

∞

James Prince Richards had survived the forty-two-month ordeal as a POW. The suffering he and the other prisoners endured was beyond measure. War is an atrocity no man or woman should have to suffer. Prince left Co-operative a young man but matured quickly, too quickly, because of what he had to experience. However, he never forgot his love of the Kentucky mountains and the people he grew up with in the coal community of Co-operative, Kentucky.

Toward the end of his life, he chose to return to McCreary County to live out his remaining days. Yearning to get as close to his roots as possible, he was able to find a small house close to Pine Knot, Kentucky. This was his last move.

His last battle was with cancer, though cancer couldn't diminish his mind and spirit. He spent many hours staring at the countryside. He never neglected to comment on how beautiful the countryside was and how blessed he was to have everything he needed.

His last words were, "I'm not afraid to die, and besides, I'm going to be with the Lord. Don't be sad. I have had a good life."

CHAPTER 19

1945

At the beginning of 1945, Stearns Coal and Lumber Company issued a statement agreeing with the President of the United States, who said the most serious problem our country faces in producing the weapons the fighting forces need and depend on is the manpower that produces the energy needed for supplying the industry power source—COAL. Everyone must devote full time to make sure this source of energy is not interrupted. Therefore, Stearns Coal and Lumber Company will not feel justified in requesting a deferment of any coal employee who is not a full-time worker each week. Any man physically able who does not give full time to producing coal can better serve this country in the U.S. Armed Forces.

    I think President Roosevelt knew the big military push was coming soon and he used his influence to remind workers not to relax, to keep working as hard as they could so the industry supporting this country's military would stay at peak performance.

In those days, it was the coal miner the federal government held in high esteem but the feeling was short lived. True, the country needed coal to run its industries. But the coal miner's wage did not reflect this high position of preeminence, and little effort was put into improving the public opinion about the men who worked back-breaking jobs, who risked everything each day shoveling coal by hand. After the war, the push to replace coal as the number one energy source used by industry started almost immediately.

∞

Back in Co-operative toward the end of January, the Company Store was broken into on a Sunday night. Those responsible entered the store by breaking a glass window. It was not known at the time, nor would it ever be, if it was one person acting alone or two or more thieves. What was stolen was fifty cents of U.S. Post Office money, cigarettes, and a few other items. Sherman Corder, on Monday morning when he came to investigate, announced he would be working the case. This pronouncement sounded good on the surface, but this case had little chance of ever being solved.

∞

The U.S. War Department notified one of the families in Co-operative that their son was MIA (Missing in Action). Mrs. Agnes Trebelo's son, Frank Trebelo, joined the U.S. Armed Forces in 1944 and received his training at Scott Field, Illinois. Frank was sent overseas in October 1944. He was a radio gunner on a bomber and stationed in Italy. Sergeant Frank Trebelo went missing over Austria. He had three brothers in the service: Private First Class Walter Trebelo, who had recently returned after three years overseas; Private Stanley Trebelo; and Seaman Ed Trebelo, who was stationed aboard the USS Guam.

It was later determined Sergeant Frank Trebelo and his crew had been forced to parachute out of the plane when it caught fire. He and the crew were captured by the Germans, and later liberated by allied forces. He was given a sixty-day furlough and visited his mother, Mrs. Trebelo, in Co-operative.

∞

Set for launching was the largest carrier in the world—the Midway. The Midway was poised to make a name for itself in the war.

∞

Negotiations between the United Mine Workers and the coal operators came to a deadlock. The vote was called by John L. Lewis for all coal miners in the U.S. The coal miners of Stearns Coal and Lumber Company were polled on whether they were in favor of an interruption of the war effort at the present time. The poll was taken on a Wednesday by the National Labor Board. The results were as follows: Barthell, out of 159 eligible votes, 103 voted yes and 7 voted no; Blue Heron, out of 148 eligible votes, 71 voted yes and 3 voted no; Co-operative, out of 235 eligible votes, 106 voted yes and 13 voted no; Worley, out of 167 eligible votes, 36 voted yes and 18 voted no; Yamacraw, out of 157 eligible votes, 69 voted yes and 3 voted no. A total of 385 yeses and 44 nos.

The vote was strictly by secret ballot with a representative of the National Labor Board at each mine. Others assisted in helping with the voting, but only as observers. Also, foremen and men in advisory positions could not vote. The vote was a resounding yes. But it was all for nothing because the War Labor Board ordered the mines and operators to continue for another thirty days under the present contract.

∞

On May 8, 1945, Germany unconditionally surrendered, and Hitler committed suicide.

∞

The seventh and eighth graders at Co-operative presented a play titled "Damsels" on June 15, Friday, at 7:30 p.m.

The cast included the following fine young boys and girls:
- Billy Jean Dolen
- Francis Lee Craig
- Helen Winchester
- Norma Jean Slaven
- Eugene Wilson
- Harold Winchester
- Wilma Gene Lewis
- Cleatus Slaven
- Burman Slaven
- Floyd Winchester

∞

Wilburn Kirby Ross received the Congressional Medal of Honor. Mr. Ross, born in Strunk, Kentucky, was the son of Ned and Maude Ross.

On June 19, Sergeant Alvin York and the Governor of Kentucky, Simeon Willis, among a list of speakers and over 300 spectators, welcomed Wilburn K. Ross home in Stearns.

Mr. Ross, a veteran of WWII and the Korean War, retired from the U.S. Army as Master Sergeant. Mr. Ross died three days before his 95th birthday.

∞

On June 21, the high school students at Co-operative performed their play titled "Best Sellers" at 7:30 p.m.

The cast included the following fine young women and men:

Characters	Players
Alicia Dwyer	Chloetine Chitwood
Edna Dwyer	Aldena Lewis
Kenneth Dwyer	Harry Nichols Jr.
Ester Gill	Ruth Kidd
Ledia Carter	Lois Cooper
Mable Shaw	Wilma Cooper
Helen Heather	Lucy Haynes
Aretha Thorns	June Joyce Blevins
Hope	Ella Mae Anderson
Talbot	Willie Thompson
Stephen Ottis	Leo Craig Jr.
Kendall Ottis	Thurston Wilson

∞

After a week of festive activities, tragedy struck the Co-operative miners. Arthur Webb Bryant, one of Co-operative Mine's hard workers, was traveling south on U.S. Highway 27. When he reached the bridge at Revelo, Kentucky, on his approach, he saw a Greyhound bus already on the bridge heading north. Knowing the small bridge could not support passing the large bus, Mr. Bryant swerved his car and plunged headlong over the forty-foot embankment, hitting the railroad tracks below. Mr. Bryant's survivors included his wife, Elizabeth; a daughter, Madeline; and two sons, Melvin and Herbert, who were both serving in the U.S. Army. Arthur W. Bryant was well known throughout the county, and the coal miners in Co-operative said goodbye to a good friend.

∞

Co-operative continued to be in the spotlight as a favorite stopping place for local candidates running for office to speak as the candidates traveled the twenty-one county precincts. Starting at 2:00 p.m. on Saturday, August 4, on the porch of the Company Store, Co-operative folks had an opportunity to meet the current candidates running for office, if they were so inclined.

∞

On August 15, the Imperial Japanese announced their surrender. The peace treaty was formally signed on September 2, 1945, bringing an end to World War II.

∞

A Co-operative young man, Private First Class (PFC) Stanley Parks, who had been a Prisoner of War (POW) for nine and a half months, was given a ninety-day furlough.

∞

A blanket of white closed out 1945, the largest snowfall in six years. The snow started on Tuesday night and continued through Wednesday, leaving ten inches of snow. All side roads closed and Highway 27 temporarily closed but reopened Wednesday afternoon. Telephone and telegraph services were completely disrupted for twenty-four hours. In places like Co-operative, it took several days to restore communication, and folks were completely isolated from the outside world.

∞

MARRIED THIS YEAR 1945

Gran Smith, age 48, and Gracie Meadows, age 38, both of White Oak Junction, were married.

∞

BORN THIS YEAR 1945

Roger Shoopman
Wanda Terry
Hershel Lee Dixon
Noah King
Ernest Troxell

Elizabeth Davis
Ronnie Keith
Rose Geneva Jones
Brenda Bell
Greg Haynes
Clifford Dobbs
Brenda Shepherd
George Coffey
Chester Leon Waters
Nelda Lewis
Fayrene Lewis
Darrell Garner Ball
Danny Eugene Anderson
Darrell Maxwell
Glenna Margaret Freeman
Damon Gibson
Gene (Blue) Dixon
David Keith

CHAPTER 20

Dynamite Fist— Beginning

Harrison Dixon's mom and dad were John Dixon and Susan Koger. Susan was a sister to Herb and Hurstle Koger. Harrison loved to drink, which continued after his marriage to Rosie Mae Flynn. Growing up in Co-operative, everyone I knew called her Rose. Harrison's three oldest sons grew up witnessing how their dad treated their mom when he was drinking, which was every weekend.

Harrison and Rose's son Don remembers when he was around eight or nine years old, his dad came home earlier than usual on a Saturday night. He was cussing mad, and he mentioned that some guy had cheated him playing cards, that the S.O.B. he had loaned money so the guy could stay in the

DON (DYNAMITE FIST) DIXON
PHOTO COURTESY OF BARBARA DIXON.

game had not paid him back. Harrison cussed and said, "His time is coming."

It wasn't long until Harrison and Rose were arguing. The argument escalated until finally Harrison grabbed his shotgun and pointed it at Rose and the kids. Rose didn't move because if the gun went off, it would kill her. On the other hand, maybe killing her would save the kids. Harrison held the hammer back with a rubber band. Rose knew if the rubber band broke, she was done for. After Rose pleaded with Harrison for several minutes, he finally lowered the gun. Rose did not try later to take away the gun; she knew if she attempted and failed, she was for sure a dead woman.

∞

By now Harrison and Rose had eight kids—Cecil, the oldest, then Hobert, Donald, Clara, James Lonnie, Roy Gene, Betty Imogene, and Hershel. Rose was pregnant with her youngest son, James Harrison Jr., born in 1946.

With all those kids, Rose delegated some of her chores to the older kids. Washing the dishes after supper fell to Don and Clara. Most every time, one of them would sling water on the other and the two would get into a scuffle. Rose decided to switch their duty of washing and rinsing, thinking the change would stop them from slinging water on each other. But her plan didn't work. Every time, the two would end up in a water fight and Rose would break up the fight and whip their behinds.

Don and Clara would run off crying and hide, and each time they'd make each other a promise, *When we get old enough, we're gonna leave this place and never come back.* When they finished crying, they'd go back in the kitchen and finish their job. They knew the dishes would still be waiting for them. They also knew their mom would not finish the dishes because it was their job. The next evening, the scenario would repeat itself. Pregnant Rose had her hands full with one-year-old Hershel, three-year-old Betty Imogene, and six-year-old Roy Gene. The oldest kids had no choice but to help.

∞

As Don grew old enough, he wanted to go wherever his dad went, even though Don shouldn't be in the places his dad went. Harrison didn't play cards every time he got together with his buddies but most often he did. Harrison and his drinking buddies' favorite hangout spot was a rock up on the bank just before getting to Guy Kidd's Grocery. Up in the woods there was a huge flat rock they used for a table. Around the big rock, the men sat on whatever they could find lying in the woods. Don had gone with his dad enough times to notice each man had his own place to sit, including his dad. One time they walked up and another man was sitting in his dad's place. Harrison stood behind the man and waited for the card game, that had already started, to end. When the man didn't offer to get up and move, Harrison said, "You're in my place."

"I like this spot," the man said.

Harrison grabbed the man under his arms, raised him up, and threw him like a 'sack of taters.' The man went rolling down the gradual grade and would have ended on the railroad tracks if not for the tree that stopped him. Hugging the tree, he let out a hurting sound. Don wondered if the man would be able to stand, but after several long minutes, the man pulled himself up, wobbling like a child trying to regain his balance. Finally, the man dusted himself off, gained his composure, came back to the big rock, and sat at another spot. The man did not say a word about what had happened, and if he was hurt, he hid it well.

Don sat on the ground behind his dad, and times when his dad was drinking beer, he'd leave a couple sups for Don. Those couple sups of beer sure tasted good to Don.

The man his dad had thrown down the hill played cards for maybe another hour. When the card game ended and before another one began, the man got up and said he'd had enough and was heading home. The man likely had enough time to get to the railroad tracks when Don's dad stood up and said he'd lost enough money. Harrison looked down at Don and said, "Come on. Better get you home."

Don wondered why his dad was leaving so soon. Getting him home at a decent hour had never stopped his dad before, but Don wasn't about to question his dad. It had turned dark, and the moon gave just enough light to see by. Down on the railroad tracks, they started walking toward Guy Kidd's. Don could see up ahead the shadow of a man leaving the railroad tracks and walking up behind Guy's store. His dad picked up the pace. When they reached Guy's, they turned and went behind the store and crossed the foot bridge. On the other side, they turned right, following the path for a short distance, and picked up the dirt road that went around under the train bridge.

Don thought normally his dad would have told him to go on home at this point since the Dixon home wasn't far from where they were. But he didn't. Occasionally Don and his dad could see the man ahead in the moonlight. His dad was determined to follow the man. Just when Don thought the man might be going to Co-operative, he headed down to walk through the school playground. His dad stopped and waited. So did Don, not saying a word so as not to make his dad mad. They watched the man go into the outside toilet. Then his dad hurriedly walked across the playground. He followed.

Reaching the toilet, his dad flung open the door and at the same time turned on his flashlight. Don standing a few steps away could see the man was sitting inside. His dad went in and quickly shut the door. If the man had not relieved himself before, Don bet he did then, with the shock of what just happened. Don heard his dad talking. Then, without warning, a pistol discharged from inside the toilet. Don thought, oh no, Dad killed the man. Within a few seconds, his dad stepped out, put his pistol in his pocket, and took the money out of his hand holding the flashlight. His dad then switched the flashlight off and they stood there for a couple minutes, I guess for his eyes to get used to the dark. Before walking on, his dad said, "I'll teach that S.O.B. to not pay me back what he owed."

Don asked his dad, "Why don't we use the flashlight?"

"I don't want that man seeing which direction we're going," his dad said.

∞

Don was too young to work as a miner for Stearns Coal and Lumber Company. So he talked to Guy Kidd about a job. Guy hired him to help Coy Whitehead deliver groceries and help around the store on Fridays and Saturdays. After a couple weeks had passed, Guy became comfortable having Don around. Don did whatever Guy asked him to do and he was very strong for his age. One Saturday night Guy asked Don to go hunting with him. Don said he would. So that evening Don walked back to the store around 8:30 p.m. By the time Don made it to the store, Guy was putting his dogs in the bed of his truck. After securing the dogs, they took off. They drove several miles to where Guy wanted to be. He stopped the truck and parked. Guy said, "Let's get the dogs out and see if they can get a scent." Letting the tailgate down, they attached leashes to the dogs, and the dogs jumped to the ground.

Guy, leaving Don with the truck, walked the dogs around the place in a large circle where the truck was parked. Guy came back to the truck, and the dogs jumped into the bed of the truck.

"Well," Guy said, "they didn't pick up a trail around here."

Guy and Don got back in the truck and drove on a couple miles and parked. Guy got the dogs out and repeated what he had done before. Again, he came back and said, "Nothing here." This happened several times. Don already knew some raccoon hunts could go on all night, so he wasn't surprised.

Finally, about the fifth stop, Guy asked Don if he would take the dogs. Guess Guy was getting tired. Don had been watching Guy and knew what to do. When the circle he'd made with the dogs was almost complete, Don decided to head back to the truck.

Suddenly, the dogs lunged on their leashes so hard it jerked his arm almost out of the socket, the dogs yelping with every breath. Don turned the dogs loose and they were gone. Don ran back to the truck, and Guy said, "They've treed. Let's go."

They walked toward the barking, which was slow going since in some places they had to cut their way through underbrush. Going up a steady grade the entire time, when they reached the dogs, they were at the face of a cliff. A tree had grown next to the rock. Almost eye level to a crevice in the rock, Guy could see baby raccoons. Holding onto the small tree, Guy reached back into the crevice to take hold of one of the babies. Guy jerked his hand back. He'd been bitten, probably by the momma Guy had failed to see. That ended the hunt. Getting back to the truck, Guy pulled out a quart jar of moonshine from under the seat and poured some over his hand. Then he took a big swallow himself. The next day he went to see Dr. Simpson.

∞

A few days passed. Bull Hines came by the store, and Guy and Bull talked up a raccoon hunt. Don was again invited. The next night they met up at Guy's store, and after they loaded the truck with the food and dogs, they took off. Getting where Guy wanted to go, he parked the truck and turned the dogs loose. They treed quickly. Guy and Don headed out walking toward the sound of the barking. Bull said he'd stay with the truck to make sure everything would be okay.

It was a long way to get to the dogs, and it was no easy thing to spot the raccoon. That tree was huge. It looked to be 150 feet tall, and the dogs weren't about to leave the tree. Finally, after a long while, Guy got a bead on the raccoon and shot him out and they worked their way back to the truck. Don put the dogs in the bed of the truck and settled back down. Guy looked at Don and said, "You hungry?"

Don said, "I could eat something." Guy began looking for the brown paper bag. When he found the bag, it was neatly folded up lying on the truck seat. Guy cussed, "Bull, you ate all the damn food and drank my moonshine!" Guy cussed some more.

Bull was sitting on the side edge of the truck seat with the door open. Guy shined his flashlight close to Bull's face, but not directly on him. Bull's face was as red as a pickled beet.

Guy cussed again and said, "Let's go."

∞

George Foster lived in Hickory Knob and on occasion walked to Guy Kidd's Grocery. From Hickory Knob, there was a path that angled off to the side, the side nearest Fidelity, but remained high along the ridgeline. It came down close to where the Crafts family lived. When the creek was low, one could cross the creek where cars crossed, but if the creek was up from a lot of rain, folks had to walk down to get on the train tracks, cross Rock Creek over the train bridge, then walk up to Guy's store.

George sat around in the store for a while; he didn't have to be in a hurry to get back home. Several people George knew came in the store, and when Guy wasn't waiting on customers, he sat and talked over a cup of coffee. George found out Guy had some fresh pork that had just been butchered; George wanted a whole ham. George paid Guy for the ham and left, heading back home.

Everything was going fine, White Oak Junction was behind George, and he was on the path heading up the mountain. Suddenly, he heard screaming. It was loud and close to him. George kept walking, cautiously looking around; then he saw it. It was like it appeared from nowhere, a wild cat directly up ahead in his path. George stopped and gently laid his ham down on a rock beside him. George didn't know what he would or could do; all the time the cat was easing toward him.

 The cat by now was way too close for comfort. George then noticed pinecones all around him. George eased down, not taking his eyes off the cat, and picked up a pinecone. George got lucky; it was still attached to a small limb. As the cat walked toward him, now on his rear legs, and lunged, George let go of the pinecone. George was thankful his aim was steady and true because the pinecone went down the cat's throat. It was a good thing the pinecone was still attached to the limb because it gave George something else to push into the cat's throat. Folks said George wasn't afraid of anything. This story convinced me.

∞

 As mentioned earlier, Coy Whitehead worked for Guy Kidd. Coy drove a log truck and delivered groceries for Guy. People would stop by Guy's store and put in their order. When Guy figured he had a truck load, Coy and Don would deliver orders all over Rattlesnake Ridge, Mount View, Bell Farm, and Bald Knob. Coy and Don started early Saturday mornings loading the one-and-a-half-ton truck before heading out to complete their deliveries, which all together took most of the day. Bell Farm was always their last stop. A few years later, in the early 1950s when the railroad tracks were pulled from Bell Farm to White Oak Junction, the railroad bed would become a gravel road; then getting to Bell Farm would be faster and people would not have to backtrack through Rattlesnake Ridge.

On one of those delivery trips, they had traveled through Rattlesnake Ridge and Cherokee and were headed over Hines Hill. When they entered the descent, Coy pressed on the brake pedal to slow the truck and put the transmission in a lower gear. Coy pressed the brake pedal again as the truck entered the steepest part of the hill, but this time the pedal went to the floor. He quickly tried pumping the pedal several times fast, but each time got the same result. Now the truck was picking up speed, the farther, the faster.

Don could see the effort Coy made to slow the truck; he didn't need to say anything. Then Coy said, "We can't make the curve." The road being gravel didn't help matters. The first curve they entered was hard to maneuver even when everything was working properly. The hill had an S curve in it and the first curve was one of those "kiss my ass" curves. Even if they survived that curve, the hill straightened some and then took a sharp left. At that point, the hill intersected with Road 1363 which meant you had to stop.

Well Coy and Don didn't need to worry about the road beyond the first curve because their truck left the road and straightened out the first curve riding over several small trees that didn't even slow the truck. Things didn't look good. Coy had to stop the truck somehow. Coy took a quick glance over to the passenger side but didn't see Don. He glanced again. Don was hunkered down on the floorboard.

Coy figured the only way to stop the truck was to aim for the larger trees. He jerked the steering wheel left. The rear end began to slide when the bed hit the first tree and the front bumper collided with a second tree. The front bumper wrapped around the tree just like it was made to wrap around trees, which forced the grille and hood to fold, which forced the fenders to fold in toward the engine. The radiator folded up like a tootsie roll and spat water out the bottom and steam out from the now folded hood. The collision forced Coy to the passenger side on top of Don who had figured the floor was the safest place, but now was thinking otherwise. But the two men walked away without injury, and they lost very little stock since the majority had been delivered. Guy eventually got the truck fixed, and deliveries got back to normal.

∞

Don had worked for Guy for approximately four years and was now old enough to work for Stearns Coal and Lumber Company but had not yet decided he wanted to. He liked working for Guy and he knew what Guy expected; more than that, Don liked slipping into the feed house for a mouthful of good moonshine a couple times a day. Guy liked keeping a jar of White Lightning around because he liked taking a sip now and then. When Don first started sipping a little moonshine, he didn't sip enough that Guy noticed, but then things changed. When Guy noticed more was disappearing out of his jar than he was drinking, he figured Don had found it. So Guy changed his hiding place. Each time, Don found it. Guy wasn't keen on Don sneaking and drinking his private stash.

Don had grown into quite a ladies' man; it was said he could charm the pants off any girl he met and women loved his quiet voice. His wild side women tried to tame but that was where the rubber met the road, as they say. Could any one woman do that? Time would tell.

It was late evening, and Don was inside Guy's store talking to Ada, Guy's wife. Guy walked in and saw Don and Ada talking. Surely in all the time Don had worked for Guy, this wasn't the first time Guy saw Don and Ada talking. I can only guess at what riled Guy. Was Don flirting with Ada? Was Ada flirting with Don? Had Guy told Don to stop drinking his moonshine only to find his jar empty when he went to take a sip that day? Had Guy just been told about Don's appeal to the ladies? Why did Don run? Was Guy holding the empty moonshine jar in one hand and his pistol in the other? No one will ever know, but something spooked Don. And Don knew this was a fight he couldn't win.

Whatever happened, the story is that Don ran out of the store as fast as his legs could carry him. As Don crossed the swinging bridge behind Guy's store, Guy emptied his .38 pistol. Don, no doubt, thought he was running for his life.

I don't think Guy aimed at Don but rather shot into the air. It was enough to let Don know their relationship was over. Dynamite Fist disappeared into the night.

CHAPTER 21

1946

Near the beginning of 1946, coal miners were on strike for almost two months. With the war now over and the restraints of the federal government lifted on companies and employees, it was time to negotiate a workable contract for all concerned.

∞

During the idle period of no work in the mines, supply trains still traveled to the coal camp stores owned by Stearns Coal and Lumber Company. It was late Sunday evening in Co-operative when two young men walked from Logan Holler on the main railroad track. It was late enough that church services were over. From Logan Holler, walking the main track took the two young men past the Lower

Camp and on underneath the coal tipple. Around the curve past the ballfield and Upper Camp, a few lights were still on in homes. Most folks would be getting ready for bed if they hadn't already. The two young men continued a steady pace walking past the Co-operative Company Store. They were in the clear now. The railroad track ended just beyond the Co-operative schoolhouse, close to White Oak Creek. There sat idle three empty coal gons.

The two men checked the brakes of each coal gon, starting with the back one and working their way to the lead coal gon. As the brakes loosened, they felt the coal gons begin to move, very slowly at first. The railroad track had a natural, gradual descent toward the tipple. The coal gons were heavy and the tipple was roughly a half mile from the schoolhouse. It was a slow ride, but the gons picked up speed as they went. When they passed the tipple, the two young men decided it was time to get off. They jumped off, one on each side. When their feet hit the gravel, they needed to run to keep their body from losing balance and taking a roll. Able to stay on their feet, when they slowed down, they watched the coal gons roll on down the tracks. Without a doubt, they wagered with each other how far the gons would travel before stopping.

The next day talk spread throughout Co-operative and White Oak Junction about the coal gons that were sitting on the main track beyond White Oak Junction. How did they get there and who would do such a thing? The prank could have caused a bad accident, but where the coal gons came to a stop, they were easily seen by the supply train coming to the stores in White Oak Junction and Co-operative on Monday morning. Several weeks passed before J. T. Hall and Jack Winchester were arrested on the charge of obstructing the railroad. The case against them could not be proven and charges were eventually dropped.

∞

In 1940, American Bantam Car Company in Butler, Pennsylvania, delivered a prototype of a GPV (general purpose vehicle) to the military, at the military's request. Knowing Bantam's limitation to provide the number of vehicles the U.S. Army would need, the military opened up the request to other vehicle manufacturers to submit designs and prototypes to be evaluated. Willys-Overland Motors in Ohio responded to the military's request and later so did Ford Motor Company in Michigan.

Although all three companies produced prototypes that didn't meet the military's exact specifications, the military decided to have all three companies make the GPVs. However, in mid-1941, the military decided standardization was important and, since Willys-Overland made the better vehicle for the money, gave the entire contract to Willys. But within a few months, the U.S. Army saw they needed more than one manufacturer since Willys couldn't keep up with the demand. They also recognized the danger of having the enemy bomb the only manufacturing plant, so they gave Ford a contract as long as Ford would build to the Willys' specifications. There was confusion about what to call the vehicle: Seep, Peep, Jeep. For several years during the war and after, the vehicle was simply called Willys.

Whatever it was called, one of them, owned by the Kentucky State Highway Department, made the trip to Barthell. On the trip, it carried Ed Hall, foreman of road construction; Cabell Owens, district highway engineer; L. C. Bruce; and G. M. Humble. The vehicle went over six miles of rugged mountain trail. When they reached Barthell, they were close to the mining tipple. Construction of the new road was set to start within days, and it would run parallel with the Ice Camp Branch.

∞

The school year was over and summer break was ahead. A young RL Terry had a job lined up, but the job required two people. RL's dad had told RL about it a few days before school was out. RL had mentioned it to a couple of his friends, but they were not interested. Walking the railroad tracks on their way home, RL asked Hobert Dixon, "What are you going to do this summer?"

Hobert said, "Nothing in particular."

"How would you like to make some money?" RL asked.

Hobert said, "Yeah, sure, but what will I have to do?"

"Cut timber," RL said.

Hobert asked, "Where?"

"Walking over the mountain to Charlie Winchester's place," RL said.

Hobert said, "When do we start?"

"Monday morning," RL said.

Monday morning, Hobert walked up to Harvey Terry's house and waited outside for RL. The Dixons lived in Logan Holler, so it was on Hobert's way to walk by the Terrys. Hobert didn't have long to wait, maybe a couple minutes, and RL walked out of the the house and down where Hobert was standing. The two boys walked up the single-lane, dirt road people used to get to the Upper Camp. The road took them up and underneath the tipple; then they turned up the hill and got onto the tram tracks and followed it up the incline. When they reached the top, which was part of Hickory Knob, they walked on close to Trapper Foust's place, making their way along the ridgeline and down the other side of the mountain. When they reached the bottom and crossed the railroad tracks, they were close to Fidelity. They walked across the swinging bridge over Rock Creek to the other side, up a small embankment and to the right, and they were on Charlie Winchester's property. When they reached Charlie's house, the lights were on, and on the front porch of his house, his old hound dog began bellowing. One thing was for sure, if anyone in the house wasn't awake, they were then.

It being the boys' first day of work, they walked to the jobsite with Charlie. Looking around, Charlie found a crosscut saw and reached it to Hobert. It was for both boys to use. Then Charlie pointed toward the general area he wanted Hobert and RL to work.

Charlie said, "Now when you get two trees on the ground, go ahead and cut them in ten-foot lengths and make sure you cut off all the limbs." Charlie looked around and there were two other men walking toward that same area he wanted Hobert and RL to work. Charlie said, "Follow them."

When the trees were cut up into logs as Charlie requested, a man with a team of mules came, hooked them to the logs, and pulled the logs over to a ramp the men had built on a wagon road off the main road. One end of the ramp was the same height as the truck bed, so when the truck was backed into position, two men with cane hooks rolled the logs up the ramp and onto the bed of the truck. When the truck was loaded, the driver took the load to Stearns.

RL and Hobert's wages were $6 a day, more money than they had ever seen. Those boys were on the job every day. There was no way they would miss a day's work on purpose. Of course, there were times Charlie had to stop the work when they got heavy rain. Those were the only times RL and Hobert missed work that whole summer.

When summer break was drawing near the end, RL told Hobert he was sorry he had to tell Charlie they had to quit next week cause school was about to start back. Charlie was an understanding gentleman and he already knew when next Friday came it would be RL and Hobert's last day.

The men lined up to get their wages on Friday; Charlie used the ramp as a chair and desk to distribute the money. RL and Hobert made sure they were the last to receive their wages.

As RL and Hobert stepped up, Charlie said, "Boys, I know school is starting back. I'm going to miss you two. Next summer if you want a job come see me."

Both boys thanked Charlie and started their walk home. As RL and Hobert were making their way over the mountain, although they were not aware, the air waves in August 1946 were filled with The Ink Spots' song "Gypsy" and Perry Como's song "Surrender." On August 31, 1946, Freddy Martin and his Orchestra took over the number one slot with their "To Each His Own."

At the time, RL and Hobert may not have heard these songs. If they did, it was likely on a Saturday night just before the Grand Ole Opry. But in those days, a radio was a luxury and not every home had one, but the next decade would see an explosion of radios, TVs, and music.

∞

In Co-operative, kids made up rhymes all the time and they became popular in the coal camp. One of the rhymes went like this: "If I had a nickel, if I had a dime, I'd give it all away, to see Sally Goodin' cut a shine." You might ask, who is Sally Goodin'? No one knew. The name fit and rhymed and that's all that mattered.

∞

Back in the 1940s, it was rare for someone's legal name to consist of only two capital letters, for example, RL. His full name was RL Terry. The R didn't stand for a name and the L didn't stand for a name. RL's younger brother's name was JT. Again, JT didn't stand for anything other than JT. My oldest brother's name is LD, the same situation as RL and JT.

My uncle Virgil Freeman's nickname was Steamboat. Steamboat loved practical jokes and loved getting one over on anybody. So one time he was around the Terry boys and he gave them a name using the two letters of their name. He probably thought the two boys would argue with him. But to his surprise, neither boy said a word; in fact, they ignored him. When Steamboat saw RL, he called him Run Lester, and he called JT John Tracy. Every time he saw the boys, he'd call them by those names. Steamboat would laugh but neither boy ever said a word back to him.

∞

One fall weekend after the school year started, a few of the miners planned a fishing trip. One of the men was RL's dad, Harvey Terry. When RL found out, he asked his dad if he could go. Harvey said he could.

Saturday, around 11:00 a.m., Harvey and RL walked up to Harley Hardwick's. At the time, the Terrys lived at the east end of Logan Holler. The three—Harvey, RL, and Harley—walked up to R. D. Wright's house. He lived in the fifth house east of the Co-operative tipple, or in the Lower Camp. The four of them—Harvey, RL, Harley, and R. D.—walked up the tram tracks behind the Co-operative Mine superintendent's house. Arnold Shoopman lived in a house nearby and was sitting on the porch waiting for them.

The five walked up the incline to the top where they were on the edge of Hickory Knob. From there, they walked out to Ezra Foust's place. Ezra was also outside waiting and joined the group. They walked on over that side of the mountain and ended up on the railroad tracks at the bottom. From there, they walked to Fidelity on the train tracks, which were higher than the ponds. They crossed the swinging bridge, turned right, and gradually worked their way up that side of the mountain. Crossing over the mountain and down the other side, they came out close to Oil Well Branch. There, they turned right and walked about a mile to the huge rock the locals named Ship Rock.

Each man had his own bag of gear he thought he'd need, and they all busied themselves setting up camp. Each of them brought a gun. The food each brought was for everyone. They made coffee in an eight-pound lard can, emptied and cleaned, of course. One of the men cut two forked sticks and drove them into the ground opposite each other near the campfire. Then he cut a sturdy straight stick to lay in the forks. The container for making coffee would hang over the campfire from this stick. A couple of skillets were brought for cooking.

A small boat was always tied up to the bank. The boat was a small, flat bottom boat only large enough for two men to sit comfortably, one on each end of the boat. Everyone who camped there used it and took care of it and always left it like they found it. As far as I know, no one ever knew who originally provided the boat.

Ezra Foust always brought his rifle. RL walked with Ezra a short distance from camp when he started shooting birds. RL wondered why he decided to shoot birds on a fishing trip. Before RL could ask, Ezra told him birds made great fish bait. "Come on," Ezra said. "You can help me set the trotline."

Ezra and RL put everything they needed in the boat and eased downstream about fifty yards and strung their line. Ezra secured the line like he wanted it, and with RL paddling, they came back across and Ezra baited each hook. When they finished, they docked the boat, tied the rope to a nearby tree, and walked back to camp.

By the time Ezra and RL got back to camp, the other guys had finished setting up the campsite and had food ready. Corn bread fritters, pork and beans, and coffee. After everybody ate, it was time for the main order of business, time for fishing. One way to keep coffee from boiling over was to lay a green (i.e., not dead) stick across the top of the can, which they did before leaving.

Their camp was positioned at the base of the Ship Rock. The rock was formed so that part of the rock extended out over their campsite, providing a semblance of a roof. The river was only a few feet away. Everyone settled into their favorite spot to sit on the bank. They cast their hooks and enjoyed the quiet solitude. Listening to nature was a large part of their fishing experience: an occasional bird chirping, the soft sounds of the river water flowing, the smells of clean mountain air, and a hint of a soft breeze moving downstream. For several hours, they were the closest they'd ever come to heaven on earth.

It was still a good while before dark when RL began hearing a subtle sound that could be a pheasant he thought. Then RL looked to his left and saw Harley hit a tree root sticking out of the water with his mining cap. Harley then looked in RL's direction, smiled, and said, "Sounds like a pheasant, don't it?"

Soon, Ezra got in the boat to check the trotline.

Harley had an old saying he'd sing out from time to time, "Shoe fly pie and apple pie, dede, I can't get enough of that good ole stuff."

Returning, Ezra secured the boat. Walking by the guys, he heard what Harley said. He responded, "Sounds like somebody's hungry."

Harley said again with a chuckle, "Shoe fly pie and apple pie, dede, I can't get enough of that good ole stuff."

"We'll have something shortly," Ezra said. "As soon as I clean and fillet these bass."

In camp, R. D. joined Ezra in cleaning the fish and then Ezra rolled those bass fillets in a mixture of flour, cornmeal, salt, and pepper. Arnold mixed up the corn bread fritters. Harvey had brought potatoes, which he placed around the edge of the fire. Someone opened a can of pork and beans to warm over the fire.

By now, everyone was sitting around the campfire, waiting because the aroma of food cooking over a campfire would make any mouth water. Fried bass, baked potatoes, pork and beans, and corn bread fritters. That was a meal that couldn't be topped. Ole Harley Hardwick would say it's this kind of a meal that'll cause you to slap your grandma and just laugh. (That was something guys would say when they were alone; it wasn't meant to be taken seriously, of course. No one would do that literally. It was a silly way to emphasize how good the food was.)

When the meal was over and everybody's tummy was full, the men talked for a while, enjoying each other's company. Harley said, "It'll be dark soon. Might as well get some more fishing in."

Everyone went back to the riverbank before it got too dark to see. Arnold had set up three small piles of wood separated by about twenty feet. The wood burning made a good light to see by. The men brought their carbide lamps, but saved them for emergencies.

Darkness fell but that didn't matter because everyone was still on the riverbank checking their hooks between casts. Those fires Arnold had set gave just enough light. So far it had been peaceful and quiet until suddenly screams broke the peaceful solitude. Everyone secured their reels and went on alert. The screams were coming from across the river.

Arnold was the first to get his carbide lamp burning, shining it in the direction of the sound. The carbide light shined just far enough to see two sets of eyeballs staring back at them across the water. The aroma of food no doubt had brought the intruders to investigate. The two cats fought for a minute, stopped to look across at the men, and then fought some more. By now, every man had his gun ready for battle. It appeared the cats were fighting for dominance; for sure, the cats didn't like each other. Although the cats were not together, the men were confident both would find their way to their camp at some point in the night. Hearing the screams as they fought brought chills to young RL, who was holding tightly onto his shotgun.

Suddenly after a moment of silence, the men heard the splash in the water. Guess they didn't have to wonder any longer when they'd get visitors. "They're coming," someone said.

By now, Harley, Ezra, Harvey, and Arnold had their carbide lights lit and shining across the river. The cats' eyeballs could clearly be seen. R. D. had not fired his carbide light yet. Someone said, "Won't be long now; the cats are halfway across." RL was holding his shotgun steady, as were the others.

Then, without warning, the two cats got into another fight, right there in the river. They were locked up together; both bobbled in and out of the river. It was evident they were trying to kill one another. Then, quiet. The men looked at each other, still on alert and wondering what just happened. They waited, half expecting the two cats to jump out of the water at the same time. And they waited. They did not see or hear the cats again. Relief. One thing was for sure, the cats had ruined fishing for the night. They sat around the campfire and talked until someone decided it was time to get some sleep. They'd fish some more the next morning.

∞

MARRIED THIS YEAR 1946

In Bell Farm, John S. Crabtree married Violet Hill.

In Co-operative, Gib Carson married Betty Bell. The children of this union were Rick, Danny Joe, James, Roger, and Melinda.

∞

BORN THIS YEAR 1946

Lonnie Jones
Jenny Blevins
Glenna Clark
Louise Watson
Judy Hardwick
Jimmy Davis
William Troxell
Jewel Tein Whitehead
Junior Shoopman
Jerry Coffey
Roger Hall
Mary Lou Hall
Frances Slaven
Hazel Shook
Howard Gibson
Bonnie Maples
Joyce Cox

CHAPTER 22

1947

Beginning of 1947 on a Saturday afternoon, ten-year-old Virgil Gibson was riding his bicycle on Smithtown Road. Ellic Foster, driving his car through Smithtown heading home to Co-operative, saw the boy up ahead on the bicycle. Suddenly the boy veered out into the road. In a panic, Mr. Foster quickly swerved his car to miss the boy, but he guided his car to the wrong side of the road. All the while, Mr. Foster was breaking the vehicle hard, trying to get it stopped. Doing everything he could, he still could not prevent hitting the boy.

Mr. Foster left his car and ran to the nearest home to call for help. Young Virgil was taken to Stearns to be checked by the doctor and immediately taken on to Somerset Hospital. The youngster suffered a compound fracture to the leg and several cuts and bruises. The car had to be jacked up in front to get it off the bicycle. Mr. Foster went to the sheriff's office in Whitley City to give his report of the accident. The sheriff accompanied Mr. Foster to the scene. Mr. Foster was released to go on home to Co-operative.

∞

Arnold Shoopman was still working at Co-operative Mine at the bottom of the incline. It wasn't that long ago Arnold and the other miners had worked out nine-foot coal, a seam of candle coal. Since the coal seam ran in such long, high strips, it had to be blasted twice. As of late, the coal seam was getting smaller and smaller. Arnold could load as many as twenty-three tons of coal a day, if he had a good room. But on days when he was in a low-coal room, he had to turn the coal.

Turning coal is where there's not enough room between the top of the coal car to the roof of the mine to shovel the coal directly over the top of the coal car. On those days, Arnold had to pitch the coal out of his room and then shovel the coal in the car, which meant handling the same coal twice. Those times, Arnold would come home and say, "Well, I just got sixteen tons today," or he'd say, "I only got fourteen tons today." Sometimes when he had to turn the coal, he could get only nine or ten tons of coal.

Occasionally, Arnold would say, "That Marion Wilson can load thirty-three tons a day; I don't know how he does it. He can load more coal than any one man I've ever seen."

∞

Frank Slaven, son of Cack and Betty Slaven of Co-operative, came home on a three-week furlough before leaving for the Marshall Islands, where he continued his service in the Air Force.

∞

The school year at Co-operative was close to ending. RL Terry, walking home from school one day, began thinking about how he would spend the summer. RL walked to the Company Store to check if his family had any mail. As I've mentioned, the U.S. Post Office was in the Company Store. RL walked in and looked to see if there was mail in their box. Since he saw no mail, he didn't have to bother the postmaster. RL turned to walk back out of the store and head on home when he overheard Othel Smith talking to the store manager, L. L. Craig, about needing to hire some men to work. RL walked on out and waited for Mr. Smith to come out. RL knew Mr. Smith and was curious what work he needed men to do. In a couple minutes, Othel Smith came out the door.

"Mr. Smith," RL said, "I overheard you tell Mr. Craig you needed to hire some men to work."

"That's right," Mr. Smith said.

RL said, "Well, I could work this summer."

Mr. Smith told RL he and his brother Howard had a sawmill over in Lonesome. "It's hard work," he added.

RL said, "I worked for Charlie Winchester last summer; I was on one end of a crosscut saw."

"Oh, well," Mr. Smith said, "you're what I'm looking for."

RL said, "Just so you understand, I can only work the summer; when school starts back, I'll have to quit."

"If you can work the summer, that'll help us out," Mr. Smith said. "If you know anyone else that will work the summer, bring them with you."

RL said, "School's out next Thursday; how about if I start the following Monday."

"OK, you be at my house at 6:30 a.m.," Mr. Smith said.

RL said, "OK."

Young RL walked on home happy, thinking about the money he'd make over the summer. Also, being at Mr. Smith's house wouldn't be a problem since he lived only four houses from Mr. Smith, and Mr. Smith's brother Howard lived just over on the hill on the far side of the gravel road.

The school year ended and Monday morning came early. RL walked up and stood in front of Mr. Smith's house. He watched as Howard crossed the creek on the foot bridge, over the railroad tracks, and up close to the Model-A Ford. RL was sitting on the running board when Howard walked up.

"Hello, RL."

"Hello, Howard."

"Othel told me you'd be with us today," Howard said.

By now, Othel Smith was walking down to the car. "RL, it's good to see you. Let's get started."

At that time, it was a small, one-lane dirt road they drove on. Willie Jones lived in the third house beside Othel, in the next house was a Gregory family, and in House 52 lived a Duncan family. The dirt road went behind the small barn owned by the Stearns Company and up a hill and underneath the tipple. Then the road headed down in front of the blue house (where my family lived at this time) and down a short hill that leveled off in front of the mine superintendent's house. The dirt road then turned right over a very small wooden bridge covering the drainage from the water spring originating up in the holler and then crossed the ballfield on the side close to the row of homes. From there, it crossed the railroad tracks at the crossing and then went down a small grade to the larger wooden bridge that spanned White Oak Creek. At the end of the bridge, the road came to a T. There, they turned left and stopped at the porch of the Co-operative Boardinghouse to pick up the rest of the crew. Now, the Model A was full inside and outside: A man stood on the running board on each side of the car. These two men held on by putting an arm inside the open window.

Leaving Co-operative, they headed up Dobbs Mountain hill and drove beyond Bell Farm, where they turned left off the main road and traveled down a long hill which started leveling out where George Gregory lived. Although George lived on the left side of the road, he owned another house on the right side of the road. Just beyond these houses was a huge barn. About a quarter mile from the barn was where the Smiths had their sawmill. At the time, Mr. Gregory owned the whole countryside, and it was with him the Smith Brothers contracted for the timber rights. Bull Hines drove the log truck for the Smith Brothers.

Driving from Co-operative to the jobsite to transport the Smith crew in that Model A took approximately one hour. The sawmill was out in the open, so if it started raining, the crew made its way to the barn for shelter. The men didn't even go to work on days when it was raining before they left home.

RL worked wherever he was needed that summer. But mainly he was on one end of a crosscut saw cutting down trees. RL was paid $6 a day, quite a sum, but like Mr. Smith told him, it was hard work. In those days, young men were not strangers to hard work; they did whatever they could do to make a dollar and were glad to get the work.

∞

Summer break had a way of passing rather fast. On the hill east of the schoolhouse, the Stearns Company carpenters poured concrete pillars, the foundation of the future Co-operative church house.

∞

Marion Wilson and Arnold Shoopman were good friends. Marion loved squirrel hunting as much as Arnold. They would get together and hunt as often as they could during hunting season. If it was just the two of them, they practically knew what the other was thinking, which came from spending a lot of time together. One night, early evening but dark, they each had their carbide lights for spot lighting. They both looked for holes high up in the trees; if they found one, they knew there was a good chance it was a squirrel nest.

"Come here, Arnold." Marion said. "I think I found one."

Arnold walked over to where Marion was standing. Marion found a safe place to prop up his gun. He then squatted down at the base of the tree. Arnold climbed up on Marion's shoulders. Marion then slowly stood up with Arnold on his shoulders. Now, Marion was a tall man, and this put Arnold high up the tree. If it was a good stretch to the first limbs, Marion would bring his arms up so Arnold could step on his hands. Then Marion would stretch his arms up as far as he could reach, which pushed Arnold a lot higher up the tree. Their system made tree climbing easy and they almost always scared up a squirrel out of its nest.

The following weekend, Arnold Shoopman, Marion Wilson, Harley Hardwick, and Willie Jones got together to go squirrel hunting. Marion once said, "There's not a tree too big or too high Arnold Shoopman can't climb when he's after a squirrel."

The guys paired off and hunted different hollers. Marion and Arnold went off together and Willie and Harley went another direction. Before dark, they all met back on the ridge and decided to do some spot lighting. Using their carbide lights, the men went together in single file to look for potential squirrel nests. They were about to call it a night when Harley spotted something high up and the other three shined their lights in the same direction. It lit up the area in the tree and they decided it was a squirrel nest.

Arnold climbed up on Marion's shoulders. Once he stood up, Marion told Arnold to step in his hands and stretched his arms as far up as he could, which put Arnold about fifteen feet up the tree. Arnold looked back at the ground and seeing the three men watching, Arnold yelled back toward the men, "Now don't yun's start shooting as soon as you see a squirrel; you might shoot me. Wait till it runs out a limb."

Arnold climbed up farther but remained lower than the nest. Arnold carried a few firecrackers for times like this, but when he didn't have firecrackers, he had makings for creating smoke to put in the hole. Arnold positioned himself just lower than the hole in the tree. All he had to do was reach up and, without effort, drop a firecracker in the hole. Arnold reached in his pocket and pulled out a firecracker, lit it, and dropped it in the hole. After the explosion, out ran a squirrel to the end of the limb and one of the men shot it. Arnold waited a few minutes for things to get quiet again.

Arnold yelled down to the ground, "You reckon there's another one?"

Marion yelled up, "Try it."

Arnold lit another firecracker and dropped it in the hole. Out scurried a squirrel on the same limb and one of the men on the ground shot it down.

Again, Arnold waited a few minutes and yelled down, "You reckon there's another one?"

Harley said, "Won't hurt to try."

Arnold did, and another squirrel came running out and one of the men on the ground shot it off the limb. Getting three squirrels from one tree, the men called it a night.

∞

Stearns Coal and Lumber Company decided to shut down the mine at the bottom of the incline in Co-operative because the coal seam was getting too small. The order came to start the robbing process.

The simplest way to describe robbing a mine is to first describe how a deep mine is worked. When a mine is opened, twenty-foot square rooms are blasted out; then the coal miners are assigned a specific room to work. If a person could look down inside the mine from a bird's eye view, it would look like a checkerboard. As miners emptied their twenty-by-twenty-foot square of accessible coal, they left the square room and moved to another room assigned to them. It's these unoccupied spaces that are worked during the robbing process. The coal miners go into the mine to the place where coal operation stopped and start working those square rooms that were left, making their way back to the face of the mine.

CO-OPERATIVE, KENTUCKY
CO-OPERATIVE MINE TIPPLE (TOP VIEW)
PHOTO COURTESY OF
THE *MCCREARY COUNTY RECORD*.

Several weeks passed with the robbing progressing at a steady, normal pace but the progress was nowhere near the face of the mine. Without warning, the roof close to the face of the mine collapsed, trapping the whole crew. The dust created by the fall inside the mine made visibility almost impossible and breathing more difficult until the dust settled some, which took a while. After getting their bearings, the miners gathered toward the rock fall and began digging.

Outside, the dust cloud created by the fall could be easily seen by anyone looking in that direction. But everyone at the tipple was busy doing their jobs and did not notice the fall immediately; however, the motorman heading toward the tipple to bring back the loaded cars saw the dust cloud coming out of the mine entrance. As he rounded the curve, he immediately stopped, and went back to the tipple and informed the tipple foreman and Cack Slaven, mine superintendent.

When they confirmed the roof had collapsed and trapped the miners, they shut down the tipple and every man rushed to the mine entrance to start digging. Cack sent the motorman to the main mine entrance, which was on the north mountain opposite the mountain where the collapse happened, to inform the men there to stop what they were doing and ride the motor car back to help.

When the men were all gathered, Cack organized three work groups. The men who lived outside of Co-operative and would be leaving on the evening train (Group 1) would start digging immediately. The men who lived in Co-operative he divided into two groups. Group 2 would start digging when the evening train left and work until 11:00 p.m. Group 3 would take over at 11:00 p.m.

Cack told Groups 2 and 3, "So right now, go home and get some rest."

"Now has everybody got it straight?" Cack asked and repeated the instructions briefly, "Group 1, start digging; Group 2, you come back when you hear the evening train come in; Group 3, you'll relieve group 2 at 11:00 p.m."

I'm sure Cack felt good about focusing everyone's minds on a purpose. This would be the way they would work until they found those men and got them out, no matter how long it took. Cack went to the Company Store and called Stearns officials to inform them what happened and what he was doing. The store had the only phone in the community.

The administrators of Stearns Coal and Lumber Company prepared for every contingency and backed Cack's decisions on dealing with this tragic event. Cack arranged for fresh buckets of spring water to be close to the face of the mine for easy access to the miners who were digging. I imagine Cack would have watched the progress for a long while. I'm sure Cack assessed what was being done and wondered if he had forgotten anything. I'm guessing when he was satisfied that everything possible was being done, he might have left his foreman in charge to walk home for a few minutes to clear his head. This is conjecture on my part.

Inside the mine on this day, thirty-eight men didn't know their fate. They, too, had divided into groups: while one group dug, the other group rested and conserved their battery lights. Under normal working conditions, the lamps would last an eight-hour work shift but not much longer.

The evening train whistle blew and Cack was at the face of the mine checking on the progress; the shift change took place. Cack asked his foreman to make sure the water buckets stayed filled with fresh, cool spring water. Cack stayed with the men; when he got tired, he found a place to sit but back far enough to be out of the way. After several hours, Cack may have gone home, planning to be back around 10:00 or 10:30 p.m., prior to the next shift change.

After the shift change at 11:00 p.m. and after standing close by a few more hours, I suspect Cack went home but he would not have gone to bed. He would have wanted to be ready at a moment's notice to get up and go. He may have tried sleeping in his chair. Sleep would not have come easy or lasted long, maybe an hour or two at most; not knowing whether his men inside the mine were dead or alive would have weighed heavy on him. He likely found himself walking back to the mine to check on the progress.

The men at the face of the mine would have had a fire going. Family members of the thirty-eight men inside the mine would have gathered there also as they could throughout the night. Cack would have stayed a long while. Likely, he would have walked back home again; he may have even tried to rest his eyes for a few more minutes; he might have made some coffee.

Walking back to the mine this time, he might have heard the morning train in the distance. Cack would have checked on the progress and would have been pleased with what they had accomplished through the night and pleased to see the men coming in on the morning train to relieve the men who had worked through the night.

Cack continued to stay just outside the mine entrance while the men from the morning train relieved the night crew that had worked since 11:00 p.m. Cack couldn't help notice how hard everyone worked. He was likely thinking that those miners on the outside digging knew it could have been them in the mine when it collapsed. Cack may have decided to walk to his office at the tipple; he had not been there since early morning the day before. Cack likely went through the motions of staying busy, knowing full well he wouldn't be able to concentrate on anything until those men were out of the mine. Sitting at his desk, Cack was praying when a frantic knock on the door came and the door swung open. Before Cack could say anything, the man said, "We broke through."

Cack rushed to the mine. When he got there, the first miner walked out. Cack walked straight to him and shook his hand, and all down the tram track on both sides were fellow miners and he jubilantly greeted every last one. Women and children who lived close enough to hear the celebratory noise came running; when their husband, or son, or brother came down the long corridor, they grabbed him, hugged him, and likely cried tears of relief. When Arnold Shoopman walked out of the dark mine, he covered his eyes briefly from the bright of day and the first person he saw when he opened them was his wife, Geneva; they walked home, arms wrapped tightly around each other.

The waiting was over, and the coal mining community of Co-operative breathed a huge sigh of relief; all thirty-eight men walked out, thankful to see the light of day.

∞

A few weeks later, Arnold and Geneva Shoopman moved their family down to the end of the Lower Camp of Co-operative and close to where Logan

Holler began. Arnold was able to rent the house next door to his brother Orville (Bug).

∞

The following month on Saturday night, November 22, on a street in Whitley City near the Jim Caylor building, Sheriff Douglas Manning was shot twice. Mr. Edward King gave himself up to officials following the shooting. His motivation for shooting Sheriff Manning and for turning himself in I could not uncover in my research. Mr. King was the son of Mrs. Lola King, former county clerk and former operator of the King Edward Café. Mr. King had been in Dayton, Ohio, working the past several months. Sheriff Manning was elected in 1944, and before that, served two terms as jailer. Sunday morning following the shooting, he underwent surgery at the Good Samaritan Hospital in Lexington, but never recovered. Coy Perkins was named sheriff to finish Mr. Manning's term.

∞

Mr. Ned Kidd received burns on seventy percent of his body when a cigarette caught his clothes on fire. His condition was critical for the duration of his hospital stay. He received several blood transfusions, which gave the family hope. However, on December 11, just over a month following the accident, his suffering came to an end. Just a few days before he died, he told his wife, Alma Jo, and his mother, Eva, he was ready to meet death. Mr. Kidd had joined the Fidelity Baptist Church at an early age. He was the son of the late Jeff Kidd, born and reared near Gregory and Bell Farm. He was employed by Stearns Coal and Lumber Company and worked at Co-operative Mine. Mr. Kidd left behind his wife and three daughters (Joann, June, and Judy), a son (Roger), four brothers (Guy, Neil, Curtis, and Bethanie), and six sisters (Amanda, Edna, Ruth, Daley, Mrs. Russell Draughn, and Mrs. Melvin Anderson). The pallbearers were fellow coal miners: Jess Chitwood, Arnold Winchester, Willard Bell, Othel Smith, Lester West, and Estil Bell.

MARRIED THIS YEAR 1947

Kathleen Crabtree, better known as Kitty, married Bill Marnhout. Kitty and Bill had three children: Mike, Randy, and Gary.

At Co-operative, Arlin Winchester, age 27, the son of Pete and Della Winchester, and Stella Smith, age 17, the daughter of Roscoe and Sarah Smith of Co-operative, got married. Stella was born and raised at Dobbs Hollow, until she was 15 years old, at which time Roscoe moved his family to Co-operative to the house next door to the Winchester family. Now neighbors, that's how Arlin and Stella met. Arlin and Stella had three children: Lee, Linda, and Angie.

Gran Smith, age 57, and Mattle Lay, age 43, both of Co-operative, got married.

BORN THIS YEAR 1947

Wanda Worley (my sister)
Beverly Keith
Eddie Winchester
Judy King
Clora Watson
Joe Haynes
Danny Bell
Jimmy Young
Darrell Whitehead
Lenna Coffey
Fayrene Waters
Larry Lewis
Bill Gregory
Joan E. Anderson
Eva Mae Haynes
Jim Douglas
Roy Whitehead
Virgil Conatser Jr.
Carolyn Crabtree
Bill Dixon
Brenda Cox

CHAPTER 23

Armless Wonder

Born Fred Thomas Strunk, August 9, 1930, at Barthell, he had two sisters, Dell and Evelyn, and a brother, Wilburn. His parents were Fred Strunk and Alpha (Dobbs) Strunk. I don't know if it was his parents or his schoolteachers who began calling Fred Thomas, Tommy, but Tommy was the name he was known by. You might be wondering what was so special about Tommy Strunk that I'd devote a chapter to his story. I have no doubt you will understand quickly just how special he really was, the man, Tommy Strunk.

You see, Tommy was born with no arms and no hands, and you might agree that was special. And for most people, that would have been the beginning and the end, but not so for Tommy; that was where his story began.

TOMMY STRUNK
SEEN HERE DRIVING HIS TRUCK.
PHOTO COURTESY OF
THE *MCCREARY COUNTY RECORD*.

Tommy was not yet four years old when his daddy, a coal miner, died. Tommy's mom moved the family to Skull Bone Tower Road, and Tommy went to Dobbs Hollow School. At that time to start first grade, a child had to be seven years old, so Tommy entered first grade in 1937.

In those early years, Tommy relied on his older brother, Wilburn, for everything. Especially at lunch time, Wilburn helped a lot—at first. But he gradually became resentful of the time he had to spend taking care of Tommy and at times ignored young Tommy. Wilburn would leave Tommy alone, and Tommy would sit and cry. At one of those times, Tommy must have figured out he was going to have to start learning how to take care of himself, so he started learning to use his feet and his toes to do things they weren't made to do. For example, Tommy learned quickly to write his name with his toes, to his teacher's surprise. After that, Tommy did all his schoolwork with his feet and toes.

At home, Tommy was constantly trying different things with his feet; he decided early on he wasn't going to give up. The things he couldn't do or thought he couldn't do, he kept trying until he could. After learning to write, he learned to play marbles and throw rocks, things he watched his friends do.

∞

Many days and weeks passed, and Tommy reached the point when he'd taken Wilburn's cruelty as long as he could. In those days, kids walked to and from school, and Wilburn was walking with several of his buddies on the way home. Tommy, walking several steps behind, watched the group of boys, and when Tommy saw his chance, he took a running leap and hit Wilburn on his side, knocking him off balance. Wilburn went rolling into a briar thicket. Wilburn's friends ran over to help him. Tommy started running as hard and fast as his legs would carry him and was near home by the time Wilburn got out of the briars and back on his feet.

∞

The kids at school were constantly bullying young Tommy; nobody would give him a chance or invite him to play games with them. The other kids were constantly saying, "How can you?" One day an older boy began picking on Tommy at recess. Wilburn would not come to Tommy's defense. When the boy got tired of harassing him, he waited until Tommy turned his back and pushed Tommy. Tommy lost his balance and fell. The boy then walked up to his friends, and they all laughed. Tommy got to his feet, slipped his right shoe off his foot, and felt a small rock under his toes. With his toes squeezing the small rock, he raised his foot and in one motion flung it. At lightning speed, the pebble hit the boy in the back of the head. The boy, almost in shock, turned and stared at Tommy as the back of his head began bleeding. A few other kids, seeing what Tommy had done, stared in amazement.

The teacher would have punished Tommy if not for a couple of other kids coming to Tommy's defense. When the teacher learned what had happened, she was amazed and could have still punished Tommy for throwing the rock at another person. The teacher chose not to because Tommy with no arms looked so helpless. The teacher's logic was that Tommy had to be handled differently, considering his circumstances. But that day was the turning point for Tommy.

That day, young Tommy's esteem among the other kids rose above everyone on the playground. After-all, who else could throw a rock with their toes. And yet, he must have looked so innocent standing there with no arms.

∞

One day at school Tommy saw a few of the guys pitching pennies. Tommy watched the whole recess break. It interested Tommy to the point he just knew he could do that, but he didn't have his own penny. He knew from watching the boys play that if he had a penny and he played and lost, his penny would be gone. He also knew if he pitched his penny closest to whatever the group agreed to pitch at, he would win all the coins.

Some days passed and Tommy was out playing. He was curious about most things but was especially curious when he saw something bright and shiny in the dirt. It was thin and might not be anything of value, but he couldn't just leave it not knowing for sure. Tommy slipped his shoe off, took hold of a stick lying nearby, and scratched the dirt around it, and to his shock, it was a nickel. It was the most money he'd ever had of his very own. Since Tommy went barefooted as often as the weather allowed, it was a good thing that day he was wearing shoes; Tommy put the nickel inside his shoe.

Several days passed, and every day Tommy practiced tossing the nickel at different targets until he felt confident enough about wagering his money.

The day came. It was morning recess. Three boys were tossing pennies. One boy ended up with all three as several other boys stood watching, including Tommy. The boy that won the pennies said,

"Anybody else got a penny to try me?" No one else took the challenge, and he singled out Tommy. "How about you, Tommy, you got a penny?"

"Nope," Tommy said. "But I got a nickel."

The boy said, "Well, all right. You afraid? You too chicken to try?"

"No," Tommy said. "I'll throw my nickel against your penny, but I'm only betting a penny."

The boy said, "Yea, sure. Besides, I don't believe you got a nickel."

Tommy slipped his foot out of his shoe, tilted his shoe, and out fell the nickel.

Wilburn, Tommy's brother, was one of the boys watching and said, "I'm telling Mom when I get home you got a nickel."

Tommy ignored his brother and tossed the nickel. The other boy tossed his penny and the boy won. He acted like he wasn't going to give Tommy his four pennies, but he finally did.

"You want to go again?" the boy asked. "I want those four pennies back."

The boy lined up and tossed the nickel and way under shot the target. Tommy won this time. They swapped money back again. Tommy had his nickel back. That very instant, the school bell rang. Recess was over. Tommy had gotten a taste of competition. He had let his nerves get the better of him on the first toss. He would not let that happen again.

At the afternoon recess, Tommy was challenged again and won three of the boy's four pennies. The boy would not toss his last penny. That afternoon when Tommy got home from school, he gave his mom the nickel and two pennies. He kept one penny for himself.

∞

As time went by, Tommy kept adding things he learned to do. He learned to feed himself. He learned to shoot a gun. He learned to hunt and kill squirrels. He learned to bait his own hook, cast his own reel, and fish. He learned to play horseshoes. All this before finishing the eighth grade. He also learned to do simple tasks like lighting matches, using a hammer and nails, brushing his teeth, and bringing in coal for the heating stove.

To get a bucket of coal, Tommy put his belt through the handle of the empty coal bucket and fastened it, then got ahold of the belt and put it over his head. He straightened up, lifting the empty coal bucket off the floor, slipped his shoe back on, walked to the front door, took his shoe off, and turned the doorknob with his toes to open the door. He then slipped his shoe back on, stepped outside, slipped off his shoe, took hold of the knob, and closed the door.

He walked to the coal pile and bent over to let the coal bucket ease to the ground. While bent over, he removed the belt off his head, and with his foot, filled the coal bucket with coal. He put the belt back over his head, straightened up, slipped his shoe on, and walked back to the door. Taking his shoe off at the door, he opened the door, slipped his shoe on, and stepped inside. Then he slipped off his shoe, closed the door, slipped his shoe back on, and carried the coal bucket close to the heating stove. He bent over, lowering the coal bucket to the floor, and bent a bit lower to let the belt slip off his head. He then slipped his shoe off and removed the belt. If the stove needed more coal, he put some in the stove before putting his shoe back on.

∞

Tommy finished the eighth grade in spring 1945. For the next two years, he did a lot of hunting and fishing and trying to figure out what he was going to do in life. Time moved slowly, and it's possible Tommy thought this was it for him. But in 1947, a friend persuaded Tommy to go to Stearns one night during the 4th of July celebration. Tommy didn't like going to places where he needed money because he had none.

When Tommy and his friend arrived, the large Stearns ballfield was full of people and lights and sounds and shows and rides and smells. The Capital City Shows were lined up around the peripheral and in the center of the large space. Games sounding like slot machines in Vegas, motors humming, people talking, kids (and adults) squealing on rides, and music blaring—sounds saturated the air. Lights on the rides and games flashed nonstop. It was a beautiful sensory overload for the miners, their families, and other county folk. Once a year they had the pleasure of experiencing the 4th of July carnival. It was a time when folks got to see friends and family they often saw only once a year. It was a massive family reunion of sorts.

Walking through the grounds a couple of times looking at all the shows, the games, and the people, a light came on for Tommy. He figured out what he was going to do with his life. Tommy asked a carnival worker, "Who's in charge of all this?" The man pointed Tommy in the direction of the manager's trailer. Tommy and his friend found the trailer and Tommy lightly knocked on the door with the toe of his shoe.

A man opened the door and looked at Tommy. "I want to talk to you about a job," Tommy said.

The man asked, "What can you do?"

"I can do anything but snap my fingers," Tommy said.

The man's face lit up and after a brief pause said, "You come back around midnight and show me what you can do."

Tommy and his friend never left the carnival grounds. They walked around a few times and decided sitting was cheaper and easier on the feet than walking, so they headed to the bleachers and sat and waited until the grounds cleared. Tommy and his friend walked to the manager's trailer. The manager came out and they walked to a tent in back, along with a few interested carnival workers. Tommy showed he could shoot a rifle and hit the bull's eye every time, drive a nail with a hammer, and sign his name with a pencil.

"Okay, okay, I've seen enough," the man said. "You got the job."

For the next fifteen years, Tommy Strunk, the country boy from Dobbs Hollow, traveled with the carnival, had his own tent, and was advertised as the Armless Wonder. And people paid to see him perform. During those carnival years, Tommy drove nails with a hammer, pitched horseshoes, struck matches, threaded needles, wrote his name and address, and performed as a sharpshooter. He hit the bull's eye so often, people watching thought it was a trick and had trouble believing what they saw.

Traveling with the carnival, Tommy visited Mexico, Canada, and forty-one states in the U.S. and earned eighty to ninety dollars a week.

∞

In 1962, Tommy came back home to McCreary County to the mountains he loved. He had always lived in areas close to Co-operative. In those early years, Tommy didn't have a driver's license but that didn't stop him from driving. It was Floyd Frasure who stopped Tommy and told him if he was going to drive, he needed a driver's license.

Tommy found out where he needed to go to get his license. The officer looked at Tommy but couldn't find anything in his manual that prevented Tommy from trying for a motor vehicle license. Reluctantly, he gave Tommy the written test; Tommy, writing with his toes, passed the written exam.

When Tommy returned for the road test, he saw it was the same officer who gave him the written test. The young officer watched the armless Tommy open the car door with his toes, get in, and close the door. In shock, the officer reluctantly got in the passenger seat. Tommy turned the ignition with his toes, put the car in reverse, and backed up. Then he put the selector in drive and drove away with his right foot guiding the steering wheel. Tommy did everything the officer asked, including parallel parking in front of the courthouse. Tommy pulled the car in the same location where he started and parked the car. Tommy passed the road test scoring in the 90s. The officer told Tommy, "If there were more drivers like you, I'd be out of a job."

∞

Tommy met the beautiful Virginia Watson, and after a period of courtship, they decided to get married. Lec Watson, Virginia's dad, living in Western Kentucky, came to the wedding. Someone asked Lec what he thought about his daughter marrying Tommy and he said, "Well, if you're going to make a mistake, you might as well make a damn big one." So Tommy and Virginia got married and remained together for the rest of Tommy's life.

∞

During the years of living back in the hills of Kentucky, Tommy drove coal trucks and logging trucks. Tommy, in his own words, described what it was like to drive a log truck down a rutted mountain road with mud a foot and a half deep: "It's tough with the truck bouncing, but I learned to do it safely." Tommy's left foot worked the gas pedal, brake, and clutch; his right foot handled the steering wheel and changed gears. He braced the steering wheel with his leg when he changed gears.

∞

During the mid-1980s, the *National Enquirer* ran a story about Tommy and the *McCreary County Record* ran two articles on the Armless Wonder. Without a doubt, Tommy Strunk was one of the most popular McCreary County citizens of all time.

∞

In the latter years of Tommy's life, he said he wasn't bitter about being born with no arms and hands. His physical impairment turned out to be his livelihood and his ticket to places he would not have seen if he'd been born with arms and hands. Tommy also said, and I quote, "When life gives you a lemon, you make lemonade."

Some of the people who knew Tommy personally may be inclined to judge him harshly, but I know these things about the man: Tommy didn't depend on others to support him, which he could have. Tommy, as a youngster, didn't adopt an attitude of "I can't," which he could have. Tommy didn't let his physical challenges plunge him into depression, which he could have. Tommy didn't want people to feel sorry for him, which he could have. Instead, Tommy had enough spunk and attitude to do what most around him would say was impossible. He set out to do, at an early age, the impossible and succeeded. That's the man Tommy Strunk was. Toward the end of his life, he said, and I quote, "I consider myself lucky."

∞

Fred Thomas Strunk died February 6, 1999.

CHAPTER 24

1948

As 1948 began, the law served notice to the community of Yamacraw. The community had voted in November in favor of the corral law, which included hogs. Some people were continuing the tradition of letting their hogs run where they pleased. These people were given notice they had thirty days to corral their hogs or legal action would be taken. I guess some people thought they might have more time before the county started slinging words around like legal action. Besides, it was a lot of extra work to cut down trees to make a pen for one's hogs. Another issue was the smell. If the owner didn't have a good-sized lot, he would have to build the pen close to the house, creating an awful smell in almost no time. The nearest neighbor also had to be considered. Everyone soon conformed to the corral law and all controversy was forgotten.

∞

In the community of Worley, on a Monday night, thieves entered the Stearns Company General Merchandise Store and got away with one hundred dollars worth of jewelry. Local officials had no suspects in the case.

∞

As of March 21, all coal miners working for Stearns Coal and Lumber Company were on strike, along with coal miners across the country. The walkout occurred when John L. Lewis who represented all coal miners, slammed the coal company operators for breaking the contract by not activating the pension fund. The dispute over method of payment was between John L. Lewis, representing coal miners, and Ezra Vanhorn, representing coal operators. The pension fund was thirty million dollars financed by a ten percent royalty on coal production. A month later, both sides agreed that work should continue while the two sides ironed out the method of payment details. Critics called the strike the most needless in recent memory.

∞

At the time of publishing my book titled *CO-OP: Coal, Community, & House 52*, I did not know Jess King's wife's name or the names of their children. Jess lived in Co-operative in House 32 in the Upper

Camp. Mrs. King was Gracie (Cooper) King. Their children were Wilma, Glen, Vella, Mary Jo, and Jimmy (Jim).

Jim King remembers that Oren Spradlin came to Co-operative Saturday afternoons, twice a month, to cut people's hair, mostly males'. There was a bench outside next to the wall of the Stearns Bathhouse. The bench was made by putting three 2x4s together side by side. They rested on five-gallon lard cans, one on each end of the boards and one in the center to keep the ten-foot-long boards from sagging in the middle when it was full of guys waiting to get a haircut. Oren, in those days, would cut hair until dark for twenty-five cents per head.

∞

In those days, every fall, Stearns Company would bring a carload of coal to Co-operative on one of the trains bringing supplies to the Company Store. On the side of the tracks opposite the store but close to the crossing, there was a small one-room building that was used to house surplus supplies for the Company Store. It was next to that building where the car of coal was dumped. The coal was free to the coal miners to take to their homes to use for heat and cooking. Each individual household was responsible for getting its own coal. The way the houses were designed on the hilly terrain, there was usually a space under the house for keeping coal and wood dry. The underpinning was boxed in with wood and a door for easy access.

Wilburn Burk lived on the hill in House 39 behind Jess King's family. The Burks had a bunch of sons and one of them was named Harrison. Harrison was mentally challenged, but he was physically strong as an ox. Many thought he didn't know his own strength, but when he played with other kids, he was very gentle with them. When Harrison saw the coal being dropped off over by the Company Store, he would head over with two grass sacks. He'd fill those grass sacks full of coal, leaving just enough room to squeeze the top together. Those grass sacks when filled with coal weighed about one hundred pounds each. Harrison would carry both grass sacks on his back at the same time up the hill to their house and could do that all day or until Mr. Burk told him to stop.

∞

A dedication service at the Co-operative New Haven United Baptist Church was scheduled for June 19 but had to be postponed. Early Sunday morning, nine train cars derailed near Burnside, and the officials that were to be present for the dedication were called out to investigate the wreckage. However, on Sunday, July 4, 1948, the dedication service took place. Southern Railway officials were on hand; they donated a beautiful church bell to New Haven United Baptist Church. After the service, a 'dinner on the ground' was provided by the ladies of the church. It was an enjoyable time of fellowship.

∞

It was a Saturday afternoon in Co-operative when Harley Hardwick walked down the railroad tracks toward the Lower Camp at the same time that RL Terry walked toward the ballfield from the opposite direction. They met just below the tipple on the

CO-OPERATIVE, KENTUCKY
DRAWING BY CHARLES DAN WORLEY OF THE
CO-OPERATIVE MINE TIPPLE AND
PART OF THE LOWER CAMP.
(LOWER CAMP WASN'T AN OFFICIAL NAME BUT
THE NAME WE GAVE THE PART OF
CO-OPERATIVE EAST OF THE TIPPLE.
UPPER CAMP LAY WEST OF THE TIPPLE.)

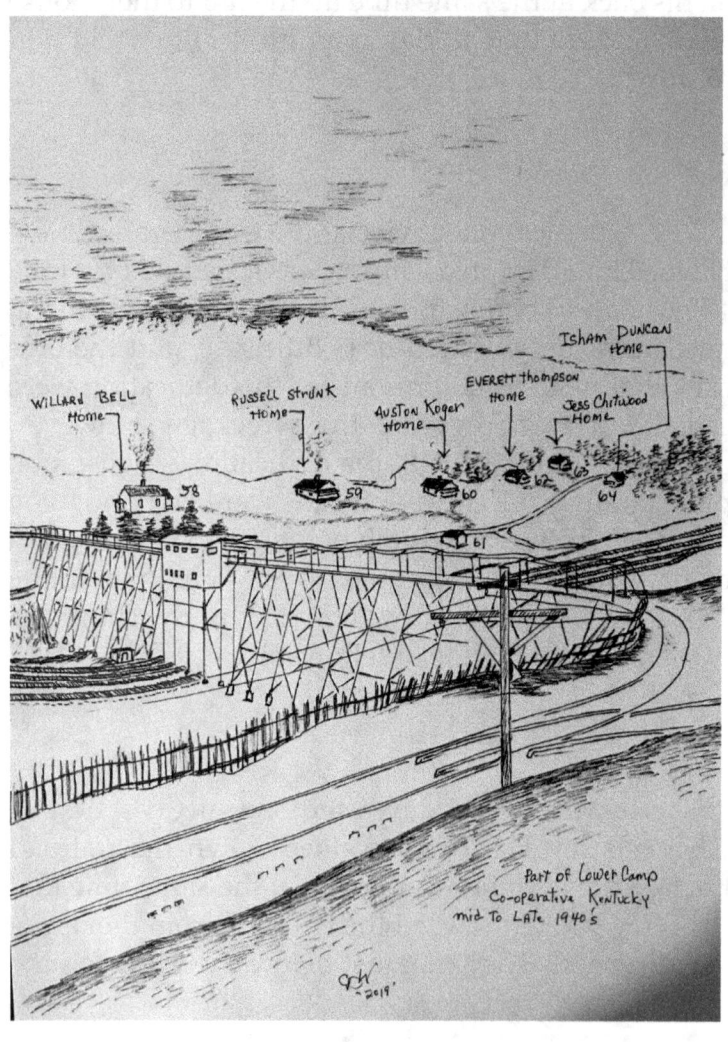

CO-OPERATIVE, KENTUCKY
DRAWING OF THE LOWER CAMP BY
CHARLES DAN WORLEY.
VIEW: LOOKING EAST FROM THE TIPPLE.

side of the Lower Camp. RL noticed Harley was carrying his cane pole. RL asked, "You goin' fishing?"

"Yeah, I was coming to see if you wanted to go," Harley said.

RL said, "Yeah, sure. Where you goin'?"

"Above Bridge 11," Harley said.

RL said, "OK. Let's go. I'll stop off at the house and get my stuff."

After stopping at the Terry home, they walked down to the head of Logan Holler and turned off to the right on the path where there were oil wells and a water spring. The path came out on the creek side behind Guy Kidd's Grocery. They crossed the creek and then walked the railroad track toward Fidelity. They crossed Bridge 11 and just beyond were the two ponds. Harley wanted to fish in the first pond. Typically, the ponds had all kinds of fish in them.

They had not been there long when Harley caught a bass and RL caught a red eye. Then they sat for a long while without catching anything. Suddenly, Harley hooked something that was so big it was like pulling against dead weight. Harley wrestled with his fishing pole so long his arms were starting to wear down. Harley turned his back to the water and started walking up the bank away from the water. As Harley started walking, whatever was on the other end of his fishing line gradually started coming to the surface.

RL then began to see what they both hoped was a big fish, but when the first little bit of the catch appeared, RL said, "Harley, you caught a turtle. It's out of the water." RL walked toward it for a closer look. Harley stopped pulling and walked back to the turtle. RL said, "That's the biggest turtle I've ever seen." Harley agreed.

The turtle had the hook in its mouth and its neck was stretched out, which was how the turtle got pulled up onto the bank. Harley made sure the line was still taut. Harley asked RL to reach him his shotgun. Harley shot the turtle's head off. Now, there wasn't anything holding the turtle on the bank. The bank was wet from the water that came out with the turtle, and Harley and RL didn't have time to react. All they had time to do was look at each other after watching the turtle slide lickety-split back into the water and disappear.

"Oh no," Harley said. "We missed out on some good eating; a turtle has seven different flavors of meat."

"Well, it's gone now," RL said.

Losing the turtle took the heart out of any more fishing for that day. They walked home.

∞

Two weekends later, some of the usual suspects talked up a Saturday night fishing outing back at the Ship Rock: Arnold Shoopman, RL Terry, Harvey Terry, Dewey Wright, Harley Hardwick, and Ezra Foust. It was early Saturday afternoon. They carried everything they needed. As the group got close to their favorite camping spot, they stopped. There were already two guys in the place where they wanted to be. Suddenly, the game warden Vole Owens came out from behind a tree and one of the two guys took off running. Vole Owens ran after him. The one remaining in the camp packed their stuff and started to leave.

Arnold said, "You don't have to leave cause of us."

The man said, "No, I have to cause I don't have a fishing license."

He kept walking and went out of sight. After a long while, Vole, the game warden, came back to the campsite and told them, "You know, I chased that man a quarter mile and suddenly he stopped. I told him running from me was going to cost him. The man reached in his back pocket and pulled out his fishing license. I asked him why he ran, and he told me his friend I left standing at the campsite didn't have a license."

Vole looked around and said, "I guess that guy is long gone?"

"Yep," RL said. "He left right after you took off running."

The game warden left, and after a good laugh, the usual suspects got busy setting up camp. Then they enjoyed some fishing while sitting in their favorite spots on the bank near their campsite. Ezra set up the trotline and docked the small boat. Now it was time for peace and harmony—fishing with friends and listening to nature.

Down the way in the distance, they could hear an occasional bird singing and the water rushing over rocks. RL saw his dad cut off his next chew of tobacco. Harvey liked to mix King Bee and a plug. He also liked to take a cut of King Bee, let it sit and dry out, and crumble it up in his pipe. That sure did top things off and help him digest an evening meal.

As Ezra settled in his favorite fishing spot on the bank, Arnold Shoopman told him, "It sure doesn't get better than this." Anyone hearing those words knew exactly what he meant. Fishing with good friends away from the noise of the world had a way of recharging a person's spirit, and a man's mind had a chance to slow down for a moment to appreciate and give thanks for being alive in the world.

Harley Hardwick started telling RL some old sayings: "Hiccup, Hiccup, right up straight up, three sups out of a teacup will cure the hiccups."

"Here's another good one," Harley said. "Beans, beans, good for your heart, the more you eat, the more you fart." RL and Harley had a good laugh.

Arnold told Ezra he was leaving his hook in the water and asked him to watch it. He was going to get supper started. About thirty minutes later, the rest of the guys left the bank, gathered around the fire, and helped Arnold finish preparing the food. After supper, they had time to get in some more fishing and get their carbide lights ready before dark. Harvey Terry fired up his smoking pipe. The aroma from the food lingered with a light hint of a good smell, and the smoke from the fire and Harvey's pipe kept the mosquitoes away.

Just before dark, Ezra left to check the trotline. When he returned, he complained he'd caught more water dogs than fish. Ezra threw those water dogs on the bank and put a bullet in the top of their heads with his .22 rifle.

Not long after darkness set in, they heard an occasional sound of a cat screaming in the distance. Then suddenly a cat screamed so loud it sounded like it was in the camp with them. They froze and began searching for where the sound came from. Then Arnold said, "Look on top of the Ship Rock." There were two sets of eyeballs looking down at them.

"Well," Ezra said, "they won't come down here. At least they never have before."

RL said, "What's that noise?"

Everyone heard it. It was a rumbling noise that lasted a good five to ten minutes. Then the rumbling stopped, and they heard the fish flopping on top of the water. After a minute or so, everything quieted down.

Harvey said, "Fishing's no good now."

"Why?" RL asked.

Harvey said, "The water has turned over."

"Everything that was on the bottom is now on the top," Arnold said. "And everything that was on the top is now on the bottom."

Ezra said, "Might as well try to get a few hours of sleep and head back in the morning."

"Might as well," Harvey said. "Fishing won't be good here for several days."

And so it went. What started out to be a good fishing trip ended abruptly without warning. But that's the way things go sometimes. It can't be helped. You just deal with it and go on. The hope is that the next time it will be better.

∞

The game warden Vole Owens continued to have a bad weekend. Shelly Crabtree was a well-known moonshiner and bootlegger. The problem was catching Shelly with any kind of evidence. Shelly lived in Lonesome but no one, to anyone's knowledge, had ever found a sign of a still. Shelly knew how to evade and move, an ole fashion game of cat and mouse. Shelly also knew without concrete evidence he couldn't be charged and fined.

Every chance Vole got, he drove into Lonesome, always parked in a different place, and scouted the woods and hollers looking for Ole Shelly. One time, Vole walked until he could see Shelly's cabin with his binoculars, and he watched the place for a long time. Shelly saw someone outside the house, but he was not close enough to make a positive identification. Vole was on a rise just beyond the tree line; did Shelly see the glare of the glass of the binoculars? A man walked away from the house in the opposite direction. Vole worked his way around through the trees and tried to follow the man. After walking a couple of hours, Vole lost sight of the man, and not knowing which direction to go, he decided to turn back. It wasn't easy; the terrain was difficult. Vole made it back to his truck as the sun was setting. Shelly always snookered the game warden. Shelly told someone, "A game warden never learns."

∞

MARRIED THIS YEAR 1948

Jess Willard Worley, age 17, and Imogene Anderson, age 16, both from Co-operative, got married.

∞

BORN THIS YEAR 1948

Faye Shoopman Jones
Ernie Jones
Gayle King
Alvin Jones
Mary Troxell
Shirley Coffey
Leroy Hall
Shirley Jean Hall
Larry Tapley
Donald Lee Maxwell
Bruce Shook

Hershel Gibson
Clinton Maples
Carolyn Cox
Mike Keith
Rick Carson
Stan Cox

CHAPTER 25

1949

Early in 1949, the community of Bell Farm woke up Sunday morning to find the Stearns Company Store had been burglarized sometime Saturday night. The thieves, or thief, gained entry by cutting through a panel in the front door. The store manager took inventory and had a list of missing items to give to the police officers. The list included shotgun shells, .22 bullets, a pair of socks, and sugar.

    A few weeks just prior to the Bell Farm break-in and toward the end of 1948, the Stearns Company Store in the community of Worley was looted and burned. The fire destroyed the building, which included the U.S. Post Office. Three men were apprehended and convicted of stealing scrip and setting fire to the building. Two sacks of scrip were later recovered near Comargo.

∞

In the auto industry, Ford Motor Company made a comeback, winning the Gold Metal Award of Fashion of New York. Ford was named the fashion car of the year.

∞

In Whitley City on a Thursday night, just past midnight, Dewey Kennedy, a deputy constable under Exroat Watson and employed by some Whitley City merchants as night watchman, stepped onto Main Street after rounding the corner opposite Burgess Drug Store to investigate a car that had stopped on the street. As Kennedy walked close to the vehicle, shots rang out from the car. The car then sped away. Kennedy pulled his revolver and managed to get three shots off, hitting the rear end of the car. Kennedy, hit once in the hand and once in the abdomen, struggled to get out of the street.

Dr. Haley in Whitley City treated Deputy Constable Kennedy's gunshot wounds. While being treated, Kennedy gave his report to the State Police. He got close enough to the car to identify J. Earl Wilson as the driver of the car and Gilbert Wilson as the one who shot him. Mr. Kennedy was then taken to Jellico Hospital. Both Wilson boys, formerly of Whitley City, lived in Whitley County and were cousins.

Early Friday morning, the police arrested both Wilson boys and charged them with malicious shooting and wounding with intent to kill. Both Wilson boys denied any knowledge of the tragedy. At the time of the arrests, officers did not know Mr. Kennedy had died at Jellico Hospital. The charge was then changed to murder. Later that morning, a car was found near Falls Road with bullet holes in the rear. Wilson had called and reported the car stolen sometime in the wee morning hours. Mr. Kennedy was survived by his wife and four-year-old son. At the trial, the Wilson boys were found not guilty of murder and were set free.

∞

The Stearns Greyhound station announced new bus rates to Somerset at $ 0.65; to Danville at $1.55; to Lexington at $2.25; to Louisville at $3.20; to Cincinnati at $3.85; to Indianapolis at $5.95; and to Chattanooga at $2.90.

∞

That summer, Ledford Clark, son of Bo and Louvada Clark, lived in White Oak Junction. Ledford managed somehow to get an old car. When Ledford got the car, it had been sitting for a long time, but Ledford wanted to see if he could get it running. People had been moving from the area of Fidelity ever since the mine closed in 1937. The previous owner of the car, no doubt, had given little thought to the old car ever running again. The man wanted $8.00 for the car, so Ledford bought the car. The owner figured some money was better than no money. Besides, if he had to get someone to move the car for him, money would be coming out of his pocket. So Ledford talked with Coy Whitehead who agreed to help Ledford get the car home. The car had two flat tires that had to be taken off the car, fixed, and put back on the car. Coy got the okay from Guy Kidd to use his truck to pull the car back home.

CO-OPERATIVE, KENTUCKY
PHOTO SHOWS PART OF THE BATHHOUSE AND
BOARDINGHOUSE. THE TINY BUILDING IN FRONT
IS WHERE RL TERRY AND THE GUYS WOULD
SIT OUTSIDE AND PLAY MUSIC.
PHOTO COURTESY OF BURMAN SLAVEN.

Ledford had been working on the car for a good while when news spread about his having a car. That was a pretty big deal in those days. A young boy with a car was unheard of. RL Terry remembers walking from Co-operative down the tracks to White Oak Junction to check out Ledford's car. It was only about a half-mile walk. From time to time several younger boys around White Oak Junction would go by and watch Ledford clean and work on the old car. Ledford's brothers also spent time helping Ledford. It was something to do for a boy. Weeks went by and Ledford's car was hardly mentioned because most felt the car would never run.

On a Friday evening, several of the guys were in the ballfield in Co-operative playing marbles when, in the distance, they heard a car getting close. It was loud. Sounded like it could use a muffler, and the occasional backfires sounded like a shotgun discharging. As the car came across the bridge, the boys playing marbles looked toward the crossing. When the car crossed the tracks and dipped down into the ballfield, it was clear who it was, but they couldn't believe it was Ledford. When Ledford parked the car, all the boys in the ballfield quit playing marbles and walked around the car, and it didn't take long for somebody to suggest taking a ride. Ledford said, "Let's go to Bell Farm and back." Most of the guys didn't want to take the chance of going that far. Plus, some of the parents wouldn't let them if they asked. However, RL Terry and Hobert and Don, the Dixon brothers, were old enough to go without parental permission. Several loaded up, and they took off with the car backfiring across the ballfield.

They stopped at Jewell Kidd's store and RL bought everybody a bottle of pop. Then they headed on up the hill toward Dobbs Mountain. Going up the steep part of the hill, the car was so loud that talking was virtually impossible. They cruised on to Bell Farm. Young and having a blast, no one noticed the sun had set, and with mountains all around, the light was leaving fast. Dusk had set in and it was almost too dark to see without headlights. Either Ledford forgot about the headlights not working or he thought they'd be back in Co-operative before dark because by now Ledford had slowed to a crawl. Yep, he was having trouble seeing the road.

Hobert asked, "Ledford, don't the headlights work?"

"Nope," Ledford said.

Hobert said, "Stop the car. Come on, RL, we'll be his headlights. It'll be fun."

"What have you got in mind?" RL asked.

Hobert said, "You got your flashlight on you?"

"Well, yeah," RL said.

Hobert whipped out his flashlight as he climbed up on the driver's side fender. RL got on the front passenger fender. Both flashlights shining made a pretty good light. It was all Ledford's young eyes needed. Ledford gave that old car some extra gas and after a few spits and sputters and two or three backfires, which had every dog within five miles howling and barking and a couple dogs chasing the car, away they went.

It didn't take long before Fred and Don wanted their turn on the fenders. After all, Hobert and RL were having so much fun and occasionally Hobert yelled, "Giddy-UP."

Ledford pulled off the road at Sherd Dobbs Cemetery and stopped the car. Don and Fred came out of the car, wanting their turn on the fenders. RL didn't mind at all letting Fred switch places with him. Fred climbed up on the fender. But Hobert on the other fender wasn't about to give up his place willingly. Hobert told Don, "Get back into the car."

Don said, "No, you get in the car."

Suddenly, Don grabbed Hobert's legs and gave him a tug. Hobert slid off the fender and lost his balance. He hit the ground in a sitting position. Hobert got to his feet as quickly as he could and came at Don with both fists swinging. Don and Hobert locked up and went rolling into the ditch line. Wasn't anything to do now but watch and hope no one got hurt. Before long, Don came out of the ditch and climbed on the fender into position. Hobert crawled out of the ditch, and as he did, his hand felt a stick.

This stick gave him a new burst of energy and confidence. He got to his feet and started swinging the stick. Don slid across the hood and got off the car on the other side. All the time Hobert was swinging that stick as hard and as fast as he could. The only thing he hit was the car fender and hood. Ledford, now out of the car, saw his chance and grabbed the stick from Hobert and threw it as far as he could. He got back in the car and started it up. Ledford looked at Hobert and said, "If you're going with us, get in the car. If not, you can walk home." Don and Fred got back on the fenders and Hobert got in the back seat with only a few cuts and bruises.

They got back to Co-operative without any more incidents. Ledford drove past the crossing and around the curve and under the coal tipple and stopped the car before going up the hill. RL and Hobert got out. It was only a short distance to where the Terrys and Dixons lived over across White Oak Creek in the Lower Camp. RL told Ledford he'd had fun. Don said he'd ride on to White Oak Junction and walk home from there. Fred stayed where he was. As the car pulled out and headed up the hill, RL and Hobert walked home. RL thought as they walked, if you get two or more Dixons together, you'll have a fight every time. With the Dixon boys, that's the way it was and would be for many more years.

∞

The next evening RL picked up his flat-top guitar and walked up to the ballfield, it being Saturday night. If some of the guys wanted to play music, he wouldn't have to walk back home to get his guitar. Just past the crossing on the ballfield side but next to the railroad tracks was a small building the Stearns Company Store used to store extra supplies. The building had a porch, perfect for sitting and picking music. RL placed his guitar on the porch and walked over to the ballfield. RL thought he might as well join a marble game while there was still daylight.

As the sunlight faded over the mountain tops of Co-operative and it was too dark to play marbles, RL walked over to the little porch of the building, picked his guitar up, and started strumming. Gerstel Bell, who lived over on the hill above the boardinghouse, heard RL and decided to join him. They wondered if anyone else would show. RL looked down the tracks toward the tipple and faintly made out a couple of people walking in his direction. RL's attention moved even farther to the right. In the ballfield, some of the guys had started a fire.

From the little porch where Gerstel and RL were, Gerstel got up and stepped across the railroad tracks on the far side and started a fire. When the fire got to going good, Gerstel ran home and brought back taters to roast a little later. The two guys walking up the railroad tracks, RL could now see, were Fred Clark and Hobert Dixon. Fred couldn't play a musical instrument but, boy, could he sing. Fred was the son of Bo and Louvada Clark of White Oak Junction, and he walked up to Co-operative on most Saturday nights. Everyone who heard Fred sing said, "If that boy had the chance, he could make it big in Nashville." Fred could hear a song one time, and if he liked it, he could sing it. He knew all the songs he sang by heart.

Everyone was welcome to join in, and when the boys kicked into a song, the sound carried all over the Upper Camp. Some of the dads who were sitting on their porches enjoying the evening, their week's work of shoveling coal over, welcomed the peaceful rest and the music. Most of the front porches in the Upper Camp had people sitting and listening to the boys picking and Fred singing. The boys would play for several hours, taking a break to eat a roasted tater. And if they needed a drink of water, they had a water pump behind the little building where they were sitting. The concert the boys put on was free to anyone who cared to listen. They'd play until around 11:00 p.m. when Fred wanted to stop because he had a long walk home to White Oak Junction.

∞

Glen Hollars, Lonnie Hollars' brother, was sweet on Jack Haynes' daughter Christine. When they became close friends and began courting, Glen drove to Co-operative every weekend. Before Glen drove to the Haynes home and picked up Christine, he'd stop by Jewell Kidd's Grocery. Usually somebody he knew was at the store to talk to. But even if no one was there that he knew, Jewell always welcomed company, and in between serving customers, she loved sitting and talking to folks. Jewell kept chairs inside around the counter and outside on the front porch so folks could sit wherever they felt comfortable.

Glen very seldom drove the same car; it was handy having a brother who owned a used car business. Lonnie Hollars Used Cars was south of Dixie. Glen would drive a car off the lot and use it for the afternoon. Glen got his nickname from something he said every time he drove a different car to Co-operative. The boys would get Glen to talking about the car he was driving; Glen had a lisp and couldn't speak some of his words clearly.

The guys would ask, "Hey, Glen, how do you like that car you're driving today?"

Glen would answer, "I gotta thirty-five-dollar kar and a hundred dollar waydough." (Glen was saying "I got a thirty-five-dollar car and a hundred dollar radio.")

So Glen's nickname became Waydough.

Another thing the boys would ask: "Waydough, is that car you're driving really any count?"

Waydough would say, "That kar I'm driving is the best kar I ever had. I could drive it all the way to Hawaii and it still would never miss a wick."

One time, one of the guys was talking about his own car and said, "You know when I'm driving my old car, every time I shift gears, I have to double clutch it."

Waydough said, "I know you're pulling my weg [leg], cause I know one of them pedals is the brake."

Before he left, Waydough would say, "See you fellers waiter. I'm going to see my waddy fwynn." (Waydough was saying "See you fellows later. I'm going to see my lady friend.")

∞

Squirrel season opened and Harley Hardwick and RL Terry wanted to go the first morning. It worked out good because opening day was a Saturday, so Harley didn't have to work at the mine. Down in the Lower Camp over on the hill across the gravel road on the north side, there were five houses and the Bells lived in the fourth house toward the tipple. Harley and RL walked by the Bell house and over the hill down the other side into the holler. There were two hickory nut trees a small distance apart. They walked to the first one and waited for daylight. The plan was that when it started getting daylight they would walk down to the other hickory nut tree.

With daylight, a few screech owls flew to a couple of trees close to where RL and Harley were sitting. RL told Harley, "If those things stay long, hunting won't be worth a dime." They waited for the owls to leave. Instead, the situation got worse as more and more screech owls flew in until one tree was black with screech owls and all of them were yelping. Harley pulled out a brown paper bag and put some salt in it and laid it down on the path and set it on fire. Within a couple of minutes every last one of those owls was gone. They waited another ten minutes before walking on down into the holler; squirrel hunting was good that morning.

∞

Three Co-operative boys were pals and loved doing things together: Buck Maples, Kenneth Waters, and Greg Gregory. In the fall when the leaves were falling, they loved going up on the mountain directly in front of Jewell Kidd's Grocery. Near the top at one particular place in the cliff, there was a separation with just barely enough room for anybody, who had a mind to, to go through but lots of room for a young boy. That crevice would be full of fallen leaves, and it had enough downward slope to make a good slide. The three boys loved passing the time by sliding in that natural passageway.

Kenneth's younger brother Chester always followed the three older boys, which they didn't like. They thought he was just in the way. But that didn't stop Chester from trying. One day, the three boys walked to the cliff and Chester tagged along behind. They climbed around on the rocks and suddenly Chester disappeared. The boys looked for Chester without any luck. Then while standing on a huge rock, they looked down and saw Chester lying on the ground not moving. The three boys rushed to him as quickly as they could. Still, he wasn't moving on his own, and they thought he was dead. Buck and Greg each took hold of Chester's ankles and dragged him off the mountain. When they reached the bottom with Buck and Greg still pulling Chester, Kenneth started crying, thinking he had let his little brother get killed while not paying attention to him.

Suddenly, Chester started kicking his feet loose from Buck and Greg's grip and jumped up and ran home. Buck, Greg, and Kenneth tried to catch Chester, yelling the whole time they'd kill him if they caught him.

A few days later, Buck, Kenneth, and Greg, after a day of roaming around Co-operative, went home. Greg's mom was waiting with a switch in her hand and told Greg he was getting a whipping. Greg pleaded with his mom, "Why? What have I done?"

She said, "I've been told you had a rope tied to a tree and were swinging out over the top of a cliff."

"Mom," begged Greg, "that didn't happen. Please, I'm telling you the truth."

Greg's mom, Della, believed him and didn't whip him.

The next day when Greg met up with Buck and Kenneth, he told them what happened and they said the same thing happened to them. The three boys always wondered if Chester told that story to their moms; they never found out for sure.

∞

Halloween was all about having fun and there was no camp ordinance when kids had to be home. Young people would have a bonfire going in the middle of the ballfield in Co-operative. Burman Slaven got an idea he thought would be fun. Burman told some of his friends and they also thought it would be fun and were willing to help. Halloween came on a Monday night, but the coal camps celebrated the holiday the last Saturday night of the month of October so it wouldn't interfere with a school/work night. To put Burman's plan in motion, the boys had to prepare before dark. When a few kids started stirring around, Burman and his helpers waited, hoping for several kids to come along at the same time.

After dark, all the kids gathered in the ballfield. Stearns Coal and Lumber Company sent a person into all the coal camps to give candy treats to the coal miners' kids. When the truck pulled into the ballfield in Co-operative, any kid who wasn't already there came running. Burman and his pals walked to the top of the tipple and got into position. Burman knew after they got their candy a bunch of the younger kids would go back home.

Burman and his pals had a washtub of water waiting on the tipple positioned over the main track below. Several kids started heading back down the tracks to the Lower Camp, but some kids waited for others to get their candy and catch up. Several were walking along, talking and eating candy, which was what Burman hoped for. He could barely see the kids but he could clearly hear them. Burman and the boys got ready. When Burman determined the kids were directly under him, they turned the tub of water on its side. The water rushed down, drenching those kids below as if they'd been in a shower.

Burman and his pals grabbed up the empty tub and hurried off the tipple laughing the whole way. The kids down below yelled and screamed and ran home. Burman and his buddies talked about that Halloween for many days after.

∞

MARRIED THIS YEAR 1949

In White Oak Junction, Tom Foster, age 22, son of Mr. and Mrs. Bill Foster, and Betty Winchester, age 21, the daughter of Mr. and Mrs. Harvey Winchester also of White Oak Junction, got married.

Back in White Oak Junction, Lester Watson, age 19, the son of Mr. and Mrs. Walter Watson, and Marie Dixon, age 20, daughter of Walter Dixon also of White Oak Junction, got married.

The week after Lester and Marie got married, Morris McKee, age 16, of Alpine, and Helen Louise Hall, age 17, daughter of Lester Hall of

White Oak Junction, got married. Morris and Helen had eight children: Jimmy, Thelma, Helena, Billy, Morris Jr., Sherry, Curtis, and Dean.

Bobby Crabtree and Clarice Lee Rose, age 16, got married.

∞

BORN THIS YEAR 1949

Junior Dixon
Terry Hardwick
Vella L. Davis
Margaret Irma Jones
Lena Shoopman
Sheila Keith
Phyllis Young
Novella Watson
Lee Winchester
Bruce Haynes
Janice Coffey
Larry Coffey
Lloyd Lewis
Jerry Gregory
Dillard Maxwell
Juanita Gibson
Shirley Whitehead
Darrell Conatser
Bob Dixon

CHAPTER 26

1950

When 1950 began and a new decade started in Co-operative, there was no indication this year would be any different from those previous.

∞

Word came to Cack and Betty Slaven that their son Cleatus, age nineteen, had reported to the Lackland Air Force Base, an enclave of San Antonio, Texas. The thirteen-week training would prepare him for entrance into one of the base's technical schools in a specific specialty. The training would also evaluate his aptitude for a vocation.

∞

The coal miners in Co-operative were working, including my dad, shoveling coal for a wage that was well earned. These men breathed coal dust all day, and I wonder how many of them thought as they walked into the mine this could be their last time. Today could be the day they wouldn't walk out, but they were satisfied to be working and didn't complained about their backbreaking job. The main thing that drove them to walk into the mine every day was that they were taking care of their families. They had no way of knowing what was looming over the horizon in Co-operative.

∞

In Whitley City, new county officers were sworn in, including the new Sheriff Tommy Roundtree. Those that operated outside the law were put on notice. His first day on the job, he arrested Alfred Slaven of Worley Hill Top for operating a moonshine still under his house. Roundtree selected McKinley Worley and Hubert Corder as his top deputies. Word was out: "Beware, boys, there's a new sheriff in town."

∞

Guy Kidd drove into the Lower Camp in his jeep. The Dixons lived in House 57, next door to Arnold and Geneva Shoopman. Next door to Arnold and Geneva lived Bug and Bessie Shoopman, Arnold's brother. Between the two Shoopman homes was a path that went back to Sid and Alti Waters' home. Sid had a fence around his yard with a gate. The fence was to keep his animals from wandering away from the house.

Geneva Shoopman was in her kitchen washing dishes. The kitchen was in the back of their house, so she had not seen Guy pull up and park his jeep in the space between the two Shoopman homes. She caught a glimpse of someone passing her window. She stopped momentarily and walked to where she could see out her back door. She didn't know at this point if the person was coming to her door, and she wanted to know who it was. Geneva could see it was Guy Kidd walking back to Sid Waters' place. Guy had a fifty-pound sack under each arm and another one he was holding with his teeth. Geneva couldn't believe her eyes. She watched as Guy got to Sid's fence. He didn't stop to try opening the gate. He turned sideways, threw one leg over the fence, and then lifted the other leg over. It wasn't unusual for Guy to make deliveries, and he was a tall, large man, but Geneva was stunned at the weight he was carrying. Geneva moved out of the doorway. She didn't want Guy to see her watching him, but after he was gone, she looked at Sid's porch and she counted three 50-pound sacks.

∞

On Monday, February 13, coal miners across the U. S., including all of Stearns Coal and Lumber Company miners, stayed away from the mines, ignoring a Federal Court order to return to work. The order came when President Truman invoked the Taft-Hartley Act. The United States Federal Act restricted the activities labor unions could do. On Monday, activity showed signs the miners wanted to get back to work—at least some of them. At the Worley Mine, Number 4, a few miners showed up. None of the miners at Co-operative Mine showed up for work. At Blue Heron, a handful of men showed up but didn't go into the mine. The two sides continued negotiations in Washington until a settlement was reached.

Out of the 370,000 coal miners in the country, I do not know how many showed up for work that Monday. The question being pondered by many was what could be done to get these men back to work if Federal Law and John Lewis couldn't. For Stearns Company, was the small effort made on Monday enough? Amidst all this turmoil, Stearns Coal and Lumber Company, one of the largest producers, posted the company's totals for the year 1949. The coal output posted was disastrous; a company spokesman said, "It's the worst year since 1911."

As March and the first half of April came and went, the coal miners in Co-operative had weathered another strike. With only a few short weeks of work under their belt, on April 25, a Tuesday, Stearns Company halted coal production in Co-operative. Mine Superintendent Cack Slaven announced as the day shift arrived, "They're shutting her down, boys." The miners thought it was just another day in the mines as they left home that morning, but they were hit with this shocking news. All these men, more than 200, depended on their job to feed their families.

Co-operative was the second Stearns mine in six months to close. Toward the end of 1949, Yamacraw Mine 11 closed. In Co-operative, a skeleton crew maintained the mine and did the necessary work like pumping water out of the mine. They needed to keep the mine ready in case Stearns Company decided to reopen the Co-operative operation.

As Stearns Company felt the sting of the Co-operative Mine closing, all agreed it was the worst setback since McCreary became a county. Since 1922, the company estimated that approximately five million tons of coal came out of the hills of Co-operative, an average of over 178,500 tons of coal per year for twenty-eight continuous years.

A Stearns Company spokesman stated the reasons the company ceased operation in Co-operative were twofold: the market for their coal was decreasing and the push for alternative fuels of gas, oil, and hydroelectric was increasing. Did the negative 1949 report, the beginning weeks of low production in 1950, and the federal order add fuel to the company's decision? I have nothing to base my opinion on, but I think they helped the company decide to close Co-operative Mine. At this point, all I have is speculation. I do know this one decision changed the landscape of Co-operative forever. As days turned into weeks and weeks into months, the miners who had hoped the mine would reopen lost hope. The coal miners who were not transferred to Mine 16 or Mine 18 migrated to other states, many of them north of Kentucky.

∞

The summer of 1950 saw several men go north to look for work and several found it at Hartzell's in Piqua, Ohio. One of those men was John Worley, my dad, who left Co-operative in March 1951 and began working at Hartzell's. He worked there until he retired. Other men like Harvey Terry, Harley Hardwick, Reese Foster, Virgil Freeman, Bob King, Oscar Jones, and RL Terry left Co-operative around October 1951. These men, including my dad, became weekend dads except RL, who a month later turned seventeen years old. Some men worked a few years, saved what they could, and came home. Some worked until they retired and came home. Some men, after a year or two, moved their families north.

The rest of the 1950s saw families in Co-operative trying to survive this new challenge they found themselves facing. The men who were transferred to Mine 16 found they had a long walk to and from work. The gravel road between Paint Cliff and White Oak Junction was not yet built, so the men walked the railroad tracks to work, in all kinds of weather, which I estimate was approximately two and a half miles one way. Sid Waters would have welcomed that short walk to work. Sid walked all the way to Mine 18 in Blue Heron. When Cack was transferred from Co-operative to Mine 18, he transferred Sid to Mine 16.

While working at Mine 18, Sid lived next door to the Wilsons in the Upper Camp of Co-operative. Leaving his home, he walked across the porch of the Company Store to the railroad tracks and followed the tracks to Logan Holler. Then he left the tracks to walk the path that went by the oil wells, which ended up at White Oak Junction above the six houses in a row facing Rock Creek. From there, he walked the wagon trail that came out behind Guy Kidd's Grocery. There he crossed the swinging bridge and walked up beside Guy Kidd's store onto the road that went toward Bridge 11. Sid then walked to Trace Branch. There he picked up a path that went up the side of the mountain that led to Ball Knob close to the schoolhouse. He walked the ridge about a mile, and then followed a path down the other side of the mountain that came out close to Mine 18 coal tipple. Mornings and evenings Sid walked that route to work and back home for just over two years in all kinds of weather. I estimate he walked 6 miles one way.

∞

In White Oak Junction, past Guy Kidd's Grocery but before Bridge 11, across the creek lived George and Artie Troxell. Their children were Luther, Denzil, Arlena, Lucille (died at birth), Ernest, William (died at six months), and Mary.

When Arlena Troxell was in the third grade at White Oak Junction, she remembers spending very little time inside the schoolhouse. Every pretty weather day, the kids played outside all day. The White Oak Junction schoolhouse was a one-room building with all eight grades in the one room. As the school year progressed, parents began asking their kids what they did all day; the children replied, "We played." The parents knew the children couldn't be learning anything if all they did was play all day. So, the parents got together and informed the school superintendent what was happening. They told the superintendent, "Either she [the teacher] goes or we send our kids to another school."

When the new school year started (1950–1951), every parent who could came to school with their child. They were happy when Mrs. Wilma Marcum introduced herself as the new schoolteacher. The parents went home happy to leave their children with the new teacher.

Mrs. Marcum, born Wilma Duncan, and her sister Bobbie were from Co-operative. Their parents were Robert and Myrtle Duncan. Robert worked for the K & T Railway. Wilma earned her teaching degree at Cumberland College (now renamed the University of the Cumberlands). Wilma's first teaching job was at Wolf Creek. While teaching at Wolf Creek, Wilma met her future husband Kenneth Marcum at the King Edward Café located in Dixie, south Whitley City.

Kenneth's parents, Claude and Marie Marcum, lived in the area that became known as Fidelity. In addition to Kenneth, born to Claude and Marie were Bill, Sheila, Barbara, Patricia, and Claudette.

When Stearns Coal and Lumber Company opened the coal mine and built the coal camp, they named the mine Fidelity. Claude was promoted to Mine Superintendent. (The U.S. Post Office kept the name Shoopman.)

Kenneth Marcum and Wilma Duncan fell in love and were married in 1950. From their union were born three children: Kent, Lou Ann, and Lecia (Lecia later married a Moreau). Mrs. Wilma Marcum taught another year in White Oak Junction before teaching a few years in Co-operative and one year in Parkers Lake.

In the late 1950s, Kenneth and Wilma Marcum moved to Lake City, Tennessee, where Wilma continued her education at the University of Tennessee.

∞

The Troxell kids walked about a mile and a half to school in White Oak Junction. On the same side of the creek where they lived, they walked a path that meandered along the terrain close to the creek. The path they always walked to and from school took them past the Craft home and Dina Watson's home. A short distance on, the trail forked; the left fork took them over a hill and to the school playground.

One morning Arlena Troxell's older brothers left for school ahead of her; several minutes later, Arlena walked the trail alone. It wasn't the first time. She knew the way very well and she had been taught to be cautious. Arlena didn't like to miss school and there was almost nothing that caused her to miss it.

Suddenly she stopped. She saw something up ahead in her path. She eased along slowly so she could get a closer look. She stopped again knowing full well what she saw was a copperhead. Now what was she going to do?

She knew she didn't want to miss school but how could she get past that snake? Then she had a thought—she started backing up slowly. When she was far enough away from the snake, she started running as fast as her legs would carry her. As she approached the snake, she jumped, hoping she had jumped high enough and far enough to clear the snake. She hit the ground running. She was scared and didn't slow down until she saw the playground. She looked back at the path to make sure the snake hadn't followed her. Arlena was over her scare when she walked into the playground, but she thought about that snake all day.

As Christmas approached, Arlena's mom, Arti, stopped at Guy Kidd's Grocery. Arti didn't let her kids go with her to the store. She shopped alone because she knew her kids would see things they wanted and she wouldn't have the money to buy them. It would hurt her to see them so disappointed. Guy Kidd's Grocery wasn't just a grocery store; the store carried a little of everything such as clothes, shoes, and a few toys for boys and girls scattered throughout the store.

Christmas Eve came and Arti gave Arlena her present. Arlena opened it and inside was the prettiest pair of red shoes she had ever seen. She fell in love with them immediately and stared at them for the longest time. She took one of them out of the box to try on and found the shoe was too small. Arti put the shoes back in the box and walked back to Kidd's store to trade them for a larger pair. The store didn't have a larger size in red, so she did the next best thing. Arti got a larger size in brown. Arlena's feelings were hurt, but she never let her mom know. Arlena wanted those pretty red shoes. It took her a long time to get over the disappointment. One thing Guy Kidd, the store owner, always did when someone bought a pair of shoes: he gave them a pair of socks as a bonus.

∞

On down where the train bridge crossed Rock Creek in White Oak Junction, the creek was quite large and very deep. In many winters in those days, the water would freeze and the neighborhood children would slip away and go down there to skate/play around on the ice. Parents would never have allowed their kids to play on the ice if they'd known because if the ice broke, a child would be a goner for sure. But to these young kids, danger was obscure. They saw only the fun and not the dangerous risk. That they were doing something their parents didn't know about made the exhilaration more enjoyable.

∞

During the following summer break, on a hot day, the Troxell kids wanted to make Kool-Aid. They looked in the pantry and found only one pack of Kool-Aid. They knew one pack would not be enough, so they decided to take it along with some sugar to the water spring. That way, it would make a lot and they could all have some. Behind the Troxell home was a hill and on top of the hill was the spring. Their dad, George, had the spring fixed so the water spilled out into a small pool and then flowed through a short pipe, making it easy to fill water buckets. The kids gathered around anxiously waiting.

Arlena was holding the pack of Kool-Aid and one of her brothers held the sugar. Someone said, "One, two, three, go." They dumped in the Kool-Aid and sugar at the same time. For an instant, the Kool-Aid colored the water and then the colored water disappeared. The younger kids said, "Oh, no! What happened?" The older kids immediately realized they'd made a dumb decision. From then on, the Troxell kids referred to the spring as the Kool-Aid Spring.

∞

MARRIED THIS YEAR 1950

In Co-operative, Obie Winchester married Ruth Douglas.

Kenneth Marcum married Wilma Duncan. Kenneth and Wilma had three children: Kent, LouAnn, and Lecia.

Leroy Waters, age 22, married Wilma Cooper, age 20. Leroy and Wilma had these children: Joe, Marisa Dawn, Jeffrey Logan, Timothy D., Lori J., Elizabeth Abigail, and Jayne.

In Co-operative, Stanley Black married Lula Gregory. Lula had four children from her previous marriage: James, Johnny, Ethel, and Helen. She and Stanley had three children together: Brenda, David, and Larry.

BORN THIS YEAR 1950

Wallace Chitwood
Billy Jay Kidd
Diane Hardwick
Linda Shoopman
Stanley Parks Jr.
Tim Bell
Thelma Keith
Lena Hall
Shirley Haynes
Kenneth Tapley
Darrell Ball
David Hall
Jim Shook
Shirley Waters
Larry Jones
Billy Jean Freeman
Diane Crabtree
Hoover Keith Jr.
Donald Dobbs
James Carson

THOMAS (TOMMY) FRANKLIN ROUNDTREE
SHERIFF OF MCCREARY COUNTY, KENTUCKY, FOR
TWO TERMS:
1934—1937 AND 1950—1953
PHOTO COURTESY OF WANDA WORLEY.

CHAPTER 27

Black Spider

Thomas Franklin Roundtree was born on January 10, 1895. His parents were Enos A. Roundtree (1860–1927) and Hannah Meadors Roundtree (1872–1962). Enos and Hannah's other children were Mary Myrtle, William Esben, Esbel Sontage, Ida Lucreta, Maude Ella, Martha H., and Enos Taft.

Dad Enos worked at Bon Jellico, Tennessee, and lived in the Pleasant Run area. The 1910 and 1920 censuses listed his occupation as farmer. When McCreary became officially a county in 1912, Pleasant Run went from being in Whitley County to being in McCreary County. Young Thomas received his education in Pleasant Run. As he grew and time passed, people started referring to Thomas as Tommy and the name stuck with him.

On September 6, 1913, Tommy married Stella Rowe and they had these children: Arnold, Gladys, Roger, Lester, James, Doyle, Thomas Jr., and M. C. (In my research, another daughter was mentioned, but I was not able to find her name.)

Tommy was not a towering figure; from photographs, he looked to be under six feet with medium weight. But from the reputation he built in his first term as sheriff, one might surmise he was seven feet tall. Before his first term as sheriff (1934–1937), he served at various times as deputy sheriff. In rural McCreary County, Kentucky, few people could afford an automobile. And many resorted to making their own firewater. (Moonshine was called many different names; firewater was one of the more colorful.) Tommy hated moonshiners and when asked why, he always gave this reason: "It takes food away from children. If one or both parents drink moonshine, children go hungry."

Tommy got his nickname—Black Spider—from folks his age and older because he wore black a lot and because he pursued moonshiners relentlessly. If he found a moonshine still unattended, he would go back with only a jar of peanut butter and a pack of crackers and he'd stay in the woods for as long as it took for the still owners to come back to finish a run or start one. Tommy always had one of his deputies drive him wherever he went. Older men who still remember have said Tommy didn't drive or have a driver's license. Whether that was true or not didn't much matter. His total force consisted of one car and two deputies. While Tommy and one deputy were out on patrol, the other deputy stayed behind to mind the office unless a situation called for backup.

Tommy earned a reputation as being one of the best sheriffs of McCreary County for all the moonshine stills he captured. It would be interesting to know the total number of stills he shut down during his two terms as sheriff. It wasn't until close to the end of his second term from 1950–1953 that the number was recorded. In this two-year stretch, Tommy captured well over one hundred stills.

In between his two terms, Tommy worked as a special officer for Stearns Coal and Lumber Company. But as sheriff for the long hours and hazardous work to capture a still, he got only $2.00 if the arrested individual paid a fine. During one two-month period, Tommy cut and sold seven hundred pounds of copper. (Moonshine stills were made of copper.) In most cases, Tommy arrested an average of two men per still. Usually, they paid a fine after pleading guilty. But every once in a while, if it was the person's first time to be arrested, he would be transferred to Federal Revenue officers.

One thing was for sure, Sheriff Roundtree knew McCreary County and its people like the back of his hand, so no one could operate a still for very long before he caught them. When the results of the election became known and folks learned Tommy Roundtree won the sheriff's race for a second term, a few men abandoned their stills and got regular jobs.

Sheriff Roundtree always wore a sports suit jacket no matter the weather. It was possible Tommy liked having all those pockets the jacket provided. Tommy liked talking about the funny things that happened on his many raids. Once Tommy was hiding in the woods when two boys came up and started preparing a batch. One of them said, "I wish the f**king law would find this outfit and bust it into a hundred pieces."

Tommy suddenly appeared out of nowhere and said, "Fellers, I believe I will." It scared those boys out of their wits. They ran but lost the race.

∞

At Yamacraw, crossing Big South Fork over the car bridge and turning left immediately as if you were headed to Co-operative, on the right was the mouth of a mine Stearns Coal and Lumber Company had abandoned.

While out one day, passing this location, Tommy said to his deputy, "Stop the car."

The deputy stopped the car. Tommy got out and told the deputy to wait. The car had rolled only a few feet past the abandoned mine entrance. Tommy walked to the entrance and disappeared inside. Tommy didn't have to walk far before he came upon a complete, working still. No one was there, but one thing Tommy knew was that somebody would be coming back. Tommy walked back to the car and told his deputy what he'd found. He said, "I smelled it when we turned off the bridge."

Tommy told his deputy to go back to the office and wait. He said, "I'm staying here. When I need you, I'll call from Keith's store." The deputy backed the car up and headed across the car bridge back to the office.

Tommy made his way up the embankment into the trees on the side of the mountain, just high enough to see the road in front of the mine entrance and most of the car bridge. Tommy was able to see any car coming and going on the gravel road below him. He was sure he wouldn't have to wait long, so he found a place and made himself comfortable. Several hours passed and only two vehicles had turned off onto the gravel road headed toward Co-operative. Then, Tommy saw an old pickup come across the bridge and slow up as if it might turn but it didn't. The driver may have stopped at the store that sits right there on the left side of the highway and on the right side if you turn toward Co-operative; in any event, the truck was out of sight.

Not long after, a man came walking down the gravel road in Tommy's direction. Tommy didn't take his eyes off the man. As the man walked directly in front of the mine entrance, he stopped and looked back in the direction from which he came. Then the man looked once in the opposite direction. Within seconds, he hurriedly disappeared into the mine entrance.

Tommy relaxed for a few minutes. He knew he had his man. Wasn't any need to get in a hurry. Taking his time, Tommy got up and made his way down the steep slope. Not making any unnecessary noise, he got to the ditch line of the gravel road. Tommy walked the ditch line to the mine entrance and carefully looked inside. He could not see the man inside but could hear him. The mine entrance went straight back about twenty-five feet, then gradually curved to the left. That's where the still was, just far enough to be out of sight. Tommy knew he had to get close to capture the man and was hoping to surprise him. The man could have a gun. Tommy had to assume he did and he, for sure, didn't want gun play inside the mine.

Tommy eased along as close to the left side wall as he could without making any noise. Tommy was lucky because the man was busy working and never once looked in Tommy's direction until it was too late for him. The man must have felt completely safe because he had his back to Tommy the whole time. The distance between the two men was no longer an issue when Tommy said, "Everything coming out all right?" The man jerked around violently. Must have been in shock. He threw the container he was holding, hitting the opposite wall of the mine shaft. The man looked as if he'd seen a ghost. Tommy said, "You're under arrest."

∞

Word got to Sheriff Roundtree that Leo Stephens was selling moonshine. He either had his own still or he was selling for somebody. Tommy decided to pay Mr. Stephens a visit. On Sandhill Road one afternoon, the sheriff with a deputy stepped up on Mr. Stephens' porch with a search warrant in his coat pocket. Just as Tommy reached up to knock on the door, he heard the stove door slam shut. Tommy opened the door and rushed to the stove. He reached in the stove and brought out a gallon of moonshine whiskey. Leo was trying to get rid of evidence but under stress of the moment forgot (or didn't know) the whiskey would have exploded and who knows what kind of damage it would have caused.

There was a small fire in the stove and the quick action of the sheriff saved the evidence. Tommy charged Leo with possession of moonshine.

∞

In the days after the Yamacraw Mine closed and people began moving out of the camp, it became easy to find an empty house to rent. The coal miners who were lucky enough to get transferred to other locations weren't necessarily forced to move if the new location was close enough to walk to.

It was common for the local guys to get together on a Saturday night to sip some moonshine and play poker. They thought it safer to gather in one of the empty houses to have their poker game; they'd also be protected from any inclement weather.

Somehow Tommy found out about the guys using the empty houses. It would be interesting to know how he found out: Did somebody mention it to him or was it Tommy's sixth sense? We'll never know.

One Saturday evening before dark, a couple of men entered an empty house on the bank in Yamacraw, not too far from the train bridge. It had been used before because the door led into the front room that had a table and eight hickory-bark woven-bottom wooden chairs. It was almost dark and one of the men lit the coil oil lamp. They didn't have to worry about anyone seeing the light from outside because they had the windows covered with cardboard. One by one the men arrived and took their usual places around the table. Every one of the men had a quart jar of White Lightning, which they put on the floor beside their chair—after taking a good swallow. The cards were brought out. They were ready. Then the door swung open and a man walked in, closed the door, and sat down. Somebody said, "All right, I'm ready to play some cards."

The card playing and the sipping began. The longer they played, the bigger the winning pot got. They played a good while before the cussing got a little vindictive. A new game commenced, and the betting started off heavy. As the game neared its climax, one of the men said, "It's about time." Then he threw his cards on the table and said, "Boys, this hand is mine."

At the same time, Sheriff Tommy and one of his deputies appeared out of a room in back and said loudly, "No, that pot is mine, and you're all under arrest."

∞

Tommy could talk about his exploits for as long as anyone cared to listen. One time, in his own words, he told of a still he had scoped out. He watched two men walk up and start preparing the still for a run when one of the men said, "Pappy said if that dang sheriff gets this one, it'll be our last one." Well Tommy got it, making it the third one he'd gotten from those boys in the last year.

At some point in his last term, Tommy said, "I'd like to get one moonshine still a week, but nowadays, they're not as plentiful as they once were."

It's a good probability no other officer, federal or state, captured and destroyed more moonshine stills than Black Spider.

CHAPTER 28

1951

In 1951, at the home of Raymond and Darkie Clark in Hill Top, Darkie gave birth to their fourth child, a daughter. Her name was Rayma Dean. In Co-operative the same morning at the home of John and Lexie Worley, Lexie gave birth to their fifth child, a son. His name was Charles Danny Worley. Charles and Rayma Dean grew up and went through grade school together and never knew they shared the same birthday.

∞

While those babies were being born, Sheriff Tommy Roundtree and deputies drove to Bell Farm early morning and caught Oliver Slavie and Shelby Crabtree red-handed. Oliver and Shelby were in the process of relocating their moonshine still nearer to Bell Farm; the still was currently located close to where the CCC camp once operated. The sheriff arrested both men and confiscated three barrels of oil and fifty pounds of sugar.

Three weeks later, Sheriff Roundtree and Deputy Hubert Corder captured a 120-gallon capacity still. It was one of the largest captured in recent memory. In addition, they confiscated 250 pounds of sugar, 15 barrels of mash, 85 empty gallon jars, and a small amount of liquor. They arrested Hollis Watters and Estil Stephens, the still operators.

The following month, the sheriff beat his still-size record of three weeks earlier. Sheriff Roundtree, federal agents, Deputy Hubert Corder, and Constable Jim Fuzz Hansford arrested Ronzo Cassidy and his two sons, Delbert and Leroy. They were in possession of a 150-gallon still. Ronzo was also charged with shooting at Sheriff Roundtree during the arrest. The still was brand new, ready for its first run. Roundtree also confiscated one hundred pounds of sugar and destroyed three barrels of mash.

Three weeks later, on Wilson Ridge, Sheriff Roundtree arrested Elihu Wilson in possession of a seventy-gallon still and destroyed two barrels of mash.

∞

In the mining industry, the 1951 report of all producers of coal showed 1950 had a slow start mainly because of strikes and cheap oil. Producers did show a steady growth according to a report by a McGraw–Hill publication, an affiliate of the *Coal Age* magazine. The overall picture showed ninety-three companies in the 100,000-over-tonnage range group, while fifty-four dropped under that, leaving a net gain of thirty-nine. The report confirmed the largest leading companies showed growth in coal production, while the smallest organizations showed a decline. The report detailed for the first time since 1947 that large producers increased their total coal tonnage.

In Kentucky, coal mining was the second largest industry in 1950, ringing cash registers for over $315 million, according to the *Kentucky Business Magazine* published by the Kentucky Chamber of Commerce. The article also stated that mine operators and coal associations had failed to make the public aware of all the products made from black gold. The story revealed an extension survey that had never been made public.

Commercial coal mining was first instituted in Kentucky in 1870 and at that time produced over 109 thousand tons. At the close of last year, Kentucky mines produced sixty-two million tons, the third largest behind West Virginia, first, and Pennsylvania, second.

In addition to the two main uses of coal—power and heat—coal was also used in nylon, paints, perfumes, inks, plastics, explosives, livestock feeds, DDT, and petroleum. In medicines, coal was used in 1) aspirin, 2) sulfa drugs, 3) vitamins, and 4) mercurochrome.

Was coal important to the country? Yes, very much so, but the coal industry did not make the public aware of the good things that came from coal. Instead, people heard only how coal produced the smoky pollution coming from big city power plants and factories. It was possible, of course, the oil industry was behind much, if not all, of the bad press coal got because if the use of coal could be diminished, oil could take its place.

Even though coal mining continued, I believe the men at the top in Stearns Coal and Lumber Company knew early on that the winds of the coal industry were shifting in the country and that coal mining as they had traditionally worked it was coming to an end. The company decided to ride it out as long as they could without a hint to the miners.

∞

One Sunday, Beatty Burks, who lived at Kidd's Crossing, traveled to Bell Farm to see Elisha Roberts. He stayed for a few days. On Thursday morning, Beatty and Elisha met up with Lincoln Burks, Beatty's cousin, and Ray Burks, Lincoln's nephew, and three Troxell boys at Sherd Dobbs Cemetery. They drank all day. Around noon, Elisha and Beatty got into an argument. Elisha threatened to kill Beatty but realized he didn't have his gun with him. Elisha and Beatty patched up their differences and appeared to be okay again.

By afternoon, they were running low on beverages. Some of the guys drove to the Tennessee state line to get more alcohol (it was legal there). The rest drove to Elisha's place in Bell Farm. From the state line, the guys brought back a case of beer and a pint of liquor to Elisha's place.

Elisha again took offense to something Beatty said. At the time, Elisha was lying across his bed and moved to get his gun. Ray Burks saw what was about to happen, and he grabbed Elisha and held him down until he thought Elisha's anger had cooled. He let him go and walked outside. Beatty walked into the kitchen with one of Elisha's daughters, and Lincoln, who had been on the porch, walked into the house and stood in the doorway that connected the kitchen and bedroom where Elisha was still resting on his bed. Lincoln was standing there rolling a cigarette. Elisha rolled over and took hold of his .30-.30 rifle. He had not noticed it was Lincoln who had walked up and was relaxed against the door. With one motion, Elisha took aim and fired a shot, hitting Lincoln in the chest. Lincoln fell forward onto the kitchen floor, dead.

Elisha got up and went outside. Still holding his gun, he walked to Melvin Dobbs' store nearby. He told Mr. Dobbs he had just killed a man and he should have finished the lot of them. Mr. Dobbs managed to take the rifle away from Elisha. Elisha hurried out and disappeared. It was later learned he had spent the night under a cliff. Mr. Dobbs immediately called the sheriff's office and reported the shooting. Early the next morning, Elisha went to the home of Mrs. Susie Jones, a neighbor of his. Sheriff Roundtree and his deputy found Elisha there around 8:00 a.m. Elisha was on his way to jail.

∞

The Lincoln Burks that Elisha killed was the same Lincoln who ten years earlier, back in late 1941, along with Hubert Burks, his sons (Charlie and Arthur Burks), Guy Smith, and Estil Smith, had been at Neil Kidd's saloon and had been drinking for a good while when Forest Gregory, son of Mr. and Mrs. Sol Gregory, walked in to do some drinking of his own.

Forest was twenty-six years old, single, and still living with his parents in Co-operative. He worked for Stearns Coal and Lumber Company at Co-operative Mine. Forest was dating a sister to his brother Marvin Gregory's wife. The Burks family allegedly did not like the potential of another Gregory in the family and discouraged the relationship.

Now what happened inside Kidd's saloon, I don't know. There may have been angry words spoken. One account had Forest attacked outside Neil Kidd's saloon; another account had him close to Copin Camp. I believe the ambush happened close to or at Copin Camp because Forest was shot with a .22 rifle. According to one source, when news of the shooting got to the Gregory family, Orville, a brother to Forest, picked him up in his car. If this source is correct, Orville was likely the one who drove Forest to the hospital. According to the newspaper, Forest Gregory died Sunday morning around 9:00 a.m. at the McDonald Hospital in Danville. Forest had two sisters—Effie and Stella—and five brothers—Marvin, Orville, Hershel, Chester, and Libern, all of Co-operative.

The night of the shooting, Arthur and Charlie Burks disappeared into the night; the rest were charged with "banding and confederating." A warrant originally charged Charlie with malicious shooting and wounding but was changed to murder. At the time, Charlie was fourteen years old. Sheriff Sam Thomas, elected in 1942, arrested Charlie at Kidd's Crossing. It was the consensus that young Charlie did the shooting. But during the trial, it was learned that Arthur was the ringleader. Arthur was captured a month later and charged with the murder of Forest Gregory. Testimonies from Charlie's trial were used against Arthur. All were found guilty.

This was the same Forest Gregory who earlier in March at Neil Kidd's saloon along with his dad, Sol, got into an altercation with Matt Coffey. Matt inflicted severe knife wounds on Forest and several cuts on Forest's dad, Sol, but Sol's cuts were not as serious as Forest's.

∞

Since Co-operative Mine had been shut down, Arnold Shoopman, along with some other men, had been working at Worley Mine. Arnold rode to work with Maynard Terry. In the summer, driving down to the mine wasn't a problem. To get to the mine, the road took a right turn and dropped over a ridgeline. It was a rapid descent to the river. Coming out from the mine was a very steep climb to the top of the ridgeline. The ridgeline was the main road through Worley Hill Top that intersected with Highway 92 West.

But in the winter, when it was snowy or icy, no one was brave enough to drive a car down that road. If one was lucky enough to keep the car on the road, there would be no stopping at the bottom of the incline. The vehicle would most likely end up in the middle of the river. Instead, what folks who drove did was stop at Calvin and Ruby Corder's place and walk a path behind their house, beside their chicken house, and through a field to the edge of the cliff. There they'd climb down ladders that were strategically placed to get to the bottom and then it was a short walk to the mine. Over time, men had solved the problem of managing the cliff. The ladders were built out of tall slender trees for the rungs. Climbing down those ladders wasn't so bad, but after working a shift, climbing the ladders up the incline was very difficult. It was well over one hundred feet to the top. Those miners did that day in and day out. Wimps need not apply. Hard work was what miners knew. Taking care of their families motivated those men to do the impossible.

∞

Occasionally on a hot Saturday afternoon, Arnold and Geneva Shoopman would gather up the kids and walk to their favorite swimming hole and have a picnic lunch and swim. They lived at the head of Logan Holler in Co-operative. Leaving their house, they'd walk down the railroad tracks, turn right onto a path, walk past the oil wells, and end up behind Guy Kidd's store. They then crossed the swinging bridge and walked to Bridge 11. At the end of Bridge 11, they turned right. There, after just a few steps, was a spring; everyone would get a drink of water.

They continued walking to just below the Fidelity Cemetery to the pond, where they loved spending an afternoon. The younger kids would swim in the lower, shallow part of the pond, but Arnold would swim all over that pond of water. A tree had grown close to a rock right beside the water; the tree was very tall and leaned out over the water. The older Shoopman boys would climb up the tree a little ways and drop into the water.

The Shoopman family was there one time when a man came up that Arnold didn't know. He could see right off that the man was drunk. The man began climbing up the rock. Arnold told the kids to get out of the water. Surprisingly, the man made it to the top of the rock without falling backwards. He even managed to stagger over to the tree and start climbing. All they could do was watch; Arnold knew he couldn't reason with a drunk. The man didn't stop. He climbed limb by limb until he reached the top and had nowhere else to go. The man couldn't have been there more than ten seconds when he fell off. The sound he made hitting the water was like a shotgun going off.

Arnold thought the fall killed the man and dove in right after the man hit the water. Archie jumped in after his dad. The man surfaced and Arnold and Archie were there to grab hold of the man and pull him up on the bank. That belly buster nearly killed the man; he lay moaning and groaning, his arms wrapped around his stomach. The man was so sick that the Shoopman family stayed near him for a long time. While walking back home, Arnold told the story to everyone they saw.

∞

BORN THIS YEAR 1951

Charles Danny Worley (me)
Rayma Dean Clark
Charles (Skeet) Davis
Charlie Gregory
Tommy King
Zadie Jones
Sheila Young
Chester Douglas
Ella Jean Jones
Jerry W. Parks
Donald Coffey
Jack Watson
Danny Shepherd
Catheryn Whitehead
Kenny Coffey
Carolyn Lewis
Logan Conatser

Glen Maples
Roger Cox
Barb Dixon

CHAPTER 29

1952

At the beginning of the year, Sheriff Roundtree, his deputies, and federal agents captured six stills in a ten-day period. They captured two in Co-operative, two at Devil Creek, and two in Sawyer. About half of the stills were operating and the rest were preparing to operate. Four people were arrested, including Arlie McCoy, Osborne New, and Frank Barnett and his wife.

Only a couple of days later, Sheriff Roundtree got word that Bonnel King of Silerville, just south of Pine Knot, was selling moonshine. Sheriff Roundtree and his deputies arrived at the home of Bonnel King with a search warrant. Their immediate search found four gallons of moonshine and they arrested Mr. King.

Before leaving the premises, Sheriff Roundtree noticed huge stones placed in a row at equal distances apart starting at the west corner of the house and going across the yard to a fence. At first observation, the rocks looked to be covering fence post holes. Roundtree bent down, turned over one of the rocks, reached in, and pulled out two half-gallon jars of moonshine. The sheriff straightened up and told his deputies to check under each stone. They did and found moonshine under every rock. Sheriff Roundtree delivered Mr. King to federal officers, who took Mr. King to London, Kentucky, for processing.

∞

Stearns Coal and Lumber Company put together a list of men currently working who had been with the company for twenty years or longer without any loss of time by accident or prolonged illness. These men started work on or before 1931 and worked through December 1951. What an accomplishment. No words are adequate to describe the respect and reverence I have for these coal miners.

Here is the list of the courageous men working and the coal mines operating in 1951:

Mine 4 — Worley

Curtis Chitwood, W. E. Roundtree, W. M. Mayfield, Jess Strunk, L. C. Vahle, L. B. Stephens, Cleo Calhoun, W. M. Duncan, Dan Cordell, Arnold Ball, Walter Wilson, Robert Keith, Virgil Conatser, Alex Patton, Lee Wilson, Cordell Storie, Lincoln Watters, Roy Leveridge, Edd McDonald, Kenneth Lawson, Ott Baker, Charlie Reynolds, Ale Wilson, Arthur Dority, Clell Keith, Edgar Thompson, N. P. Owens,

Jerome Anderson, J. W. Wilson, Jasper Ross, Jeff King, Fitz Simpson, Maurice Blevins, and Gran Smith.

Mine 18—Blue Heron

Burl Wilson, Jasper Tapley, Wyman Ross, Arnold Ledbetter, Maynard Wilson, Ellis Lewis, Raymond Foster, Dewey Privett, Henry Watters, Millard Watters, J. Ed Stephens, W. E. Walls, Lawrence Ross, Logan King, Elbert Perry, A. S. West, Clarence Watters, Elmer Coffey, Clarence King, and J. O. Pierce.

Mine 1—Barthell

Arnold Shoopman, Oscar Bell, Jess Neal, Herman Johnson, W. M. Thompson, Mitchell Simpson, Stanford Sampson, Tom Marler, Bill Crabtree, Milford Vahles, Lincoln Coffey, Arthur Stephens, C. D. Rose, and Emby Kidd.

Mine 16—Paint Cliff

Jake Haynes, Sid Watters, Dester West, Harrison Dixon, Osborn Worley, Luther Phillips, Logan Flynn, C. V. Marcum, W. M. A. Smith, W. M. Gregory, Cecil Nelson, and Marcus Phillips.

∞

In Co-operative, Bug and Bessie Shoopman and family lived in Logan Holler. Bug lived beside his brother, Arnold. This year Bug bought a place on Hickory Knob from Burton Owens. Mr. Owens had bought the place from Frank Cooper and Frank had bought the property from Columbus King. At one time, Mr. Columbus King owned all of Hickory Knob.

CO-OPERATIVE, KENTUCKY
THE COMPANY STORE
PHOTO COURTESY OF ROGER CHITWOOD.

∞

On June 14, 1952, in Co-operative, it was cloudy and rained throughout the day and through the night. It rained hard at times but would then slow to a mist and then rain hard again. The morning of June 15, folks woke up to more hard rain mixed with thunder and lightning. The rain would stop briefly, then start again. As night set in, the rain, thunder, and lightning showed no signs of slowing. Sleep did not come easily that night. The lightning cut through the dark and flashed inside uncovered windows, lighting up rooms as if the lamps were turned on. The thunder was so loud, it rattled the windows. Sometime in the early morning hours, the hard rain slowed to a mist and then stopped. The thunder and lightning continued but faded before daybreak.

Usually after a good rain, the air has a fresh, sweet smell, but not the morning of June 16. People began waking up and starting their day. As they ventured outside, they were hit with a smell in the air that was different. They knew something was wrong. But it was still too dark to figure out where the smell was coming from. As the morning became brighter, folks could see smoke but still weren't sure where it was coming from. It was summer break for the kids and several of the older ones ran toward where they saw the smoke. When they found out for sure what was happening, many of the kids ran back home to tell their moms and dads, and on the way, yelled "the store is burning" to anyone outside to hear them. Many people, of course, could see the fire from where they lived. Even in Logan Holler, word had spread the Company Store was on fire.

As soon as the Shoopman boys, who lived in Logan Holler, found out the store was burning, Roger and Archie walked up to the car bridge, close to the Company Store. The creek was swollen close to maximum capacity with all the recent rain and was very close to touching the bottom of the car bridge. They saw items floating down the creek that came from the store. Archie and Roger sat down on the upper side of the car bridge letting their feet dangle over the side, thinking they might catch something coming down the creek. Roger's feet weren't down as far as Archie's because of their age and size difference, but it was a good thing they didn't trap anything as fast as the current was moving. It could have hurt the boys' legs bad. Roger stared at the water for a little while and became mesmerized and told Archie, "Arch, we're going up the creek ninety miles an hour."

"You better not look at the water," Archie said. At that instant, Archie turned to look at Roger as Roger fell in headfirst. The water carried Roger under the bridge, and Archie hurried to the lower side of the bridge. Archie saw Roger surface. He jumped in to try to save Roger. The water was now carrying both boys downstream; the current was so strong and swift that Archie couldn't get to Roger. He lost sight of him. Archie had no choice but to give up trying to find Roger. He was in a struggle for his own life. Archie was close to the tipple when he managed to make it out of the water.

Archie immediately began running along the bank frantically trying to find his brother. He saw Roger's head pop up out of the water, then drop back under, then pop back up again. Roger was reaching for anything he saw to grab. He finally latched on to a water birch that hung out over the water.

Archie was on the wrong side of the creek to help his brother, so he ran down to the foot bridge and crossed it to the other side and came up to where Roger was holding on tight. Roger was trying to hand walk toward the bank. The water was moving so fast that it had his body fully stretched out in the water, fighting him to let go of the birch so it could give him another ride.

Archie got to his brother and managed to get a good hold of his arm. With every bit of strength they had together, they finally pulled Roger out of the water and onto the bank. It was a close call. They both could have easily drowned. They lay down on the bank for a well-deserved rest and to give thanks. Roger occasionally coughed up a little water.

Suddenly Archie had a thought and sat up. At the same time, Roger looked up and asked, "Arch, what are we going to tell Mom? We're both soaking wet."

Archie said, "The truth."

"Lord, no," Roger said. "When Daddy gets home, he'll whip us half to death."

Archie said, "Now Rog, I'm going to tell her part of it, not all of it. I'm going to say you got too close to the water and your foot slipped, and as you fell into the water, I grabbed you and I got wet helping you out."

"I don't know," Roger said. "That doesn't sound much like the truth."

Archie said, "Well, it's the best I can think of. I can't tell her we almost drowned. She'd never let us around water again."

They both sat there a little longer staring at White Oak Creek when Archie said, "Come on. Let's go. We need out of these wet clothes."

When the boys entered the yard, their mom, Geneva, was standing on the porch staring at them. As they walked up the steps and onto the porch, Geneva asked, "What happened? Did you both fall in the creek?"

"Yes, Mommy," both boys said at the same time. "It was an accident," Archie said.

Geneva said, "Both of you get in the house and change clothes. Bring me the wet ones and I'll hang them on the line to dry."

Relief came over both Archie and Roger as they turned to walk into the house. They didn't have to lie to their mom.

"Archie, did you see the fire?" Geneva asked.

Archie stopped in the doorway and said, "Yes, Mommy, it's bad. It's the store."

That morning, families living closest to the Company Store like Sid and Alti Waters (Marion Wilson knocked on their door to alert them) were the first to awaken to the horrific news. Sid was the son of Moses Waters and Melinda Winchester, and Alti was the daughter of Will Gregory and Ada Koger. Sid and Alti's children were Ella Mae, Kenneth, Janice, Chester, Fayrene, Shirley, Paul, and Mary Louise.

The older kids, once aroused from sleep, got up to investigate what the excitement was all about. A lot had already happened by the time daughter Fayrene went to the porch that morning. She was on the front porch for a long time. With their house positioned on the hill above the boardinghouse, Fayrene had a front row seat. Fayrene's vantage point allowed her to see everything, the fire engulfing the building and people running frantically but keeping their distance from the fire. She saw people over on the railroad tracks and on every porch, everyone up by now.

She couldn't see the car bridge, though, because the bathhouse blocked her view. She also didn't see Eli Logan, the store manager, pull up and park on the road, down from Marion Wilson's home. Traveling into Co-operative still required driving through Rattlesnake Ridge and through Dobbs Town and down into Co-operative since the road from White Oak Junction to Paint Cliff was not yet finished.

All people could do was watch. Although Fayrene didn't see Eli arrive, others were standing on the road and watched Eli pull in and stop his car. Some said when he got out of his car, his complexion was as white as a ghost—in shock, I'm sure—several thoughts likely rushing through his mind: How did the fire start? Would he have a job? Where would he go from here? How long would he be out of work?

In the days following the fire, Stearns Coal and Lumber Company estimated their loss at $40,000. To put this figure in perspective, the average cost of a house in 1952 in the U.S. was approximately $9,000. Stearns Company decided it would not rebuild the store. The boardinghouse had been sitting idle since Co-operative Mine closed. The company would use that building for the Company Store instead. Stearns Company used the ground floor and had the store up and running in a couple of weeks.

It was the consensus after the fire consumed the building that it was a good possibility lightning had struck the building and started the fire. There was no way to prove or disprove the theory. The large building was a total loss. Although Stearns Company suffered a major loss, still the company had to feel thankful for the longevity of the building. Built between 1920–1922, it had stood for a thirty-year run without a major incident. In comparison, the Mc-

Creary County Courthouse in Whitley City lasted only twenty years before fire destroyed it in 1951.

While Stearns Company worked on setting up the store, Co-operative families went to either Jewell Kidd's Grocery, on the west end of Co-operative, or Guy Kidd's Grocery in White Oak Junction. At stores in the county not owned by Stearns Company, the miners and their families could trade their scrip at ninety cents to the dollar.

∞

Several weeks later, the store burning still weighed heavy on the minds of people in Co-operative. Summer was still in full swing. Kids were enjoying the remaining days of summer break.

Larry Bell and Buddy Nichols were good friends. At the time, both families lived in the Lower Camp. The Nichols (our neighbor) lived in House 50, just down from where the tipple was, and the Bell family lived in House 58, across the creek and gravel road and up on the hill. Buddy and Larry were walking the rails of the railroad in the Lower Camp to see how far they could walk before losing their balance and stepping off. It was something fun all the kids in Co-operative did. They made it all the way to Logan Holler and started back.

When they got near the Shoopman home, they saw Arnold in his garden. The houses in Co-operative were not bunched up close together and so had good-sized yards. Arnold had a fence around his small garden to protect it from varmints. The garden wasn't all that big, but big enough for a few rows of corn and vegetables and one row of watermelon. His garden was close to the back porch. In Arnold's row of melons, one was getting big and Buddy commented on it, "Hey, Arnold, that melon looks like it's ready to pick."

"It will be in a few days," Arnold answered. "I'll get it then."

Larry and Buddy walked on, and Arnold didn't see the boys anymore that day. A couple of days later, it was by accident Arnold saw Buddy and Larry walking down the path in his direction. The path behind the houses was made by people walking to and from the spring to get drinking water. The fence Arnold had around his garden was wire mesh about four feet high. Arnold decided to watch the boys to see what they were up to.

Where Arnold was standing, Buddy and Larry couldn't see him. When the two boys came close to Arnold's fence, they stopped and looked around. After a few minutes, the boys thought the coast was clear. Larry took hold of the fence, hugging the top of the fence. Anyone seeing him would have thought he was trying to lie down on it. Then he rolled over to the other side. Arnold eased out the back door and went into his corn patch. Larry still couldn't see Arnold.

Arnold suspected the two rascals were after the watermelon they were eyeing the other day. And a few minutes later, his suspicions were proven right. Larry worked his way close to the watermelon. He took one last look around, then hunkered down. As Larry reached to take hold of the watermelon, Arnold reached down and took hold of Larry's shirt collar. Larry had not noticed that Arnold had been doing some sneaking of his own. Arnold said, "I don't know whether to whip you here or take you over to your dad and let him whip you."

"No, no," Larry said. "Don't take me home. Daddy'll kill me."

"All right, Larry, let's go over to the fence. Hey, Buddy," Arnold said loud enough for Buddy to hear. When Buddy got closer, Arnold said, "Now, boys, if you both will promise me you'll leave my garden alone, I'll let you go." Arnold added, "But if it happens again, there won't be any more talking. I'll either whip you on the spot or take you both to your moms and dads." That scared those boys half to death. Larry and Buddy didn't know that Arnold would never have whipped them. That was the end of Buddy and Larry attempting to bother Arnold Shoopman's garden ever again.

∞

In the Upper Camp, Arnold and Mae Winchester bought a television. In those days, to get any kind of reception in Co-operative, you had to have an antenna on top of the mountain. (Remember, Co-operative sat in a narrow valley between mountains.) Arnold stretched antenna wire up the side of the mountain behind his house to the top of the mountain, where he anchored his antenna. Everyone in the camp was curious about this new technology, but some people wouldn't impose; however, some just had to see it, like young Chester Waters. The Winchester family welcomed Chester into their home to watch TV. Chester, at the time, was about seven years old and had never watched TV before.

Chester watched for about thirty minutes and suddenly jumped up and ran out the door, across the ballfield, over the car bridge, across the gravel road, and up the hill to their home, yelling, "Mommy, Mommy." Alti, Chester's mom, quickly made her way out of the kitchen to the front door. They collided in the doorway. Chester said, "Mom, get out the winter coats. It's going to snow. I seen it on the Winchester television."

∞

BORN THIS YEAR 1952

Braville Hall
Linda Winchester
Brenda Black
Mildred Gibson
Joyce Hall
Ellen Shook
Ruby Jones
Gary Bowden
Jerry Tapley

CHAPTER 30

1953

In 1953, another Co-operative young man made his community proud while serving his country. Espy C. Haynes, seventeen-year-old son of Clell and Millie Haynes, was completing his AP Airmen Basic Training course at Lackland Air Force Base.

Lackland, located near San Antonio, was the gateway to the Air Force. Lackland, at the time the largest Air Force Base in the world, prepared men and women for entrance into the U.S. Air Force. The base was not only a human resources research center but also an officer's candidate school. The technical training helped the Air Force place each candidate, based on a thorough scientific evaluation of their aptitude and inclination, in the vocation and career best suited for the individual.

∞

Back at home in McCreary County, Stearns Coal and Lumber Company announced the closing of Mine 4 and Mine 18. Notices were posted that at the end of March both mines would cease operation. Mine 4 in Worley had operated for forty-nine years and employed an average of 170 men, and during its run had produced 7,854,599 tons of coal. Mine 18 at Blue Heron opened in 1938, employed an average of 140 men, and in fifteen years had produced 2,738,737 tons of coal. This action crippled the economy of McCreary County. R. L. Stearns, president of the company, based his decision to close the two mines, reluctantly, on the conditions of the market. He stated the company's losses were heavy even in the winter months when coal prices were one dollar higher per ton than in summer months. Mr. Stearns pointed out that if something drastic didn't change in the market to lower the cost of producing coal, deep mining in McCreary County would soon come to an end.

When April 1 rolled around, the once mighty empire of Stearns Coal and Lumber Company had been reduced to one mine, Mine 16 in Oz. Mine 16, then known as Paint Cliff, employed approximately sixty-five men. These men were under contract until the end of November.

∞

Daily life in Co-operative and White Oak Junction continued but the landscape was changing minute by minute. Several miners were lucky enough to get some work at Mine 16. Other miners became weekend dads as they were forced to find work in other areas of the county or other states; still other miners moved their families to places with work opportunities.

Even though the mine in Co-operative shut down in 1950, the Stearns Company kept a skeleton crew on to maintain the mine in case it decided to start it up again. A few men still held out hope that Co-operative Mine would start back up. However, the fate of the coal mine was about to be decided without anyone knowing. The decision made at the meeting of the Board of Directors on April 2-3 crushed all hope. Present at the board meeting were Chairman of the Board, J. E. Butler of Danville; President, R. L. Stearns; James Bennett of Tucson, Arizona; R. W. Henderson of Stearns; E. E. Barthell of Ludington, Michigan; Isaac Hilliard of Louisville; and William C. Duvall of Cincinnati.

The board had no choice but to look at the crisis facing the company, the coal industry particularly. They looked at each item that made up the cost of doing business. When they saw there wasn't any room to alleviate some costs—in fact, a few items they projected would go even higher—they gave management the directive to liquidate physical assets in Worley Mine 4 and in Co-operative Mine. These two mines had, in the past, produced an average of a 1,000 tons of coal each day and employed approximately 310 men combined.

No action was taken on Mine 16, which was still operating, or Mine 18, which had recently been closed. The board decided to let the near future in the market decide the fate of those two locations.

Co-operative sprang up in the middle of the forest like a flower in springtime in 1920–1922 and with that one decision, the board at the April 2–3 meeting put the lid on the coffin and drove in the final nail on the place of my birth. Though it would take several years for Co-operative to die completely, I can say definitively the 1950 closing of the mine and the 1953 Board of Directors' decision marked the end of Co-operative, a community of good people, a way of life.

People on the outside likely looked at us in Co-operative and said we were just a bunch of poor people who would never amount to a hill of beans, but they were wrong. I don't measure being poor by not having a penny, but when a penny is all one has, it becomes the fuel mixed with desire and a pinch of determination to reach for something better. That's what I took away from my experience and my rich heritage of living in the community of Co-operative, Kentucky.

Other communities like Co-operative were feeling the same pain; Thursday, April 30, marked the closing of the Company Store in Barthell. Judge Edward Barthell Sr. was an officer of Stearns Coal and Lumber Company; the community of Barthell was named after him. The last manager of the store was James William Shoopman, known as Bill. Bill started working for Stearns Company in 1916 and worked in Fidelity, Worley, and Barthell. Fidelity shut down in 1937, and Mr. Shoopman may have been the last store manager there. The Stearns Company Stores still operated in Co-operative, Worley, and Blue Heron.

A crew of men, representing Hyman-Michaels Company of Chicago, hired by Stearns Coal and Lumber Company, came to White Oak Junction to dismantle ten miles of the K & T Railway between White Oak Junction and Bell Farm, which included Gregory, Fidelity, and Exotus.

∞

Summer break started for the kids in Co-operative—a time of celebration. The children who walked home were talking and laughing and having fun. At least a few boys were racing each other. Some of the kids would see each other the next day and were making plans—would it be a ball game or a game of marbles? But for now, the first order of business was to get home and out of the school/Sunday-go-meeting clothes.

Mom was waiting for me. She always wanted to see my report card first thing. When you advanced into the next grade level, your summer break was that much sweeter. Not bragging, but I never knew the heartbreak of being held back to repeat a grade. Many years later, I learned that Mom kept all my report cards, grades 1–12.

∞

Larry Bell, the son of Willard and Burnett Bell, lived in the Lower Camp across the creek and gravel road and up on the hill. Archie Shoopman, son of Arnold and Geneva Shoopman, also lived in the Lower Camp. Larry was older than Archie and loved to pick on him—and he did quite often. Now Archie wasn't one to make mad. Even on the last day of school, Larry smacked Archie on the top of his head as he ran past him on the way home.

A couple weeks went by, and Archie had an idea that would be fun if it worked, and it gave him something constructive to do to pass some time.

Carroll Worley (my brother) walked down to spend some time with Archie as he often did in those days. They were good friends. Archie told Carroll he had an idea, and it would be fun if it worked. Carroll said he wanted to help. So, Archie, Carroll, and Archie's younger brother, Roger, went up to the tipple to look for potential boards they could use. They found a couple nice ones they thought would work and took them back to the Shoopman house to begin work. They managed to drive a round piece of wood deep into the ground and tamped and hammered rocks in the ground around the post securing it solid, leaving about a foot and a half of the wood above ground.

They then needed a wide, flat board for the next part of Archie's idea, which Carroll and Archie were lucky enough to find at the tipple. After determining where the center of the board was, they used a poker Archie's mom kept by the cookstove to accomplish the next task. Archie put the poker back in the fire until it was glowing red and used it to burn a hole in the center of the flat board. Then they poured water over the hole to cool it down and stop the smoking. The wide board was a good ten feet long. It took both Carroll and Archie to place the board on the post. Archie let go of his end and grabbed the hammer to drive a large nail through the hole of the board into the post.

Now the board would stay off the ground if someone was on each end of the board to keep it balanced. To make sure it was going to work, Archie and Roger climbed on the board, and Carroll got it to spin by holding on to the small board they'd nailed on one end. Carroll ran one complete circle and let the board go. It kept spinning several times after Carroll let go. It worked like Archie hoped. Stopping the rotation was no problem. It just took one of the boys to let his feet drag on the ground. Archie was thrilled. He got off the board to let Carrol have a turn.

Larry Bell had walked the railroad tracks toward Logan Holler and on the way back saw the boys playing and walked up to see why they were having so much fun. Larry stood nearby and watched Carroll, Archie, and Roger take turns on Archie's new invention. Archie invited Larry to take a ride.

When the board stopped spinning, Archie got on one end and said, "Come on, Larry. Let's take a ride."

Larry walked over and got on the other end of the board. Carroll got it spinning, not too fast at first to give Larry a chance to get comfortable. Suddenly, Carroll pushed as hard and fast as he could and jumped out of the way.

Archie got himself an idea and waited for the right time and jumped off. When he did, the end of the board where Larry was sitting slammed into the dirt and Larry went rolling like a sack of taters down the yard and into a briar patch. Those briars broke skin everywhere they came in contact, drawing blood to the surface in a couple of places. Briar patches like to hug you and not let go, which is what they did to poor Larry. Larry began crying as he worked to free himself. When he got free, he came at Archie fighting mad. Archie grabbed the slop bucket and hit Larry on the side of the head. Slop scraps went everywhere and a good part of them on Larry. Lord, Larry was mad. He went home just a bawling. Archie, Carroll, and Roger stood and just died laughing.

A few days later, Archie, Carroll, Roger, and Larry, and some other friends were playing a softball game. What happened in Archie's yard was forgotten. It was a new day.

Later that summer, Larry Bell's family moved out of Co-operative.

∞

Also later that summer, the Shoopman family moved to House 56, the yellow house. It was the only house painted yellow in Co-operative. Everything they owned, they carried to the new house. Children carried what they could. Arnold carried the washer on his back. After taking everything loose off the cookstove, Arnold somehow managed to get the stove on his back and carried it to the yellow house. Not long after they moved, they bought their first refrigerator.

∞

The Korean War was halted as delegates from both sides and the United Nations came together in a short ten-minute ceremony to sign the armistice agreement, marking an end to the three-year-and-one-month proxy war. The official date and time of the signing was July 27, 1953, at 8:00 p.m. (EST). Four weeks later when the death toll was released, America had lost 142,277 brave soldiers.

∞

On Monday, December 7, under the new union pay scale, not one man showed up for work at the only mine Stearns Company had operating. The contract between United Mine Workers and Stearns Coal and Lumber Company had ended Friday night, December 4. Stearns Coal and Lumber Company posted the new pay rate to continue operation. The posted pay rate was $14 per day to work inside the mine.

Mr. Stearns released a statement detailing the situation of the coal market and how the company arrived at its present condition. In his statement, Mr. Stearns explained why their timber operation had become a sideline when the federal government stepped into the picture. The federal government wanted to take control of all the timberland in Eastern Kentucky for the Cumberland National Forest. This meant most of the Stearns Company land holdings were taken over by the government at prices fixed by the courts. Stearns Company was allowed to keep only the mineral rights. With the loss of timber, the company lost a big part of its business in McCreary County. Banking on harvesting future crops of timber to offset the decline in the coal market was no longer possible.

As the year ended, Mine 16, owned by Stearns Coal and Lumber Company, remained idle. The only coal operations in McCreary County were these:
- Bobo Denham strip mine at Marsh Creek
- R. B. Campbell Coal Company strip mine near Holly Hill
- Shelt Smith Truck Mine in Yamacraw
- Walker Mine at Alum Creek operated by Clem Swerts of Whitley City

∞

BORN THIS YEAR 1953

Sheila Worley (my sister)
Reba Clark
Roy Shoopman
Doyle Keith
Jerry Watson
Reba Ruth Coffey
Brenda Coffey

Diane Maxwell
Carol Sue Hall
Dean Ball
Geneva Gregory
Norma Jean Conatser
Lois Ann Hall
Gene Maples
Darlene Judy Maxwell
Carroll Rose Jr.
Merita Bowden
Brenda Cox
Carroll Dixon

CHAPTER 31

1954

As the year 1954 began, Stearns Coal and Lumber Company had its back to the wall. Coal mining at present was at a standstill and timber was running out.

One by one Stearns Company coal camps were slowly disappearing. The company began selling the houses, and families were forced to move. Fidelity camp was the first to go in 1937. I believe Fidelity was the company's second largest coal community in its prime with seventy-two homes, a bathhouse, boardinghouse, and store, and two tipples.

The largest of them all was Co-operative (my community) in its prime with eighty homes, a bathhouse, boardinghouse, store, and huge tipple. This year, 1954, Co-operative had already lost thirty-four of the eighty homes, and the families that remained in the camp paid rent at $2.00 per room, per month. That meant my family's rent was $8.00, unless we were charged for the food pantry which was a large walk-in space with shelves on both sides and under the small window at the end. Instead of the sound of coal being loaded, the sounds heard in Co-operative were homes being torn down by Stearns Company carpenters.

Castello (Cack) Slaven, superintendent of Co-operative Mine, which closed in 1950, was heard saying, "If the sounds of hammering were from building in Co-operative instead of tearing down, it wouldn't be so sad."

The Stearns Company Stores remained open and operating only in Co-operative and Blue Heron. The mine in Blue Heron that went on a standby basis March 27, 1953, had once employed over one hundred men; now the Company Store served only four families.

∞

Sometime in the night on February 4 at Mine 18, Blue Heron sub-station, thieves stole approximately 2,000 feet of copper feeder line wire, the main haulage line near the mine (seven west) opening. Thieves stripped the wire on the spot. With copper selling at thirty-two cents a pound, Stearns Company officials valued the loss at $800.

Just a few days later, Stearns Company received more bad news: the company's proposal to strip mine in Cumberland National Forest had been entirely rejected.

∞

On February 20, the President of Stearns Coal and Lumber Company released a statement informing employees of Mine 16 in Paint Cliff that the wage proposed last December was still in effect. Within days, a committee representing the majority of Mine 16 employees notified Stearns Company the employees would resume work in accordance with the December proposal. On March 4, the committee signed a two-year local union bargaining agreement, and on March 10, the employees went back to work.

On April 1, the McCreary County Miners Union negotiated a back-to-work contract at Mine 18 in Blue Heron; the employees who were working at the time the mine was put on standby in 1953 had priority. The scheduled date for work to begin was Thursday, April 8.

Just like that, Stearns Company was back in the coal business with approximately sixty-five miners at Mine 16 and over a hundred miners at Mine 18, with the potential for new markets to open up. With this positive change came a welcomed announcement: Kentucky Utilities (KU) announced it was building a coal-fired steam plant that would need 1,090,000 tons of coal per year. The future was starting to look brighter for Stearns Coal and Lumber Company.

∞

Winter was still trying to hold on, and school in Co-operative had several weeks before it would close for summer break. Arnold Shoopman's dog and a couple of other dogs somehow killed one of Marion Wilson's pigs. When the Wilson boys found out one of the dogs belonged to the Shoopmans, Gerald and his brother Doyle Wilson started calling Archie and Roger Shoopman "pigs" or "piggy," in not a kind way. This went on for several days, and Archie was getting tired of it and madder by the day.

One cold morning a light snow mixed with ice fell, and during the day, it became slushy. Walking home from school, Gerald walked by Archie and said, "Hello, piggy." He walked on ahead of Archie a few steps. Archie reached down and got a handful of slush and began squeezing it into an ice ball. Archie threw the ice ball at Gerald, hitting him on the side of the head and mostly on the ear. Gerald grabbed his ear and ran down the railroad tracks as fast as he could go crying. Gerald told his dad, Marion, that Archie hit him with an ice ball. It no doubt gave Gerald an earache. Gerald's mom and dad thought it might have damaged Gerald's hearing.

The next morning at work Marion was mad and began telling Arnold, Archie's dad, what Archie did to his boy.

Arnold said, "Yeah, I know all about it and I gave him a whipping for it." Arnold continued, "But the reason Archie hit your boy—you don't know the reason, do you? Gerald didn't tell you, did he?"

Marion said, "Well, no. What's the story?"

"Ever since the dogs killed your pig, your boys have been calling my boys pig and piggy, and it happens every time they see my boys. Well, Archie got tired of it."

Marion said, "I didn't know anything about that."

"Yeah, and if they don't stop," Arnold said, "I'll kill every one of your pigs."

Marion said, "Now, wait. I'll take care of this when I get home today."

Arnold and Marion were good friends and this was the first time anything had come between them. They didn't talk anymore that day, nor did the subject ever come up again. Gerald and Doyle never called Archie and Roger pig or piggy again. I don't know what Marion did when he got home, but whatever it was, it worked. That was the end of it.

∞

School was out for the summer and the Co-operative kids were enjoying those leisure days of doing pretty much whatever they wanted to do aside from their chores required at home. Even though it was summer, their mom's cookstove still needed something to burn if any food was to be cooked. That meant keeping wood and coal handy by the stove and, on wash days, carrying water, usually from the closest spring.

One day, Archie and Roger Shoopman and JT Terry went out exploring along the incline. In those days going up the incline was a bit of a challenge. The incline was very steep. The boys made it to the top and walked out a ways and found an overhanging cliff. They decided it was a good place to camp. They went searching for things to burn and rounded up a good supply of dried out limbs and made a pile close to the cliff. They figured to spend the night they'd need something to eat and some means to cook.

On the hike home, Roger said, "Yeah, we're going to need food, but what? You know Mom won't let us carry anything out of the house."

JT said, "Let me work on that. I have an idea."

Before separating, they agreed to meet up after supper. When the time came, Archie and Roger walked past the Terry home looking intently for signs of JT. But no one was about. Archie told Roger, "Let's wait on the tram track above the tipple."

When they got up there, JT was there, waiting for them. JT stood up holding a grass sack half full of something. "What you got in the sack?" Roger asked.

"Taters," JT said. "Tonight, we'll roast taters over the campfire." And that's exactly what they did.

After that first night, some of their other friends joined in the fun. The usual suspects were LD and Carroll Worley (my brothers), Roger Chitwood, Kenneth Waters, Chester Waters, and Jimmy Hardwick. There could have been others. That summer, the boys of Co-operative experienced freedom, friendship, and independence in the wide-open spaces on top of the incline.

They always had plenty of taters to roast provided by JT Terry. The rest of the gang never knew exactly how JT was getting all those taters. Not that it was a concern to them. The boys were happy to have something to eat those nights they camped.

But it wouldn't be until later in life when the Co-operative community was a memory that Roger and JT, by circumstance, ended up working at the same location. It was there when the two men talked of those days of growing up in Co-operative that JT revealed to Roger he had gotten the taters from his dad's garden. JT said his dad most likely knew he was getting them but never let on.

∞

The summer break came to an end and the new school year was well under way. In those days lighting fires with matches was common and every home had matches. Matches, made of wood, were about the size of toothpicks, and they came in a small box and on each side of the box were strikers for convenience. Some kids would save those small sticks after they'd been used and cut off the charred ends. After collecting a bunch of them, kids played a game with them by taking turns stacking them.

Someone with creative ability like Archie Shoopman could build things with the clean sticks. One Sunday afternoon, it had been raining and was too wet to play outside, so Archie started assembling his match stems and created a stick man, complete with eyes, nose, and mouth. It looked pretty good; Archie called it his "Buckeye Man."

The next day Archie decided he'd take his stick man to school and show his teacher. Getting to school, he had a few minutes before the first bell and some of the kids were curious and had to have a closer look. One of the kids was holding the stick man when Jimmy Maples suddenly snatched it out of his hands and took off across the playground. Archie flew mad and reached down and picked up a rock and threw it as hard as he could. It hit Jimmy in the back of his head. Blood squirted down the back of Jimmy's shirt and Jimmy went to crying and threw the stick man to the ground. Archie ran over and retrieved his Buckeye Man. Jimmy told Mr. Farley, the principal, and Mr. Farley paddled Archie for throwing the rock.

At the next recess, some of the boys kidded Archie about getting a paddling but that didn't bother Archie. He said, "It was worth it. I'll teach Jimmy to grab my Buckeye Man." Archie had no more trouble with his stick man.

∞

In Whitley City, three men were charged with stealing the copper wire Stearns Company had lost to thieves back in February. The police were clued when the three men tried to sell a large quantity of copper.

Alfred Slavey, Claude Cooper, and Bones Perry were sentenced to six months in jail.

∞

As the year slowly came to a close, the season for raccoon hunting was projected to be good, at least according to Hoover Keith. On a hunt with Luther Phillips on Little South Fork, Hoover and Luther caught two river raccoons. One was a twelve pounder and the other, a fifteen pounder. This kind of news encouraged a lot of men to go raccoon hunting, like Guy Kidd, who loved an all-night hunt.

∞

MARRIED THIS YEAR 1954

James Howard Blevins married Ella Jean Hill. James and Ella Jean had four children: Marsha, Steve, Joy, and James Jr.

∞

BORN THIS YEAR 1954

Zoe D. Davis
Donna King
Charlotta Ann Coffey
David Black
Kathy Young
Dovie Watson
Mary Louise Waters
Paul Gregory Waters
Clara Jones
Marsha Blevins Thrash

Pearline Gregory
Clem Ball
Lonnie Gibson
Donnie Gibson
Teresa Freeman
Jerry Whitehead

CHAPTER 32

1955

Since the U.S. Forest Service rejected Stearns Company's proposal to strip mine, R. L. Stearns appealed to Benson, the U.S. Secretary of Agriculture. Benson appointed a three-man committee to study the situation and report back to him. Mr. Stearns was not happy with Benson's decision to appoint a committee and sent a letter to Secretary Benson expressing his thoughts. In the letter, Mr. Stearns wrote candidly that Secretary Benson as the federal representative should accept the responsibility of making the decision on his appeal instead of passing it on to a committee that had no responsibility to the people.

∞

Harley Hardwick was one of several men who went north seeking employment after Co-operative Mine closed. He found work and became a weekend dad, but not for long. After two or three years, he returned home to resume work in the coal mines.

Harley and Arnold Shoopman were good friends. One weekend, they talked up a fishing trip. When Roger found out about it, he asked his dad if he could go.

Arnold said, "Now, Son, we plan on staying out all night."

"I don't care. I want to go," Roger said.

Arnold said, "It's okay with me if your mom says it's okay."

Saturday came and Arnold and Roger met Harley by the Co-operative schoolhouse playground. It was early afternoon. Harley said, "Arnold, I'm sure glad you brought us a cook."

"I can't cook," young Roger said.

Harley said, "Well, you sure can't fish. Why…a fish'll drag you in the river."

"You just wait and see," Roger said.

They started out walking the path to Hickory Knob, around two and a half miles, and the path led them close to the Hickory Knob church house. From there, they walked the road to Grandma Worley's place and picked up the path behind her house and down that side of the mountain to Exotus.

In those days, wasps built their nests on the sides of trees. Harley loved using baby wasps for bait. Harley was not afraid of them. He'd walk right up to a nest, the nest covered with wasps, and lean his rod and reel against another tree; then he'd run his hand under his shirt to his armpit and swab it a couple times. Then he'd reach up and take hold of the nest. Every last wasp would fly off like they were scared to death. Harley would pull the nest off the tree with the baby wasps inside. That nest could be four inches across. He would put it in his bag and walk on. Harley never once got stung.

After they set up camp, the first order of business was fishing; after all, that's why they were there. After a bit of fishing, since camp was within a few feet of the bank, Harley looked at Roger and said, "Let's step back to the campfire. I bet you could eat something. I know I could."

Harley pulled out the bologna. Using his pocketknife, he cut three-inch blocks. He then quartered the block and put a piece on the end of a stick and reached it over to Roger to hold and got one ready for himself and held both over the fire. When the bologna got brown, Harley told Roger to try it. Harley ate his and said, "Now, boy, that'll make you wanna slap your grandma."

Arnold came over and the three of them enjoyed several minutes of quiet serenity, eating their roasted bologna and listening to the sounds of the water and nature. Arnold and Harley were doing something they loved and were able to forget about the backbreaking work of digging coal, at least for a little while. And food seemed always to taste much better out in the wide-open spaces. It was a good outing. Seems like when you're doing something enjoyable, time goes by too quickly, which is exactly what happened in this case.

∞

On Monday, July 11, Shelt Smith opened his new mine operation in Co-operative. He had negotiated a contract with the McCreary County Miners Union. Hobart Stephens was the timekeeper for the operation. Mr. Smith hoped to work a maximum of fifty men and produce fifty tons of coal per day. The coal was removed by truck, then taken to Paint Cliff and transferred to coal gons.

∞

Arnold Shoopman got up one Saturday morning and said to Geneva, his wife, "Let's take the kids fishing today. Besides, seems like it's been a long time since you've been fishing."

"Sure. Where do you want to fish?" Geneva asked.

"Let's go down to White Oak Junction. It's close and we haven't been there in a while," Arnold said.

After breakfast, Geneva busied herself getting together everything she figured they'd need. It didn't take long to walk to White Oak Junction; it was only a half mile or so. Walking down the railroad tracks a short distance, the family turned right leaving the railroad tracks and walked the path that went by the oil wells. The path brought them out below the swimming hole in White Oak Junction. Geneva told the kids to go play and she and Arnold would be over by the big tree fishing from the bank. They were no more than forty to fifty feet away from the concrete pillar that supported the train bridge. It was there the kids loved to play. It was sandy just like a real beach.

Arnold and Geneva wet their hooks and fished for about forty minutes. Geneva stopped fishing and bent down to wash her hands in Rock Creek. She decided to walk back and round up the kids for the picnic dinner she had brought. Arnold said, "I'll come, too. I'm hungry."

After everyone ate, the kids went back to playing in the white sand close to the train bridge and Arnold and Geneva went back to fishing. The younger kids loved building things in the sand.

All of a sudden, they heard a loud voice say, "Get out of the way, you S.O.B." All eyes looked toward the train bridge. A horse came around the curve, running as hard and fast as it could go. The kids ran screaming to get out of the way of the horse and narrowly escaped the pounding hoofs. Sitting on the horse was Obe Winchester, and when he saw the kids, he cussed some more, "You little S.O.Bs." Obe had to be drunk because when he wasn't drinking, he would never risk hurting a child.

Seeing his kids almost trampled to death, Arnold threw down his rod and reel and broke into a run, trying to head Obe off. Where Arnold and Geneva were fishing, Obe had to come past them. But the horse was in full gallop, so Arnold didn't quite make it. If he had, he would have knocked Obe off his horse. The kids had never seen their dad this mad. Roger overheard his dad say, "If I had a gun, Obe would be one dead man right now." Unaware, Obe, too, had narrowly escaped. Geneva packed up. Arnold fetched the rods and reels. And they walked back home, no longer in the mood to fish.

∞

A little over two weeks later, Dovie, Obe Winchester's wife, came to the Shoopman place riding that same horse that Obe was riding when he nearly ran over the Shoopman kids. This time the horse was gentle. Dovie got off the horse and tied the reins to the handrail of the steps. By now Arnold and Geneva had walked out on the porch. Dovie told Arnold and

Geneva she hadn't seen Obe in about two weeks and there wasn't a bite of food in her house. She asked, and you could tell it was hard for her, "Would you have anything to give me?"

"You wait right here," Arnold said immediately.

Geneva and Dovie sat on the porch talking while Arnold was in the house. In the pantry, Arnold pulled out two grass sacks and filled them with canned food and taters and tied the grass sacks together and carried them around front where Dovie's horse was standing. Arnold positioned the grass sacks in front of the saddle, one hanging on each side so they balanced each other. Dovie thanked both Arnold and Geneva as she climbed on the horse.

Arnold said, "If you need more food, you come on back." Dovie would have tried to pay Arnold if she had had any money. Obe had drunk up all their money. Dovie knew the Shoopman family was large and Arnold had a lot of mouths to feed, so she must have felt she had nowhere else to turn.

One thing Stearns Coal and Lumber Company didn't do was fire a man for having a drinking problem as long as he didn't drink at work.

∞

Stearns Coal and Lumber Company lost its appeal to the Secretary of Agriculture to strip mine the land it held mineral rights to. Secretary of Agriculture, Ezra T. Benson, gave his decision to his assistant, E. L. Peterson. The three-man committee was also involved in the decision. A press release by a spokesman for the Department of Agriculture stated, "It's not in the public interest to strip mine on National Forest Land." The committee determined that strip mining 1,000 acres would disturb an additional 2,500 acres with spillage, contouring, and roads being continuously built as the work progressed. If the decision had been in the company's favor, would the company have stopped its two deep mining operations and converted to strip mining? Also, would the company have gone back to the places where they had closed mining operations, like Co-operative? If that had happened, Co-operative would not be recognizable today. Strip mining would have completely changed the shape of the mountains.

In the previous year, 1954, as many as 1,000 coal mines closed in several states. Only a few short weeks later, the head of United Mine Workers Union and the president of Coal Operators, Henry Moses, negotiated the largest increase in pay in union history. It called for an increase of fifteen cents an hour, time and a half pay for Saturday work, and double pay for Sunday work.

Stearns Coal and Lumber Company did receive some good news before the year ended. The Tennessee Valley Authority announced its coal contracts for the upcoming year and Stearns Company was awarded a contract for 173,800 tons of coal.

∞

On the mountain north of Co-operative, in the area of Rattlesnake Ridge, Mount View School year started with forty-four students and A. O. Lee as the teacher. The Mount View softball team defeated Wolf Creek by a score of 25–2. The Mount View Tigers softball team members were Boyd Phillips, Larry Phillips, Lloyd Thompson, Vernon Thompson, Leland Haynes, Leo Tucker, Smilie Keith, Luther Phillips Jr., Melvin Godsey, Herbert Jones Jr., Clyde Tucker,

James Keith, and Cedeous Coffey. One player, Ronald Tucker, didn't get to play because he was sick.

∞

Roger Shoopman thought his dad might want to go fishing one Saturday. So he set a minnow trap in White Oak Creek. Saturday came and, sure enough, Arnold was ready to get in some fishing. Roger was ready, too. Roger told his dad he had a whole jar of minnows, and Arnold said, "We can go and fish for a few hours and be back before dark."

This time, it was just Roger and his dad. Roger carried the jar of minnows the whole way. There was a big pond that was close to where Charlie Davis lived. So the pond was called the Charlie Davis Hole. That's where Arnold said they'd try. As they walked down the path close to the bank, a water bird chirped and flew out over the water. As that happened, Arnold unknowingly brushed against a wasp's nest on the side of a tree.

Those wasps covered Roger, stinging him mostly on his face, elbows, and knees. Roger threw the jar of minnows and started slapping wasps. The jar landed on a pile of rocks in the shallow part of the water and minnows went to jumping everywhere.

In those days, Arnold chewed Prince Albert tobacco. He put tobacco juice on the stings, which helped draw out the venom. But it didn't stop the hurt. Roger couldn't fish. He hurt too bad. Instead, he walked out and sat down in the cool water and that seemed to help ease the hurting some. Arnold didn't fish as long as he might have. After about an hour, they walked home.

MARRIED THIS YEAR 1955

As soon as RL Terry was released from active duty in the Army, he continued his courtship with Faye Winchester. Both families still lived in Co-operative. RL, age 21, and Faye, age 18, got married. Della Winchester and Dessie Nichols stood up for the couple. RL and Faye had two children: Lynn and Dester.

BORN THIS YEAR 1955

Gloria Worley (my baby sister)
Boris Haynes
Linda Davis
Robbie Shoopman
Betty Watson
Darrell Hall
Jeannie Dixon
Elda Conatser
Geraldine Maples
Randy Lee Jones
Ella Dixon
Connie Dennis
Joe Waters

CHAPTER 33

Dynamite Fist— Conclusion

Don Dixon's self-esteem and pride showed through when he was a boy, which was evidenced in the first few times Rose, his mom, sent him to Guy Kidd's store to buy an item. When he reached the store, Don would not go right in. He would wait on the porch for a few minutes listening for other customers who might be inside. Playing barefooted with friends and being around family barefooted was one thing but having folks in the Company Store see him barefooted embarrassed him, so if Don heard someone talking inside other than Guy or Ada, Guy's wife, Don would wait until they left. There were a few times Don couldn't wait some people out. If one of Guy's friends came by just to talk and have a cup of coffee, he was forced to go in, get what his mom sent him to get, and leave as fast as he could. But if possible, Don would wait outside on the side of the building until customers left.

As Don grew, he became more adventurous. He walked the railroad tracks one afternoon to see what lay west beyond White Oak Junction. Don had heard about Co-operative. He wanted to see the place for himself. As he walked through Logan Holler and came around the last curve, straight ahead about a half-mile stretch, he saw the coal tipple. The valley opened up which had to be breathtaking to a young boy. Don went all through Co-operative, looking and taking it all in. The camp was much bigger than White Oak Junction.

Don walked all the way to Jewell Kidd's Grocery before turning around. He had lingered longer than he realized. By the time Don made it back to Logan Holler, it was dark and all Don could clearly make out were the rails that illuminated from the smallest amount of moonlight. Don's eyes now becoming acclimated to the dark saw something come out of the woods ahead of him and start walking on the tracks. Whatever it was, the distance between them remained the same. The thing never slowed to let Don catch up, not that he wanted to. If Don picked up the pace, the thing picked up the pace. When Don reached the porch of the Dixon home, whatever it was ran off. Don was relieved to be home.

∞

One day, Don Dixon and Bob Shepherd walked to the swimming hole and Bull Hines and Lester Watson were there getting ready to go out in the flat bottom boat. Bull said they were going frog gigging, did Bob and Don want to come along. Don had never done frog gigging before and it sounded like fun, so he said, "Yeah, sure."

They started out and drifted along the current. Where the train bridge crossed Rock Creek was deep water. How it happened no one remembers, but the little flat bottom boat flipped over, and they had to swim to the bank. Don became sick and then got pneumonia and came close to dying. During that same time, he also got a kidney infection and swelled up like a toad. Don was bedfast for several weeks. When he recovered, he walked to visit Henry Ridner. It was the longest distance Don had walked since beginning to feel better. Don was sitting on Henry's porch as the sun was setting and frog gigging came up in their conversation. Don said, "I'll never do that again."

Henry said, "Don, you know what those frogs are saying?"

"No, I don't," Don replied.

Henry said, "On the far side of the bank, the frogs are saying 'new neighbors, new neighbors.' And, on this side, they're saying 'moved in, moved in.'"

Both Don and Henry had a good laugh. People who knew Henry knew one of his favorite sayings was "Yeah, boy." So naturally after he stopped laughing, he said, "Yeah, boy."

∞

Don and Hobert, his brother, got into their dad's carbide and put some in a can. They then went into the woods. Don told Hobert, "I've heard others talk about using carbide to make an explosion, and I wanna try it."

Don got everything set up and walked back a safe distance when Hobert said, "Ahh, that ain't gonna do anything." And Hobert walked over and squatted down over the can. About that time, the explosion went off and tattered the seat of Hobert's pants, and he went to rolling in the dirt trying to cool his rear end down.

When they got home, they thought they might have gotten lucky because their dad wasn't home yet from work. But that didn't stop Rose, their mom, from tanning their rear ends. Hobert thought he shouldn't have gotten a whipping since it was his bottom that got the brunt of the explosion, but his mom explained that since he was older than Don, he should've known better. Hobert's rear end was still numb from the explosion, so he never felt the whipping.

∞

Close to where the train bridge crossed Rock Creek was a cave, and water from Rock Creek spilled into the cave. It's said the other end comes out near the gravel road where the S curve is located. Well, one day, Don walked to the swimming hole. As he walked under the train bridge, Lester Watson was there with the flat bottom boat and said to Don, "I'm taking the boat into the cave. Wanna come along?"

Don wasn't afraid of anything (except maybe frog gigging) and said, "When do you want to?"

Lester said, "How about right now? I've got everything I think we'll need."

They both figured out, once they started, there wouldn't be any changing their minds. Easing the little boat close to the entrance, Lester lit his dad's carbide light. The boat was positioned with the current. Inside they went. Going through the entrance, they didn't have to duck their heads, but deeper inside, there were narrow, low places barely big enough for the boat to go through. Some of the places and things they saw were amazing. There were rooms so large they could get out of the boat and walk the banks. There were catfish with light blue eyes. There was one place so small the boys had to push the boat through. When they came out the other end, they sat on the bank of Rock Creek and pondered what they both had just done. Lester said, "That was fantastic."

"Sure was," Don said. That was all the two said. After a long rest, they carried the boat back to White Oak Junction.

∞

After the Dixon family moved up to the Lower Camp in Co-operative, many an evening Rose would walk out on her front porch for a little rest before dark. In the summertime, she'd ask one of the kids to get a gnat-smoke going. Then she'd want the boys to get their guitars and play some music for her. Hobert, Don, and Roy Gene all played and took turns singing. It wouldn't be long till the neighbors would gather in the front yard. They'd be sitting on the railroad tracks and on porches next door listening. People would stay close to the Dixon home as long as the boys played music, and they did until late in the night many times.

∞

Time was moving and when Don got a job with Stearns Coal and Lumber Company, he bought himself a car. Most Saturday afternoons and evenings he spent drinking and driving the gravel road through Co-operative as fast as he could go. The Harley and Imogene Hardwick family lived past the schoolhouse heading toward Jewell Kidd's Grocery across the creek on the left side of the road. Imogene raised chickens and it was common for her chickens to wander across the gravel road. If Don happened by, you could guess what happened if chickens were in the road.

Imogene started missing a few of her chickens and was very upset over it. After all, they laid eggs for the family and would become food themselves when killed. She didn't know how they had disappeared. Until one day Imogene was outside hanging up clothes to dry, and Don Dixon came down the road driving fast and slinging gravel and almost hit one of her chickens. It was a narrow escape.

A couple of days later, Imogene was in Jewell Kidd's Grocery and Don stopped to get gas. Imogene was leaving as Don was starting to walk in and they met in the doorway face-to-face. Imogene said, "You S.O.B., Don Dixon, you've been killing my chickens, driving up and down the road like a maniac."

All Don could think of to say seeing Imogene was so powerfully mad, "Well, I'm just trying to feed my family."

Hearing that made Imogene even madder and she said, "You piece of shit." She let the screen door slam and walked on home.

∞

As time went on, Don began dating Joan Chitwood. No one could blame him since Joan sure was pretty. Joan was working for Jewell Kidd at the store and Don stopped on Halloween night to see Joan. Bruce Shook and a couple of his friends were at the store. Don had been drinking and he thought the boys were there to take Joan trick or treating, but, in fact, they had stopped just to talk and hang out for a while. Bruce bought the smallest container of Vaseline in the store. He went outside while everyone was talking and smeared it all over Don's windshield.

Of course, it was a prank. Bruce didn't think anything bad would come of it. When Don finally left, he thought he couldn't see clearly because he'd drunk too much. Don made it past Raymond Clark's place and the curve was too steep to maneuver going fast, and he lost control of the car. The car came to rest in the creek with the headlights pointing to the sky.

Down in the ballfield, a bunch of Co-operative boys had gathered around a campfire and heard the crash. Roy Gene said, "Oh, no, I know that's Don." And he went running toward the lights.

Don was hurt bad. He was alive but unconscious, one eyeball laying out on his cheek. The family rushed Don to the hospital. He survived the crash, and after several weeks of recuperation, Don and Joan continued dating and eventually got married.

∞

Rose Dixon moved her family to the Upper Camp in Co-operative. Her husband, Harrison, Don's dad, had been dead several years. He was a victim of a rock fall inside the coal mine. Don stopped by to see his mom. While he was there, Hobert and Roy Gene got into an argument and were starting to physically fight. Don got between them, broke it up, and told them, "Don't be fighting in Mom's house."

Don and his mom were in the kitchen talking when they heard Hobert and Roy Gene fighting again. Don picked up a couple of cans of cream and hurried into the front room. Hobert saw Don and knocked Roy Gene to the floor and broke to run. Don went after him, going down several steps to the ground and through the yard. Hobert was running as hard as he could across the ballfield. Don, running hard also, waited until now to throw a can of cream at Hobert. It was hard to hit Hobert with both of them running and the can of cream missed wide. Don threw the other can of cream with the same result, so he stopped running. Hobert kept running as hard as he could, thinking Don was still after him. Don picked up the cans of cream and walked back, gave them to his mom, and left.

∞

Don drank a lot when he wasn't working, but when he was on the job, he worked hard, did dangerous work, and stayed sober. Don worked nightshift at Co-operative Mine. One Friday night, a rock fall happened and a piece of the rock hit Don's right toe, smashing the steel in the toe of his boot into his toe. He felt some discomfort, but finished his shift, and on the way home, he stopped and got a half gallon of moonshine to sip. When Don got home, he lay down on the couch but didn't take his boots off. He would go to the doctor the next morning.

He got a couple of hours of sleep, and when he woke up, blood had seeped out over the top of his boot. On Saturday morning at the doctor's office, when Don pulled off his boot, the doctor found the toe next to the little toe hanging by a small piece of skin. The doctor cut off the hanging toe and sewed the loose skin to the toe next to it. Don's toe injury healed eventually, but he suffered walking for quite a while.

∞

One Saturday many weeks later, Don had been drinking most of the day, and that evening, he decided to visit Walter Jun Hill. Jun was gone, so Don stayed a while with Velva Dean, Jun's wife, and then left. On his way back through Co-operative, Don recognized Jun's car sitting beside the road, so he stopped. Walking up to the car, he saw Joan, his wife, sitting in the passenger seat talking.

Don asked, "What do you think you're doing, Jun?"

"Sitting here talking," Jun said.

Don said, "I just bet you've been talking."

"I'll whip your ass," Jun said.

Don said, "Well, I can't stop you from doing that, but I can open the door for you." Don opened the car door, reached in, and grabbed Jun by the shirt. He jerked him out of his seat and onto the ground. The fight was on. Don took his own guilt and anger out on Ole Jun.

The next day at work, going into Co-operative Mine, Lester Watson said, "Don, what in the world did you do to Jun Hill?"

"I don't know what you're talking about," Don said.

Lester said, "Jun is laying down in Oneida Hospital, his head swelled up bigger than a watermelon. He says you done it." Don didn't make any comment and went on to work.

Don and Joan would later divorce, but not before children Millie, Jessica, and Chad were born. Don and his brother, Hobert, spent a couple of years running from the law, trying to escape paying child support, but Dynamite Fist's reckless ways finally caught up with him.

When the police caught up with Don, he spent some time in the big house. Getting out of jail, Don went to Western Kentucky and worked for Peabody Coal Company. It was there Don met and married Barbara Simpson, and they had two boys: Donald Jr. and Jeremy. Barbara also lived through many rough years with Don because his love for the wild side kept reappearing.

But when Don became a Christian, his life changed. Dynamite Fist and the wild side disappeared. Instead, he spent his time being with family and fishing. Don's love for music continued but changed to playing and singing gospel music. Donald Dixon became Dynamite for the Lord.

CHAPTER 34

1956

In 1956, William Carroll Haynes, age seventeen, the son of Jake and Elsie Haynes of Co-operative, Kentucky, was in San Antonio, Texas, at Lackland Air Force Base. Haynes was completing his Air Force Basic Training that prepared him to enter a career field. The community of Co-operative loved that another one of their own was doing good while serving his country.

∞

Good news came to the miners working for Stearns Coal and Lumber Company when the McCreary County Miners Union signed a three-year contract granting the miners a $1.50 raise per day. The agreement also gave a ten-cent royalty per ton starting April 1 that would increase to twenty cents by July.

R. L. Stearns Jr., president of Stearns Coal and Lumber Company, announced more good news. At Mine 16, the company was opening a second seam of coal. Only about a half mile of tram work would need to be added to connect the two seams. The second seam was called Mine 2 and would be mined mechanically using joy equipment with the coal transferred to the current tipple. For the men currently working, this news meant the potential for many more years of continued work. The new mine was scheduled to open at the beginning of 1957.

∞

One morning, Gabby Gregory stopped by Jewell Kidd's Grocery to get gas for his truck. He also went into the store and picked up a couple of items and paid for them. While there, Gabby and Neil Kidd (store owner) talked for a while and Gabby found out Neil was heading out to get commodities for the store. Gabby knew Neil would do some drinking before coming back, so Gabby told Neil he'd go along to keep him company, and Neil welcomed having someone go with him. Gabby told Neil he needed to go home first and when Neil got ready to leave, just to stop by and pick him up.

About an hour later, Neil left the store and drove around Rattlesnake Ridge to pick up Gabby, and they drove to Jellico Grocery in Oneida, Tennessee. There, Neil loaded everything he needed in the bed of his truck. On the way back home, Neil wanted to stop for a beer when they reached the Tennessee/Kentucky state line. A few hours later, Neil was ready to go, but Gabby wasn't. Gabby wanted to stay longer to keep drinking. Gabby could be a little contrary when he got to drinking. Eventually, they left for home.

Driving around Rattlesnake Ridge, when Gabby's house came into view, Gabby took out his pocketknife and opened one blade without Neil noticing. As Neil slowed the truck down to a stop to let Gabby out, Gabby reached over behind Neil and, in one quick motion, cut Neil's back from shoulder to shoulder. The blood poured, but with the large amount of alcohol in his system, it wasn't clear if Neil knew what Gabby had done because Neil drove on home. When Neil pulled in front of the store, he was so weak he now knew something was wrong and didn't know if he could walk. Neil pushed on the horn for about a minute. He then managed to get the truck door open and ease out of his seat. Jewell thought Neil was blowing the truck horn because he needed help unloading, so she sent someone out to help. When he saw Neil was bloody from his neck to the seat of his pants, he ran back to the store door, yelled for help, and ran back to Neil. A couple of other guys came running out, and they got Neil to a chair on the front porch.

When Jewell saw Neil, she was frightened to death but didn't let on. All she could think to do was grab towels and wrap them around Neil. She asked one of the men to drive Neil's car and take him to the doctor in Stearns. I don't know who was at the store that day but possibly Arlin or Arnold Winchester or maybe Joel King (few men in Co-operative owned cars in those days, but these men did). Someone drove Neil to the doctor in Stearns and then on to the hospital.

Jewell said she'd be right behind them. Jewell asked one of the other men to drive her. Jewell went behind the counter and came out putting her pistol in her apron. RL Terry was there that day and saw and heard everything. Jewell said to whoever was driving her, "If Gabby Gregory is home, I'll kill that S.O.B."

When Jewell and the man driving pulled up in front of Gabby Gregory's house, Jewell got out and checked the front door. The place was quiet. No one came to the door. They drove on after Jewell was satisfied she wasn't going to see Gabby.

Neil had lost so much blood the hospital kept him for about a week before he could return home. For a long time, Neil carried his pistol, hoping to run into Gabby one more time.

Where was Gabby? Folks learned later that Gabby left for Indiana and would not return to McCreary County to live.

∞

Weeks later, Neil's oldest son, Bob, now fifteen years old and large for his age, had been driving around Co-operative, making grocery deliveries. One Saturday, RL Terry stopped by Jewell Kidd's store, and Harley Hardwick and RL began talking about going fishing. Bob heard the conversation and said he'd like to go. "We'll take Dad's truck," he said.

Harley said, "Yeah, sure. That'll save us a lot of walking."

Bob said, "Let's go today and camp out tonight."

"What time do you want to leave? Cause I'll need to go home and get my stuff," RL said.

"What time can you get back?" Harley asked.

RL looked at his watch and said, "It's almost 11:00 a.m. now. Let's meet here around 2:30 p.m."

Everybody agreed. At 2:30, they were back at the store. When they got loaded, there were two additional boys: Bob's younger brother Billy Jay and Donald Lee Maxwell, a friend of Billy Jay's. They drove up to Bald Knob and over the land the Kidd family owned and down the other side of the mountain and on to Harley and RL's favorite fishing spot. Somewhere along the way, Donald Lee lost a shoe while riding in the back with the tailgate down.

Harley and RL told the boys what happened on one of their camping trips at this spot when they were almost attacked by wildcats, so they'd better stay close to the campfire. But Billy Jay couldn't be still, and he went off exploring alone. Donald Lee wanted to go along, but having lost one shoe, he wasn't about to go away from camp.

Billy Jay was on a high bank behind their camp. Harley looked toward Bob and RL and winked. Then he screamed like a cat. It scared Billy Jay, and he came running. He was running way too fast down the embankment and stumped his toe. He fell. Billy Jay's momentum started him rolling. When he stopped, he was under the truck. Billy Jay was a large boy, and it took him longer to get out from under the truck than it did to go in. They didn't have any more trouble with Billy Jay wandering off the rest of the night.

∞

Weeks passed. Rankin Parks and Bob Kidd spent a lot of time together playing games. Bill Doolin lived across the creek behind Jewell Kidd's Grocery. Bill also had a place up on Troublesome, his old home place, and that's where he'd go to make moonshine. One Saturday, Rankin and Bob figured out Bill was gone. Now, Bill had a horse named 'Bob' and Ole

Bob was in his corral eating. Rankin and Bob thought it'd be funny if they moved Ole Bob's trough so Ole Bob couldn't get to his hay. Rankin and Bob hid to watch Bill's reaction when he came home. When Bill came home, he was furious. He walked to Jewell's Grocery and voiced his opinion and asked if she'd seen any strangers around walking on the road. Jewell told him no, and Bill went back home.

The boys waited for Bill to leave the store and went running into the store to tell Jewell what they'd done to Bill's horse. "And, boy, was he mad," they said.

Jewell said, "Yes, he just left here madder than a wet hornet." Out of the corner of her eye, Jewell saw the deputy sheriff's car pull up in front of the store. Jewell thought it would be funny to get one over on the boys. "Yeah, Bill said he'd called the law. Look who just pulled in. If I were you two, I'd slip out the back and hide out because if the deputy doesn't see you, he can't arrest you."

Bob and Rankin disappeared out the back, down the steps, and across White Oak Creek. The boys hurriedly walked up in the woods, where they stayed the rest of the afternoon.

The deputy sheriff walked into the store and ordered the Jewell Kidd Special—a bologna sandwich. The special included thick-sliced bologna, tomato, onion, and mayo. Before wrapping the sandwich, Jewell always placed a cracker on top of the onion and then placed the top piece of bread. The deputy also got himself an RC Cola and left. But not before Jewell found out what he was doing down in this part of the county. The sheriff's office had word of a moonshine still he was sent to check out.

Jewell had to smile after the deputy sheriff left. It was slick how she had pulled the wool over Rankin and Bob's eyes and gotten them out of her hair—for a while at least.

∞

MARRIED THIS YEAR 1956

One of Co-operative's most eligible young girls, Miss Frances Chitwood, daughter of Dewey and Kizzie Chitwood, and James Anderson, son of Mr. and Mrs. Jerome Anderson of Pine Knot, became engaged. The couple planned a quiet wedding, but when word spread, it became a double-ring ceremony at the First Baptist Church of Whitley City with Pastor Ralph Whicker performing the ceremony.

George Shepherd, age 26, son of John and Millie Shepherd of Co-operative, married Fayrene Terry, age 21, daughter of Harvey and Hattie Terry of Co-operative. George and Fayrene had two daughters, Connie and Karen.

James Jones, age 29, son of Ephraim and Ollie Jones of Slavens, married Oma Freeman, daughter of Steamboat and Emma Freeman. James and Oma had eight children: Tommy, Clyde, Mary, Kathy, Anita, Janie, Wayne, and Joanne.

∞

BORN THIS YEAR 1956

Kay Clark
Jack Kidd
Thomas Oscar Jones

Sandra Keith
Larry Black
Denzil Jones
Dicie Mae Hall
Kevin Douglas Bell
Steve Blevins
Lois Gregory
Wayne Shook
Bennie Whitehead
Judy Maples
Merrill Bowden
Rick Cox
Dawn (Waters) Strunk

CHAPTER 35

1957

At the beginning of 1957, the Commissioner of Mines and Minerals, James Phalan, sent a directive to all operators in Kentucky: All 3,000 operators must be licensed and pay an annual fee of fifteen dollars. A new form would accompany the annual report. The form was to be completed and sent in, even if the mine was abandoned or only partially operating.

From this small beginning of requiring operators to be licensed and pay a fee, today, the requirements have increased to a checklist of eleven items. For one, the fee has increased from $15 to a base of $300. Now the relicensing fee is based on tonnage. The fee starts with $300 plus $100 for each additional 100,000 tons of coal, up to a maximum fee of $1,500. Also, two notarized, up-to-date maps of the mine certified by an engineer licensed in the State of Kentucky must be on file. Could a small operator survive as it once did?

∞

The community of Co-operative lost one of its beloved citizens, Marion Wilson. Marion came from Harlan County to Co-operative when the mine opened and was one of the first men to work in the new mine. Marion's hard work earned him the position of motorman, and when Co-operative Mine closed, he was transferred to Mine 16. All his children came home when he became ill: Denzil from Muncie, Indiana; Thurston from Kokomo, Indiana; Eugene from New Castle, Indiana; Doyle and Gerald of Co-operative; Joyce Dobbs from New Castle, Indiana; and Lou of Co-operative. After a twenty-eight-day illness, Mr. Marion Wilson died on February 16, 1957, at the very young age of fifty-one.

∞

On March 1, John E. Butler, while on vacation in Florida, suffered a cerebral hemorrhage. Born in Canada, he moved to Ludington, Michigan, at an early age and was educated there. He attended the University of Michigan. When Mr. Butler joined Stearns Coal and Lumber Company, his goal was to make sure all the company's coal camps had a means of educating their children. Mr. Butler also loved sports. When he became too old to play the more rigorous sports, he made golf his game and helped inspire youngsters in Stearns and Somerset to play the game of golf. Mr. Butler became general manager and later president of Stearns Coal and Lumber Company.

∞

A family of McCreary County now living in Sidney, Ohio, Oscar and Beulah Worley lost their four-month-old daughter Kathy Ann. They brought her back to McCreary County for her final resting place.

∞

Rebecca Worley (my paternal grandma) of Hickory Knob, widow of the late Reverend Will Worley (my paternal grandpa) became ill. Their oldest son, Uncle Howard, and his wife, Aunt Mary, of Marion, Indiana, came home to spend several days with Grandma. Uncle Howard, like many others, was forced to leave the Co-operative area to find work when Co-operative Mine closed in 1950.

∞

In Co-operative, Old Man Winter wasn't ready to turn loose, and a hard freeze with a light snow fell overnight. The next day at school during the first recess, some kids checked out the creek to find it frozen in most places. At the blue hole, some kids took the dare and got on the ice. Others followed. Some saw the potential danger and weren't about to get on the ice and, of course, were called chicken.

At lunch break, Clinton Dobbs wanted to be the first to hit the ice but failed to recognize the temperature had warmed a few degrees. When Clinton stepped on the ice, his momentum would have carried him all the way across except for one problem: The center of the creek was melting and when he got close, the ice gave way and he disappeared. Lucky for

Clinton he came back up through the hole he made, and his brother Harold and a couple of other boys helped Clinton out. They rushed him inside the classroom where he stood next to the potbelly coal stove and dripped dry.

∞

Several weeks went by. A few weeks before spring finally arrived, Reed Foster was found dead around Hickory Knob. What happened to him remains an unsolved mystery.

Coy Whitehead, of White Oak Junction, fell in love with Dolly, Reed Foster's widow. Dolly wasn't ready for a relationship and didn't want much to do with Coy, but she was polite when Coy was around. Everybody knew Coy was head over heels in love with pretty Dolly.

Alfred Laxton, who lived over on the hill above the Co-operative ballfield, had his wife, Lula, write a letter to Coy as if she were Dolly. In the letter, she asked Coy to meet her on the hill above the boardinghouse by the water tank the next Saturday, about dark. The boardinghouse had been converted to the Company Store after the original Company Store burned to the ground, and the water tank was a man-made water supply for the Upper Camp.

Lula let Alfred use one of her dresses, and on Saturday evening, Alfred walked over to the water tank with three or four of his buddies. It was almost dark. Alfred put the dress on over his clothes and got in place. It was time for Coy. Alfred's buddies hid behind some trees when they heard Coy climbing the hill. When Coy reached the top of the hill, all he could see was a light-colored dress. Disguising his voice,

Alfred said, as he began walking toward Coy, "I've been looking forward to this."

"Lord, I have, too." Coy said immediately. As he pulled in close, reaching for the arms he thought belonged to Dolly, Coy puckered to lay a kiss on Dolly, but lucky for him he had not closed his eyes. Now he was close enough to see a beard on the face he was about to kiss.

Coy jumped back. By now the guys who had hidden behind the trees had stepped out and were laughing so hard they were holding their stomachs. Alfred couldn't hold back any longer. He, too, began laughing.

"I'll kill you," Coy said as he turned to walk over the hill. Before Coy got out of hearing distance, he gave Alfred one last angry outburst, "You S.O.B."

Alfred bent over double, laughing that much harder.

After a few days passed, cooler heads prevailed. Coy never tried to retaliate on Alfred, though no one would have blamed him if he had.

∞

Summer was in full swing, school was out, and Archie and Roger Shoopman walked to White Oak Junction. They had walked down the railroad bed but walked back on the gravel road. On the hill close to House 64, Archie pulled a stick weed out of the ground beyond the ditch line. As the boys continued walking along, Archie broke off the clump of dirt and root. Those stick weeds grew fairly straight and were good throwing sticks.

When electricity came to Co-operative, the electric poles and wires were placed close to the creek. The gravel road was higher in most places than the electric wires, as they were now where the road leveled off past House 64. Archie happened to look to his left and noticed the wires were level with where they were standing. Archie threw the stick. That thing sailed beautifully and came down on both wires as if it were placed there. Immediately, white and blue sparks started shooting out from the wires, reaching up to about eight feet in the air. The wires burnt through, and when they hit the ground, they set the dry grass on fire. The fire spread fast.

Archie and Roger went running as hard as they could go toward the car bridge. Getting close, they stopped running and walked across the bridge and backtracked down the railroad tracks toward home. They could see black smoke high in the sky and several older guys running toward the smoke. As the boys came close to home, they saw men over across the creek fighting frantically to put out the grass fire. Archie and Roger walked up on their front porch, sat down, and watched as the men finished putting out the blaze. No one ever knew what caused the wires to burn and fall.

∞

Some weeks passed. Arnold Shoopman told Geneva, his wife, he was going spotlighting. Roger heard his dad and said he wanted to go. Arnold got his miner's cap with the carbide light and his trusty shotgun, and away they went. Arnold decided to go up the holler and on up the incline. By the time they reached Hickory Knob Church, Arnold had killed five rabbits. It was before church service and a bunch of folks had gathered and were standing around talking outside the church building. Arnold knew everyone. Somebody asked, "You got rabbits?"

"Yeah," Arnold said. "Take one if you want one."

Someone said sure they wanted one; then someone else wanted one. Arnold stood there talking and gave away all five rabbits. When Arnold was ready to leave, he told the men he'd see them later. As they walked away, Roger said, "Daddy, we ain't going to have any rabbit."

"Don't worry," Arnold said. "I'll get you one on the way home."

Roger and his dad backtracked the same trail, and as they walked along, Arnold paid close attention to both sides of the path. When they arrived back home, they had four rabbits. That was a total of nine rabbits Arnold killed just walking to Hickory Knob and back.

Standing at the Hickory Knob Church giving his rabbits away was just one example of the giving heart of Arnold Shoopman.

∞

Three weeks later, Lizzie Strunk retired after almost thirty years of service with Stearns Coal and Lumber Company. Her last duty was managing the Stearns Hotel. Ms. Strunk's successor was Delbert Ross of Revelo. Mr. Ross said he planned to continue serving the same quality food as Ms. Strunk had served and the Stearns Hotel had a reputation for.

∞

In Co-operative, Neil and Jewell Kidd owned Jewell Kidd's Grocery. Neil suffered from chronic high blood pressure and for the past three weeks had been ill in Somerset Hospital. Thursday night, November 14, Neil died, leaving behind Jewell and five children: a daughter, Joyce, and four sons, Bob, Lindell, Billy Jay, and Jack.

The day of the funeral services, the White Oak Creek was high due to recent rains. The casket containing Neil's body was put in the bed of his brother Curtis's pickup truck to take to Co-operative New Haven United Baptist Church, where Neil was a member and the service was to be held. Reverend Willie Marcum and Reverend Wheeler Blevins presided over the service. Neil, only forty-seven years old, was the son of the late Jeff and Eva (Marcum) Kidd.

∞

MARRIED THIS YEAR 1957

At Bell Farm, Woodrow Koger, age 27, married Clora Dobbs, age 20, from Dobbs Mountain.

∞

BORN THIS YEAR 1957

Mary Theresa Coffey
Wanda Watson
Russell Jones
Patricia Ann Chitwood
Cindy Coffey
Hubert Jones
Dale Shook
Nola Gibson
Christine Conatser
Della Dixon

CHAPTER 36

1958

In 1958, Kentucky held onto its ranking as the number three state in the U.S. in producing bituminous coal, according to the National Coal Association. The news came in advance of the official U.S. Bureau of Mines report for 1957 that reported Kentucky produced 75,746,000 tons of coal. The report put Kentucky over the 2.5 billion mark of its all-time record of coal output. Previous estimates put this number at about four percent of the state's rich coal reserves. At the production rate in 1957, it would take 800 years to deplete the coal riches in Kentucky.

Stearns Coal and Lumber Company leased its rights to oil and gas to a company out of Shreveport, Louisiana—the Barnwell Production Company. The lease totaled 128,000 acres: 71,000 acres in McCreary and Wayne Counties and 57,000 in Tennessee, all west of the Big South Fork River. Part of the property bordered the oil belt in Wayne County and ran through White Oak Junction in McCreary County. Already in existence were a few active oil wells brought in a few years earlier by Pigeon Rock Oil Company. It was understood by both parties that Barnwell Company would test some deep wells and map all progress as it occurred.

The first oil well drilled in Kentucky within the boundary of McCreary County is credited to Martin Beatty, who was drilling for salt on Bear Creek in 1824. According to settlers, a small quantity of the rock oil was bottled and sold to occasional travelers for medicinal purposes. The Stearns Company, of course, retained its black gold (coal) mineral rights.

∞

Mr. R. L. Stearns Jr., president of Stearns Coal and Lumber Company, requested Robert (Bob) E. Gable become his personal assistant. Mr. Gable, son of the late Gilbert Gable and Pearline Dean Stearns, received his Industrial Engineering degree from Stanford University. He had spent two years in the U.S. Navy after college. Bob represented the fourth generation of his family to work in Stearns Company management. He and his wife lived in Stearns.

∞

In an interesting development to the north of McCreary County, the Governor of Kentucky visited Burnside for a dinner meeting held jointly by Somerset and Burnside. At the meeting, the deed to Bunker Hill Island, later changed to Burnside Island, was presented to the governor by Colonel Eugene J.

Stann, Chief of the U.S. Army Corps of Engineers of Nashville, Tennessee. The U.S. Army Corps of Engineers had created the island by constructing the Wolf Creek Dam.

∞

Only days after Steve Gregory got married, his brother Edgar Gregory, age sixty-six, a coal miner and farmer, died suddenly at his home near Co-operative. Besides Steve, Edgar had four other brothers (Tom, Melvin, Ola, and M. Gregory) and one sister (Martha). Edgar's immediate family who survived him were his wife, Lue (Bell) Gregory, two sons (Princeton and Edgar Jr.), and three daughters (Lexie Dobbs, Clova Dobbs, and Vela Gregory). Stanley Davis conducted the funeral service.

∞

The Stearns Theatre, at the end of April, announced that the first big musical film starring Elvis Presley, titled *Loving You*, would show May 2, 3, and 4. The shows were surefire sellouts. Local people and those from the surrounding areas would come out to see Elvis even if they had to walk miles—and many did.

∞

At Jewell Kidd's Grocery in Co-operative, the passing of Neil only a few short weeks before was still fresh on everyone's mind. Bob, the oldest son in his teens, felt his role was to take his father's place. He started handing out orders to his siblings, and when they didn't go along with his demands, he was ready to throw his weight around. Bob at his age was bigger than most grown men, and the brother next to Bob was Lindell. Lindell was tall but didn't have Bob's weight.

One day, Lindell and Bob were out playing in the backyard, throwing rocks at each other. In order to play this game without getting hit, you needed a barrier to hide behind, so Lindell made his way across the creek and got behind the hog pen for cover. At some point, Lindell must have thrown a rock that came close to hitting Bob. When that happened in the game, the person almost hit tried even harder to get even.

Lindell ran out of rocks and waited several minutes. He likely thought Bob was also out of rocks or wanted to stop playing the game. So Lindell climbed up on the fence that corralled the hogs for a much-needed rest. Meanwhile, Bob, holding one last rock, had been working his way closer to Lindell. When Bob looked up from hiding and saw Lindell in the clear, he had his chance and threw his rock, hitting Lindell square between the eyes. Lindell fell backwards into the hog pen, landing in the slimy mud. The fall knocked the breath out of him, and it took a moment for him to try and work his way out of the mess he was in. Lindell raised his upper body off the ground and took hold of the fence to help pull himself up.

The hogs were all running around in the pen squealing their heads off except the boar hog. The boar hog had been sizing up Lindell. He attacked and rammed Lindell on his hip. By now Bob had made his way to the fence, and using a long stick he'd picked up off the ground, prodded the hog and drew his attention away from Lindell. That gave Lindell enough time to climb over the fence to safety.

Lindell was able to walk by holding his side, his complete backside muddy, his side bleeding, and a pumpknot in the middle of his forehead. Jewell, seeing Lindell in this shape, kept a cool head. The main thing was to get Lindell to the doctor. She'd find out each boy's part in this disaster later. Lindell got over the attack from the boar hog, although it left a bad scar he carried the rest of his life.

Bob continued issuing orders. Bob made Lindell deliver groceries more frequently than he did, and if the store needed restock items, Bob sent Lindell to Stearns Wholesale. When Lindell went to Stearns, Bob would tell him to run down to the Tennessee State line while he was out and pick him up a case of beer. Lindell wasn't supposed to be driving. He was not old enough to get a driver's license. Lindell knew if he ever got caught he'd be in big trouble, so one day when Bob told Lindell to go pick up some beer, Lindell told Bob, "If you want it, go get it yourself."

That instant, Bob struck Lindell across the jaw on the right side of his face. Bob used the back of his hand and hit Lindell with such force it loosened one tooth and broke another one. Jewell had to stop her work in the store and hire someone to take her and Lindell to the doctor. She was fuming mad and had no choice but to leave Bob in charge of the store.

While Jewell and Lindell were gone for several hours, Bob enjoyed being in charge, but he didn't like doing the work. He remembered Joyce, his sister, was in the living quarters. Bob found Joyce and said, "Come into the store and wait on customers while Mom is gone."

Joyce said, "No. Mom told me you were in charge and had to take care of the store."

Bob pulled a pistol out of his pocket and said, "Now, I said, get in the store."

Joyce did exactly that because she knew her brother better than anyone else, and she knew he couldn't control his temper. Joyce worked in the store all afternoon. When Jewell came home, Joyce told her everything. That was the last straw for Jewell, and she told Bob she wanted him out, gone, and "I mean right now."

Bob knew his mom meant business. He grabbed a change of clothes and left.

I don't know exactly where Bob went, but he stayed gone for about three weeks. I think, and these are my thoughts only, Bob stayed with his Uncle Curtis up in Bell Farm. Because for him to be gone that long, and I estimate he was around seventeen years old, I figure he must have stayed with a close relative. When he came home, he brought gifts for everyone and apologized. For Bob to do that, he had had a change of attitude. It's possible his uncle gave him a good heart-to-heart talking to. From that point on, Bob was a changed young man. He quit trying to take his dad's place, which no one could do.

∞

On Saturday, September 27, Shelt Smith, prominent McCreary County coal operator, died at his home in Dixie. Mr. Smith had lived all his life in McCreary County and had employed many men as a coal operator. Before Mr. Smith was a self-employed businessman, he was mine superintendent for Stearns Coal and Lumber Company at Co-operative Mine back in the 1930s. Mr. Smith was survived by his wife, Beckie (Jones) Smith; a son, Lewis; two daughters, Sophia and Florence; and two brothers, Gran of Co-operative and George of Winfield, Tennessee.

Stearns Coal and Lumber Company General Manager R. W. Henderson resigned his position Friday, December 12, effective December 15. Mr. Henderson had been employed by Stearns Company since 1903. The announcement cited ill health as the reason. Dr. Frank Thomas took Mr. Henderson's position as general manager.

∞

MARRIED THIS YEAR 1958

In Co-operative, Steve Gregory married Alma Ruth Haynes.

In Hill Top, James Roger New, age 19, married Vina Jean Winchester, age 16.

∞

BORN THIS YEAR 1958

Lynn Strunk
Faron Clark
Jerry Shoopman
Ruby Maples
Tom Jones
Linda Cox

CHAPTER 37

1959

Indulge me for a minute while I go off track (pun intended). Two railroad heros that deserve a spotlight—albeit brief—because they are rapidly fading from the U.S. landscape are the steam engine and Casey Jones. There's nothing quite like the sight of a steam engine with its bloom of smoke chugging through the tree growth of a countryside. And the sounds. Sometimes called Iron Horse, the steam engine made huffing and hissing sounds unrivaled by any other train.

It's only when we look back on the life of Casey Jones that the magical essence of it drifts into the mythical wonderment. Born March 14, 1863, as John Luther Jones in Western Kentucky, at seventeen, he got his first job in Cayce, Kentucky, Fulton County.

His early tie to Cayce is how he got his nickname Casey.

He worked himself up the ladder from helper to telegraph operator with Mobile & Ohio before he was thirty years old. Casey worked hard, going through all the steps to become a passenger engineer on the Illinois Central Railroad. His work ethic drove him to be the best engineer, and he was proud, too, that he always got his train to its destination on time. His reputation helped get him the top assignment: old 382, the Cannon Ball.

The morning of April 30, 1900, was far from magical for engineer Casey Jones. In the early morning hours on that spring day, rolling through thick fog near Vaughan, Mississippi, the Cannon Ball rounded a curve when Casey saw a freight train a few feet ahead on his track. Casey ordered his fireman to jump while he remained in his cab. Although he was unable to prevent a crash, he, however, managed to keep his load on the tracks, saving the lives of all the passengers in twelve coaches.

Casey's burnt body was removed from the wreckage and buried at Jackson, Tennessee, the place he had called home later in life. Other engineers passing the cemetery always saluted with a blast of their whistle, honoring the engineer of the Ole Cannon Ball, Casey Jones.

∞

Stearns Coal and Lumber Company lost its master mechanic, Mr. W. S. Bill Schick, to retirement. Mr. Schick, from Burrville, Tennessee, started working for Stearns Company back in 1906. He started as a helper in the shop. Over time, he learned every job from the ground up and in 1943 became master mechanic. Over the course of his fifty-two years with Stearns Company, he watched the town grow from its humble beginnings to the thriving community it had become. Mr. Schick was active in local civic and religious activities in various capacities. He had the distinction of working for Stearns Coal and Lumber Company his entire work career.

∞

Bill Shoopman came to McCreary County in 1913 from Fentress County, Tennessee, and started working at the Stearns Company Store in the Worley coal mining community. He was later transferred to Fidelity and was store manager there through 1938, when the mining operation closed. Mr. Shoopman then transferred to Barthell, where he worked another eighteen years in the Company Store until Barthell Mine closed in 1953. Then he moved to the Blue Heron Company Store. Altogether, he worked for Stearns Coal and Lumber Company for forty-six years. He, like Mr. Schick, retired this year.

∞

Sunday, June 14, Ada Kidd, wife of Guy Kidd of White Oak Junction, drove to Wayne County with her daughter Lois Ann and neighbor Mrs. Linda Winchester and Linda's daughters Mary and Lizzie Craft. The purpose of the trip was to visit the Kidd Graveyard in Wayne County. On the return trip near the Wolf Creek Bridge, the car, with Mrs. Kidd behind the wheel, crashed into a rock cliff on the curve prior to reaching the bridge.

Mrs. Kidd, Mary Craft, and Lizzie Craft were found unconscious at the scene. Daughter Lois Ann was apparently unhurt. However, everyone in the car was taken to Somerset City Hospital where a short time later Mrs. Winchester died. Mrs. Winchester, age seventy-five, the widow of Frank Winchester, was born in Wayne County. She was the daughter of George and Susie Powell. Mrs. Winchester was survived by her children: Virgil Craft, Ruth Foster, Ethel Anderson, Dovie Foster, Lizzie Craft, and Mary Craft. The funeral service was held at the White Oak Junction Church with cousins Earl and Stanley Davis officiating.

∞

In spring 1959, a year after Arnold and Geneva Shoopman moved their family to Hickory Knob for the second time, Arnold put out a big garden. After all his work of preparing the ground and planting, it didn't rain for several weeks. Arnold's garden was getting baked hard, especially the potato patch, so the potatoes weren't coming up.

Geneva's dad, Dewey Wright, came up to visit from Tennessee and stayed several days. The first day, Dewey went out and walked around the garden. The next morning after breakfast when Arnold went to work, Dewey asked Geneva if they had a mule. Geneva said, "No, but Bug has one."

Dewey walked over to Bug's place and asked Bug if he could use his mule. "Yeah," Bug said. "Don't care a bit."

"Do you have a harrow?" Dewey asked.

"Yeah. What are you going to do with it?" Bug asked.

"Use it on Arnold's tater patch," Dewey said.

Dewey took the mule and harrow over to Arnold's garden and began working. That evening when Arnold came home from work and Dewey was still going around and around in the tater patch, Arnold went in the house, mad and cussing. "That old man is going to ruin my tater patch," Arnold said. "I won't have a tater. He's out there tearing up every tater I've got."

Geneva said, "I tried to tell him. He acted like it made him mad, and you know how he is. It's his way or no way." Arnold didn't say anymore.

Arnold went out and sat down on the porch, still mad. While sitting there on the porch, it had to cross Arnold's mind how much hard work he'd put into planting four sacks of tater seeds. Arnold got up and went back inside where Geneva was and said, "That old man has ruined the whole crop. I won't have a tater."

Geneva knew when Arnold was this mad it was better not to say anything. After a little while, Arnold calmed down some. There wasn't nothing could be done about it now. Might as well forget about the tater patch.

Not many days passed, and the potatoes Arnold had planted started showing green sprouts. Before he knew it, those taters got turned loose growing and the crop turned out to be the best Arnold had ever raised. Arnold had more taters than he knew what to do with. They stored all they had room for and gave away the rest. Arnold changed his mind about Ole Dewey and said to Geneva, "That ole man sure knew what he was doing." Geneva had to laugh.

∞

Back in the early days, the only way soda pop came to the stores was in glass bottles. The bottles had a value of two cents each when they were returned to the store. So, in effect, when buying a soda pop back then, you were buying what was inside and renting the bottle. Most people in rural areas wouldn't return each bottle as they became empty. To cut down on walking trips to the store, folks would take several bottles at once. So it was with Bo Clark.

(In this story, two names—Gorge and Carti Doxell—have been changed to protect the innocent.) One Saturday afternoon, Bo Clark walked to Guy Kidd's Grocery carrying a grass sack full of empty pop bottles. Now, beside Guy's store on the west side was the feed house. The building was about twelve feet by about fifty feet and sectioned off into four individual rooms. The building was strictly for feed and storage, and it was a good place to hide a jar or two of moonshine. The moonshine was used only for medicinal purposes, of course.

Across the creek and up close to Bridge 11 lived the Gorge and Carti Doxell family. Now Gorge and Carti walked to the store that day and arrived about the same time as Bo but from the opposite direction. Bo heard talking in the feed house and figured that's where Guy would be and started walking to the end of the feed building where the doors were open. Bo stopped when he saw Guy and a couple of men step out. One of them was Black Bird Coffey who came out waving his pistol.

Bo had moved his load of bottles off his back and set the sack on the ground, still holding the top of the sack. Black Bird asked Bo, "What you got in the sack?"

"Pop bottles," Bo said.

Finding out the sack contained bottles, Black Bird fired one round into the sack. Bo turned loose of the sack and stepped away from it. Gorge and Carti, standing several feet away, saw what just happened.

Gorge pulled his pistol from his overalls and would have shot Black Bird, but his wife, Carti, grabbed Gorge's hand and the gun discharged and grazed Carti's hip. By now Guy had secured the door of the feed house and was about three steps from Black Bird. Guy put his hand in his pocket. It's a good bet Guy took a hold of his pistol and said, "Black Bird, put your pistol away while you've got the chance."

Black Bird put his pistol in his pocket and brought his empty hand up to show Guy. Looking at the man with Black Bird, Guy said, "You get him out of here and I mean right now."

Guy hurried to Carti, who was now sitting on the ground leaning on her husband, Gorge. Guy couldn't see the wound, but he could see she was bleeding pretty bad. He looked at Gorge and said, "Let's put her in my truck and get her to Stearns." Carti received emergency treatment and the ambulance took her to Somerset City Hospital. She was released the next day.

∞

Weeks later, the excitement of that day at Guy Kidd's store had faded from memory. Bo and Louvada walked to Co-operative, heading to Jewell Kidd's Grocery. The fastest route to Co-operative was to walk the railroad tracks as Bo and Louvada had done many times. Bo had nicknamed Louvada "Ping," so every time they walked the tracks, Bo would say, "Crossties and rails, Ping."

It was a very hot day, and when they got to Jewell's, Louvada dropped into the first chair she saw on Jewell's porch. Louvada took a hold of the bottom of her dress and began using it as a fan. She raised her dress tail high and said, "It's hot"—several times.

∞

A few weeks later, a long-time resident of White Oak Junction, Reverend Benny Whitehead died, leaving behind his widow, Ida, four sons (Elmer, Eugene, Robert, and Coy), and five daughters (Ethel, Alice, Zona, Levisa, and Stella). Mr. Whitehead had been an ordained minister for fifty-one years.

∞

Millard Crabtree, a coal miner and resident of Co-operative, had been disabled in the Co-operative Mine more than seven years earlier. Mr. Crabtree died at the Miners Hospital in Middlesboro, Kentucky. Millard was the son of Manuel and Tabby (Duncan) Crabtree. Mr. Crabtree's survivors included his widow, Theola (Kidd) Crabtree, one daughter (Susie Dixon), and three sons (Kelly, Bobby, and Roger). At the Co-operative New Haven United Baptist Church, Reverend Harvey Terry and Reverend Earl Davis led the funeral service.

∞

Just a few days later, Bell Farm lost Thomas Alford Coffey, age seventy-nine. Mr. Coffey was the son of the late Henry and Sarah (Dobbs) Coffey. Mr. Coffey was a farmer and timberman.

∞

MARRIED THIS YEAR 1959

Earl Bottoms, age 22, from Knifley, Kentucky, married Helen Worley of Co-operative.

∞

BORN THIS YEAR 1959

Donald Ray Bell
Barbara Watson
Donna Ball
Gary Coffey
Linda Gibson
Jerry Wayne Conatser
Linda Jones Byrd
Clyde Jones
Tina Dixon
Jeff Waters

CHAPTER 38

The Life and Times of JACK SMITH

"Yeah, believe I would."
the words of Jack Smith,
the most famous homeless person I've ever known

In and around Co-operative, the only homeless person I knew of was Jack Smith. Jack, son of Jim and Susie Smith, was born November 15, 1920. Jack had two sisters, Mary Smith and Burnettie (Smith) Watson.

Burnettie was married to Harvey Watson. Burnettie and Harvey had eleven children: Nancy, Clotine, Lena, Joyce, Rita, Bertha, Ken, Charlie, Leroy, Harvey Jr., and Sullivan. They lived in Jamestown, Tennessee, and when Burnettie could, she'd take Jack home with her, clean him up, and buy him a new out-

JACK SMITH
PHOTO COURTESY OF DONALD COFFEY.

fit of clothes. But, of course, Jack wouldn't stay with her. Jack's sister Mary was married to Veto Smith (a different strain/family of Smiths) and they had a daughter, Nicky, and a son, Mickey.

Jack was born in Dobbs Hollow and went to grade school there. Gib Troxell, a classmate of Jack's, said of Jack later in life, "Looking back to when we were in school, Jack was very smart in school." So what happened to Jack between then and later in life? It was said, Jim, Jack's dad, hit Jack in the head with an axe handle when Jack was a boy. Did this alter his thinking somehow? Was this the reason Jack gradually turned to nature, which he was in tune with?

Or was it the story told to me by a long-time friend and neighbor of Jack's niece Nancy? According to Wilma, the older boys told Jack they did bad things to guys when they were drafted, which scared Jack something terrible. Jack started running and hiding every time he heard visitors approaching. His hiding away gradually turned into Jack's staying away longer periods of time, isolating himself from everybody. When Jack did start coming back out of hiding, he'd go from house to house, doing outside work for people in exchange for a meal or a pack of cigarettes. This way of life Jack embraced, as he loved being alone in nature. I, without any evidence to support it, lean toward this reason for why Jack Smith lived his life the way he did.

∞

Jack was seen many a night by several different people walking the gravel roads through Co-operative, Rattlesnake Ridge, and Bell Farm or down the old railroad bed through what was once Fidelity. It was not uncommon for Jack to climb a tree and sleep the night away on a tree limb. Jack loved the great outdoors. I never heard of Jack being bitten by a dog or any other animal or snake. It just didn't happen.

Jack's demeanor was polite and easygoing. He never hurt any animal or anyone. When Jack talked, it was always with a soft, kind voice. Jack never displayed anger with anyone, and he could sense anger in other people. If he thought people might be hostile toward him, Jack would walk great distances to avoid them and the situation.

Rubin and Tamzie Maxwell lived in Bald Knob. On occasion, Jack would stop by their home. Tamzie would give Jack a cup of coffee, and as he left, she'd give him a small bag of food.

In Jack's late teens and early twenties, many folks who saw him on the road would stop and offer him a ride, and in those days, he would get in the car with anybody. Not everyone was considerate, however. Some people drove Jack many miles beyond where he wanted to go. Of course, Jack would then have to walk all those miles back. After a few times of this happening, Jack wouldn't get in the car with just anyone; he would ride only with drivers he knew very well. Even then he might refuse the ride.

When Jack was fairly young, if he was walking a gravel road, when a car was heading toward him, Jack would stop and walk backwards until the car passed him. Then Jack would start walking forward again.

One time Jack was walking on the road and Richard Dobbs stopped and offered him a ride and Jack got in the car. Jack would not ride across Yamacraw Bridge, so he got out of the car and walked across the bridge. On the other end, he got back in the car and they went on.

∞

Everyone in Co-operative and the surrounding areas in those days used wood and coal for heating and cooking. If Jack saw a pile of wood in the yard near a house, he would stop, especially if he knew the people. Jack busted many piles of wood for Gabby Gregory in exchange for food and a place to lay his head at night. Usually, he slept in the tool shed. In cold weather, Jack would go inside and lie on the floor next to the heating stove.

Leo Dolen was married to Jack's niece Clotine. They lived on Wilson Ridge. Jack spent a lot of time with the Dolens, and if Leo had a wood pile, Jack wouldn't stop until he had every piece busted and ready for the stove. Several years later, the Dolens moved to Worley Hill Top in a house Harvey Corder moved out of, but that didn't stop Jack from visiting even though it was many miles to walk.

∞

Linn Gibson recalled seeing Jack laugh one time. Jack happened by their home one morning and Linn's Grandpa Bill (his full name was William Riley Winchester) offered Jack a cup of coffee. They were all sitting on the front porch and Bill's wife, Ruby (Coffey) Winchester, brought out the coffee. Bill looked at Jack and said the reason he married Ruby was to get a little sugar with his coffee. Jack laughed and said, "You'd've been better off to drink it black."

∞

Josh Hines remembered his mom and dad cleaning Jack up and feeding him. His dad had cut a tree down and he told Jack not to try and bust it up. The wood was so hard the wood maul would bounce off when hit. Josh's dad had to run an errand for something, and when he got back home, the wood was busted and Jack was gone.

∞

Oftentimes, Jack would find a place off the road out of Bald Knob where the morning sun would shine on the spot he was sleeping. Times when Johnny and Wilma Maxwell were heading to town, if they saw Jack, they'd stop to make sure Jack was all right and ask if they could give him a ride. Most of the time, Jack would say no to the ride. Wilma said they had sat and talked with Jack many times and "he was very smart, made more sense than a lot of educated people."

Roger Winchester also lived in Bald Knob and drove a school bus. On his way home, if he saw Jack walking the road heading up the mountain, Roger would stop and offer Jack a ride. If the weather was cold, Jack would get in and ride as far as the church house.

∞

One hot summer day, RL and Faye Terry took the kids for a picnic lunch down on the bank of Rock Creek. They stopped at Koger Holler, the place below the bridge where Bald Knob Road intersected with Road 1363. The creek there had a little something for everyone, places shallow enough for wading (many liked driving their vehicles in the water for a bath) and a place deep enough for swimming. After a few hours of playing, the family gathered in the shade of the trees for a sandwich and a soda pop and conversation.

Jack had walked from Bald Knob and was walking across the bridge. Slowly and quietly, Jack walked close to the Terry family and stopped about ten feet away. RL recognized him and said, "Hey, Jack, come on over. You wanna pop?"

"Yeah, believe I would," Jack said. Jack downed the pop in about two sups.

Faye asked Jack, "Would you like a bologna sandwich?"

"Yeah, believe I would," Jack said.

RL got Jack another pop. When Jack finished the sandwich and pop, he asked, "Anyone have a cigarette?" At the time, Faye was still smoking. Usually, people would give Jack the rest of their pack of cigarettes, as Faye did. Jack then walked on toward Co-operative.

∞

For some of us, it was rare to see Jack at all. In my thirteen-plus years in Co-operative, I can recall seeing Jack out walking only twice. I'm sure there are others who have many memories of seeing Jack. To some of us, he was mysterious in a way. Jack was appreciative of anything anyone wanted to give him. If food, clothing, or shelter wasn't offered, Jack went without and he'd walk on alone. Donald Coffey remembers smoking many a pack of Marlboros with Jack while sitting on Donald's front porch in Rattlesnake Ridge.

∞

Jewell Kidd, owner of Jewell Kidd's Grocery in Co-operative, at least once a year gave Jack a complete outfit of clothes, including a pair of socks and shoes. Several churches in areas near Co-operative would leave their doors unlocked in case Jack happened by and needed to get in out of the weather.

∞

Jack always walked on the side of the road until later in life. I don't know why or when, but Jack started walking in the middle of the road. One night RL Terry and Rudolph Couch decided they'd go snake hunting. RL was driving his pickup truck, and in White Oak Junction, he turned off Road 1363 onto Junction Road and drove past Guy Kidd's Grocery heading toward Bell Farm.

It was dark and RL was driving his truck only about ten miles per hour and it was a good thing. Coming around a curve just before getting to the Fidelity area, up ahead someone was standing in the middle of the road. RL eased closer and the person stepped over to the shoulder of the road. When the headlights of the truck got within a few feet, RL could clearly see it was Jack Smith. RL said to Rudolph, "There's no need stopping. Jack will not get in a vehicle at night."

Driving on, RL and Rudolph talked about how Jack had lived virtually his whole life in the woods and had never been bitten by a snake, something they couldn't understand. Here they were in the safety of the vehicle looking for a snake they could kill.

∞

Jack would stop at Randle and Josephine Coffey's house and chop up their wood and stack it. Jack would often spend the night, and the next morning, Josephine would fix him breakfast. Jack loved fried potatoes. Josephine would fix Jack peanut butter sandwiches to take with him when he left.

One particular night after the Coffeys moved to Rattlesnake Ridge, Jack worked a long time chopping wood. It was cold and Jack spent the night. The next morning when Randle got up, he noticed Jack had dropped a cigarette in the night which burned a tiny hole in the rug. Randle told Jack, "Don't lay down to sleep with a cigarette." Jack must have been very tired from chopping all the wood for that to happen because he was always respectful of others' property and appreciative of the kindness of others.

∞

People from Stearns, Worley, Hill Top, Yamacraw, Paint Cliff, Rattlesnake Ridge, White Oak Junction, Bald Knob, Co-operative, Dobbs Mountain, Bell Farm, and down through Rock Creek knew of Jack Smith. Jack was welcomed in any home. Everyone knew Jack was a gentle man who lived a simple life.

Jack did everything he could to help others. He would work all day busting wood and be satisfied with a glass of water and a plate of food. Jack was a rare person. He was free from the bondage of materialism. He lived his life free from having "stuff" around him. Jack didn't own a TV or radio to bombard his mind with false or negative ideas. Jack lived free of everything he couldn't carry with him. What Jack owned he carried with him as he walked those dusty gravel roads.

Jack was last seen walking the gravel road past Sherd Dobbs Cemetery heading toward Co-operative. As the days turned into weeks without anyone seeing Jack, the people who saw him regularly became worried and began searching for him. The McCreary County Rescue Squad and others devoted a lot of time in a diligent effort to find Jack Smith. The White Oak Junction Church was a command center for the search. New Haven United Baptist Church in Co-operative was also used.

After searching for a couple of months, people stopped. Four years later, a body was found by a squirrel hunter in a shallow grave with only the feet and hands exposed. The location was toward Bald Knob at the top of the first hill, a short distance to the right on a dirt logging road about one and a quarter miles on the shoulder of the dirt road. It was determined the body was Jack Smith.

The remains of Jack Smith were buried in the west corner of Sherd Dobbs Cemetery. A graveside service was held and members of New Haven United Baptist Church attended. Pastor Everett King conducted the service.

Some of Jack's most famous sayings were "Bet you don't got a Marlboro, do ya?" ... "If it's not too much trouble." ... "Yeah, believe I would."

∞

Ole Jack Smith, the only
homeless person I ever knew!

BORIS HAYNES
FAMILY PHOTO

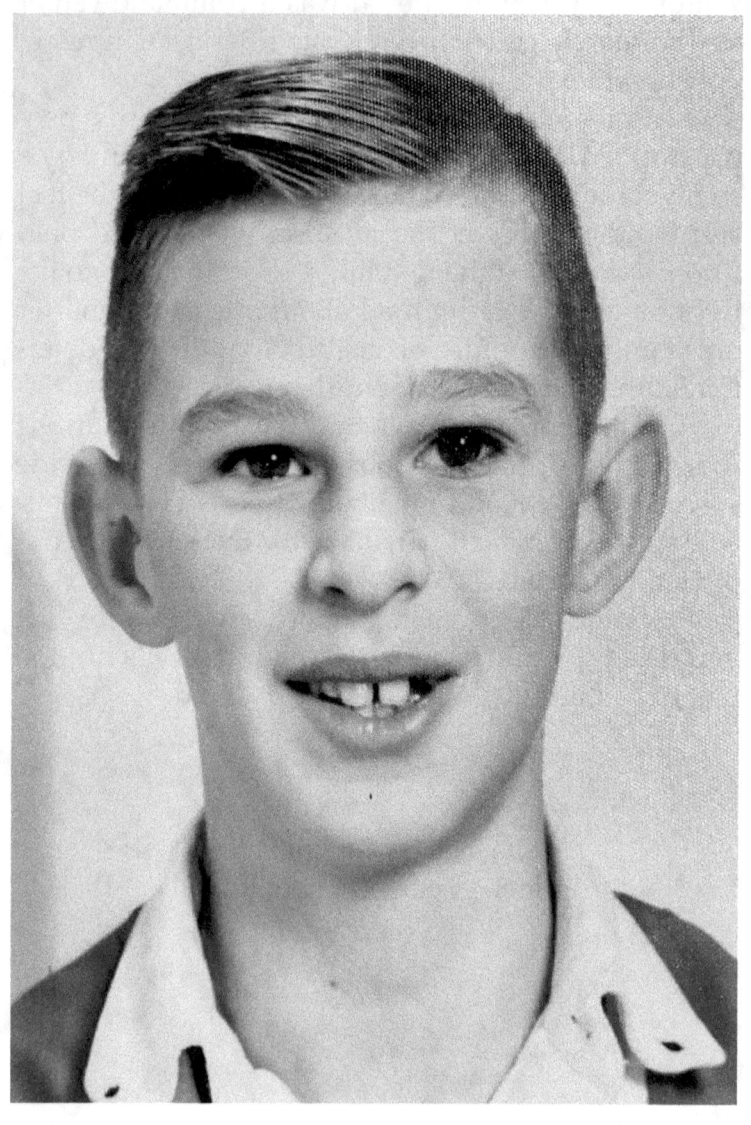

CHAPTER 39

1960
and Boris Haynes

In spring 1960, I was finishing third grade. It was a good year in the life of a boy in Co-operative. Since Stearns Company shut down Co-operative Mine back in 1950, only one small coal operation existed in Co-operative: Shelt and Gran Smith with around fifty employees. Gran continued after his brother Shelt died. Even though many families had moved away, still, several families lived in Co-operative. By now all of the one-room schools in the surrounding communities had closed and the students were being bused to Co-operative, grades 1–8.

∞

Behind the home of Joel and Eula King's family, in a two-story house, lived the Jake and Elsie Haynes family. Above the first row of houses positioned on the south side of the ballfield was a row of four houses. In the home closest to the Haynes family lived the Cecil and Dorothy Dixon family. Naturally the kids of the two families played together and were at each other's homes often. The youngest Haynes child was Boris, a son. This year, Boris was five years old and was still learning the ways of the world.

One day Boris was playing in the Dixon yard. Diane Dixon told Boris she had a dime and asked if he wanted to walk to the Company Store with her. Kids in Co-operative welcomed any chance to go to the store. So the two children walked over. Eli Logan, store manager, was behind the counter. At the end of the long showcase were potato chips, candy, chewing gum, and other snack items.

While they were looking in the showcase, Diane dropped her dime. They watched it hit the floor and roll behind the counter. Diane alerted Eli and said, "Eli, I dropped my dime and it rolled behind the counter. Can I get it?"

"Sure," Eli said.

Eli walked to a section of the counter, about three-feet long, and raised the top section and opened the gate making a doorway to walk through. The two kids walked behind the counter looking for the dime and Eli went on with his work. Eli may have been putting up stock, because where the dime lay was a carton of Kool-Aid (every kid's favorite drink) about half full. Diane said to Boris, "I'll get one if you will." Boris being so young didn't realize taking something without paying for it was stealing and may not have ever heard the word. It was likely Diane didn't know either. Both Diane and Boris got one pack of Kool-

Aid. Diane bought something with her dime and they left.

Walking toward home, Diane started eating her Kool-Aid dry. Boris thought eating Kool-Aid like that wouldn't be good. Plus, it didn't make sense. Boris went home and gave his pack of Kool-Aid to his sister Gay. Gay got a container with water and mixed up the Kool-Aid. Boris's mom, Elsie, saw what they were doing and asked, "Boris, where did you get the Kool-Aid?"

"Over at the store," Boris said.

Elsie asked, "How did you pay for it?"

"I didn't, Mom," Boris replied.

Elsie then asked, "Did you charge it to your daddy?"

"No, I just got it," Boris said.

Boris's brother, Joe, was either walking through the kitchen or was standing nearby waiting for the Kool-Aid to be ready. Elsie looked at Joe and said, "Joe, you march your little brother back to the store and tell Eli."

Going into the store, Joe said, "Eli, Boris has something to tell you."

Boris was scared. What he thought a little while ago was okay, he was beginning to understand was a bad thing. Boris couldn't say a word; he only stared at Eli. Joe waited about a minute and said, "He stole a pack of Kool-Aid a while ago. Mom said to put the charge on daddy's bill."

Eli said, "That boy didn't steal anything."

"Oh, yes, I did," Boris blurted out. What started out as innocent ignorance turned into the worst feeling Boris ever felt. This experience would stay with Boris for the rest of his life. He never stole again.

∞

Most kids typically went barefooted in Co-operative in the warm months. It was acceptable behavior; so it was with a young Boris. Behind the Haynes home, at the base of where the hill started up, flowed a small stream of water that came from a spring up in the holler. The water made its way down between the King and Chitwood homes. The King boys went fishing all the time and their dad, Joel, made a minnow box he kept in the water from the spring.

That morning, Boris wandered close to the minnow box and accidently stepped on a discarded broken fruit jar. That sharp glass cut Boris's foot open. Boris went running toward home, the blood gushing. His dad, Jake, saw Boris and grabbed him up in his arms and sat down on the porch steps. He took out his handkerchief and wrapped it around Boris's foot real tight. Jake and Elsie loaded up Boris in the vehicle and took off toward Rattlesnake Ridge.

Boris knew when his dad turned left after crossing the bridge they were going to Aunt Alice Bell's house. In emergencies, like cuts and scrapes, Aunt Alice was the family doctor. It didn't take long getting to her house, and inside, Aunt Alice slowly and gently removed the handkerchief. Aunt Alice walked over to her stove and took out some soot, came back, and put a thick coat on the cut and the bleeding stopped. She waited a few minutes and wiped off the excess soot and put some blue liquid on the cut and bandaged the wound and tied some material around Boris's foot. Three to four weeks later, Boris's foot was healed.

∞

Boris was beginning to walk without the bandage on his foot when Ross Long and his wife came to visit. Mrs. Long was Elsie's cousin and came to visit once a year in the summer. The Haynes house being a two-story with the bedrooms upstairs, two of the windows of connecting bedrooms overlooked the roof of the porch. Boris's brothers had gotten up before Boris woke up that morning and he had to pee real bad. The window was raised, so Boris peed out the window. The water hit the roof of the porch and dropped off to the ground. Boris had no way of knowing his dad and Ross were sitting on the porch drinking a cup of coffee.

Boris went downstairs and walked out on the porch and stood close to his dad. Ross pointed to the other end of the porch and said, "Boris, how come on that end of the porch it was raining a few minutes ago?" Boris looked at his dad and knew he could be in trouble, but his dad had a smile on his face and Ross began laughing. That moment, his mom, Elsie, came to the doorway and said, "Boris, get in here and eat your breakfast." Boris walked inside. His mom saved him from an awkward moment.

∞

A few weeks passed and his brother Bruce wanted Boris to learn the game of marbles. Bruce, the brother just older than Boris, knew Boris would be starting school the next year and he needed to know the game. Bruce took his little brother into the kitchen, and they played on the floor. Bruce showed Boris how to play marbles and at the same time let Boris win a jar full of marbles. The jar likely was a pint jar with a screw-on lid, otherwise used for canning. The marbles probably had been used many times and

Bruce didn't care for his little brother having them. Besides, it made Boris feel good thinking he had won them. Boris was proud of those marbles. He washed and dried them and put them back in the jar.

The next day, Boris and Bruce and a couple of the Dixon kids were playing in the front yard. Joe, the brother older than Bruce, came out of the house holding Boris's jar of marbles. When Boris saw his marbles, he said," Hey, those are mine."

"All I want to do is count them," Joe said.

Boris replied, "Well, you can count them, but you better not play with them."

Immediately Joe went out in the yard and found a good smooth place, poured the marbles out on the ground, used a stick to make a circle around them, and started playing with the marbles.

Boris screamed out, "I told you not to play with my marbles." Boris headed toward the porch and was probably going in to tell his mom. As Boris stepped up on the porch, he noticed his dad's hammer lying against the wall. Boris, as mad as he was at that instant, reached down, picked up the hammer, and threw it at his brother. The hammer hit Joe in the head and he fell back as if he'd been shot. Boris ran in the house and hid. Bruce, standing not far from Joe, ran in behind Boris, grabbed him, and whipped him.

Elsie, hearing the commotion, hurried to the front door. Seeing Joe lying on the ground, his head nearly covered in blood, she grabbed a towel and ran to Joe. When she started wiping away the blood, she found the wound and applied pressure. This was another trip to Aunt Alice.

Joe got over his headache and the wound healed but the scar remained. A few years later when Joe came home from basic training in the Army, his hair cut short, the scar was clearly evident. Much later, when the two brothers remembered that day back in Co-operative, Boris jokingly told his brother, "Joe, if I'd known how you'd turn out, I wouldn't have hit you so hard."

∞

It was late summer, and it wouldn't be many days till a young Boris would be starting school. Jake took the boys to Bell Farm to see Oren Spradlin to get a haircut. Oren was a cousin to Elsie as well as the U.S. Postmaster and manager of his own store. Oren had each of the boys sit in a chair that was already on the porch. Oren used hand clippers that pulled out more hair than they cut. Boris sure was thankful to hear, "Well, you're done, Boris." After all that hair pulling, his dad had to pay Oren twenty-five cents.

∞

While Boris was getting ready to start first grade, tragedy struck Stearns Coal and Lumber Company. The company was considering reopening Worley Mine 4 to extract the remaining coal and asked three men to go in to inspect the condition and make their assessment. Manager Morris Blevins, Foreman Ottis Tucker, and General Foreman Eugene Laferty walked into Mine 4. When enough time had elapsed that the men should have been out of the mine, Cack, mine superintendent, became concerned. He and his son Don Slaven went in to look for the men. They found their bodies and had them brought out. All three men had carbon monoxide light detection on their belts, but none were turned on. The detection is a safety light that will turn on when the oxygen level drops below sixteen percent.

After this tragedy, a careful inspection was made of Mine 18, and it was determined carbon monoxide was seeping into Mine 18 from Mine 4, making it unsafe. The operation at Blue Heron Mine 18 was closed.

∞

The school year got under way and everything was going great for a couple of weeks. One morning all the Haynes kids walked to school as usual. The older kids walked on to the big building. Boris saw a lady dressed in all white get out of a car. She even had some white thing on her head. Boris had not seen the lady before, so he asked one of the other kids who she was. That's the school nurse; she's here to give everyone a shot.

The McCreary County nurse, in those days, was Mrs. Mae Sergent. In years past, it would take her a month to visit all the rural schools.

When Boris heard shot, he knew he didn't want a shot. So when the first bell rang, Boris was walking around the curve on his way home as fast as his young legs would go. Boris rushed through the front door of the Haynes home. It startled Elsie and she said, "What are you doing home?"

"I'm not going to school," Boris said.

Elsie said, "How come?"

"They're up there giving shots," Boris said.

"Now, Boris," his mom said, "you have to go to school."

Elsie made Boris's sister Jane take him back to school. Jane waited until Boris got his shot. Getting a shot can be a traumatic experience for a young child, and so Boris did what many did. He whined and cried until Jane took him back home.

∞

As winter became a memory and spring began to share some warm days, it was recess at Co-operative School and every child was outside playing. The older boys from the upper building (grades 5–8) had a baseball game going and a few of the smaller kids, not playing, stood and watched, as did Mr. Sam Perry, the principal.

There was a good chance Boris's two older brothers were playing in the game, so Boris walked up to watch. Mr. Perry, at the time, had hunkered down on the sideline. Boris, interested in the game, hadn't noticed Mr. Perry and walked up close to him. When Mr. Perry noticed Boris standing beside him, Mr. Perry convinced Boris to hunker down in front of him. Mr. Perry didn't want Boris to get hurt by accident. Mr. Perry's act of kindness made such an impression on young Boris that he never forgot it. At that moment, Boris felt he and Mr. Perry were the best of friends.

All through the years as Boris grew up, he thought a lot about that day and recognized how doing something nice for a child was likely to make a memory they'd never forget. On the other hand, being mean to a child had the same effect. They'd never forget that either. Mr. Perry's action was the catalyst that helped shape Boris's character and attitude toward others: Being nice to others has lasting positive consequences, he learned. Boris was able to share his memory with Mr. Perry later in life; he told Mr. Perry how his loving generosity that day had made a positive impression on him as a small boy, an impression that had continued all these years.

Mr. Perry exemplified the kind of teachers who taught us in Co-operative. For a man or woman to drive a dusty gravel road for miles to get to the school, a school with outdoor toilets and a potbelly stove for heat, they had to love teaching. They had a genuine desire to see young people develop into productive men and women. You can read more about Mr. Perry in my book *CO-OP: Coal, Community, & House 52* published in 2020.

∞

Usually, in Co-operative, Sundays meant going to Sunday School and church. For those who may have forgotten, the church bell rang to remind everyone where they should be. One Sunday, Boris came in from outside and told his mom he believed he'd go to Sunday School.

"No, you're not," Elsie said.

Boris said, "How come?"

"You're too dirty," his mom said.

It was common for kids in Co-operative to play in dirt, and Boris's mom knew there wasn't time to get Boris cleaned up and for him to walk to the church and get there on time. Elsie didn't want the people at church to see him dirty. Elsie told Boris again, "You're not going to Sunday School."

Boris went back out in the yard to play and after a few minutes walked out of the yard and down the hill and headed to the ballfield. Boris walked across the ballfield to the creek and threw rocks in the creek at the car bridge. He ambled along the creek up the dirt road throwing an occasional rock in the creek. New Haven United Baptist Church sat (and still does) on a hill overlooking the schoolhouse and creek and the dirt road that used to be the railroad bed. That's where Boris found himself chunking rocks in the creek when he heard a voice calling his name, "Hey, Boris."

Boris turned and looked up toward the church. There were a lot of people gathered outside the church talking. Then Boris spotted Gerald Wilson looking at him. Gerald yelled, "Boris, come on."

"I can't," Boris said.

Gerald replied, "How come?"

"Mom said I'm too dirty," Boris said.

Gerald said, "You come on up here."

So, Boris walked up the hill as Gerald walked down to meet him. He put his arm around Boris and said, "You're never too dirty to go to Sunday School." Gerald walked inside with Boris.

When Sunday School was over, Boris walked back home happy about how the morning had gone. In Sunday School, Boris and the others colored a project the kids got to take home, so Boris never gave it any thought and walked through the door at home. Elsie saw the paper, and she knew where Boris had been.

"Boris," Elsie said, "I told you not to go."

Boris said, "Well, Mr. Wilson told me to come on." Elsie gave Boris a whipping for disobeying her.

∞

The school year still had several weeks left before summer break. Boris walked to school by himself; his brothers and Gay had walked on ahead. As Boris walked along, in the curve of the road over to the right on the big rock sat Jackie Davis. Boris said, "Jack, what are you doing?"

"I'm not going to school today. I'm going to lay out. Do you want to lay out with me?"

Boris said, "Yeah." It sounded like a good idea, but Boris didn't know what laying out meant. So Boris and Jackie hung out there all day on the big rock across from the church house. When the last bell rang, Jackie said, "Well, it's time to go home now."

Boris walked home and went inside. Elsie asked, "Boris, did you learn anything at school today?"

Boris said, "I didn't go."

"What do you mean you didn't go?" his mom asked.

Boris said, "Me and Jack Davis laid out on the big rock all day."

I can just see Elsie drop her head, slowly shaking it (likely, she was hiding a smile). She probably said to herself, "What am I gonna do with this boy!"

Still, she had to give him credit for telling her exactly what he'd done. As always, Boris never lied to his mom.

∞

BORN THESE YEARS 1960, 1961, 1962

BORN 1960

Andy Watson Jr.
Mary Lou Jones
Shirley Maples
Mary Jones

BORN 1961

Ila Clark
Lisa May Jones
Angie Winchester

Mike Ball
Anita Coffey
Johnny Wayne Dixon
Kathy Jones
Tim Waters
Roger Carson

BORN 1962

Stanley Watson
Anita Jones

DAMON GIBSON (L) AND WALTER DIXON JR. (R)
PHOTO COURTESY OF WANDA GIBSON.

CHAPTER 40

Walter Dixon Jr. and Damon Gibson

At Mine 16, both Bob and Neiler Coffey worked night-shift at Co-operative Mine and both shared a passion for the television show *Gun Smoke,* which aired Monday nights. When this one season (I'm not sure which one) began airing new episodes, the two men devised a plan where they would take turns missing work on Monday nights. That way, they both could keep up with what was going on; the one watching the show would tell the other one what happened the next day at work.

The Coffey brothers' plan worked for several weeks until Cack Slaven, mine superintendent, began noticing one of the Coffey brothers was missing work each week on the same night. Cack decided to confront the two men at the same time. One day just before the miners started their shift, Cack walked up to Red Rose, the foreman, and told him he wanted to see both Bob and Neiler Coffey right now. Red walked in with Cack and showed Cack where the two men were inside the mine, preparing to start work. The two men were not that far apart, so it took only a couple minutes to get them together. When they came face-to-face with Cack, they had no idea what Cack wanted to talk about.

"Now, men," Cack said. "I've noticed it's become a routine with you two; one of you misses work every week on the same night, Monday. Now I want to know the truth. What's going on?" Both Bob and Neiler admitted why they'd been missing.

Cack said, "I'm telling you both you'd better be at work from now on or you both are gonna be sitting home watching television every night. Now get back to work."

Both Bob and Neiler went back to work and that was the end of their plan and Cack's problem.

∞

The community of White Oak Junction was positioned to the east of Co-operative just over a half of a mile. At one time, White Oak Junction was a self-sustaining mining community, complete with store, U.S. Post Office, and school. Things had changed as they had in other coal mining communities owned by Stearns Coal and Lumber Company. The Company Store had closed in White Oak Junction around 1949 and store manager Eli Logan was transferred to the Company Store in Co-operative. The school at White Oak Junction continued through the spring of 1953.

The fall of 1953, the school was closed, and the children were transferred to Co-operative.

Walter Dixon Jr. was the son of Walter and Lexie Bell Dixon. The other children born in this family were Marie, Patsy, Ella Mae, and Thomas Howard. Walter Sr. died about two months before Walter Jr. was born.

Walter Jr. was in the second grade in 1953. This year would be the last year for the White Oak Junction school to be open. The teacher asked one of the boys to go ring the bell for class to start back at the end of recess. As the bell began to ring, it came loose and fell through the floor to the ground, leaving a large hole in the floor. A few days passed, and the bell disappeared. Several weeks later, they learned Guy Kidd bought the bell and donated it to White Oak Junction Church.

∞

Walter Jr. finished grade school in Co-operative. The summer after completing the sixth grade in 1957, Walter got a job working for Guy Kidd, helping to deliver groceries. Walter said he didn't get paid anything. It was something to do, and he went along for the ride.

That same summer, Charlie and Clara Gibson's family moved to White Oak Junction into the house Eli Logan's family once occupied. Charlie Gibson and Clara (Young) Gibson's children were Bill (Willie), Willard, Charlene, Virgie, Lois, Harold, Damon, Hershel, Howard, Lonnie, Donnie, Juanita, Linda, Mildred, and Nola.

When Walter Dixon and Damon Gibson met, they became friends—and eventually best friends.

∞

Walter Dixon's sister Marie, married to Lester (Red) Watson, lived beside the Gibsons. Red's brothers, Luke and Jess, were much older than brothers Walter and Thomas (Tom) Dixon, and the two older boys were not nice to the Dixon boys. Many times, Walter and Tom had to carry water from the spring, located past Guy Kidd's store heading toward Fidelity about two miles. Luke and Jess would wait until Walter and Tom were halfway back home and take the water buckets from them and pour the water into their own buckets. Walter and Tom each carried two buckets and they would have to walk back to the spring and fill the buckets with water again.

After one of those incidents, the following day, Walter walked to see his sister Marie. When Walter arrived, Luke and Jess were standing in the yard and told Walter that Red and Marie were gone. The boys asked Walter if he would help them. They said their door was locked and asked Walter to climb through the window and unlock the door. Under the overhang of the roof was a huge hornet's nest, which Walter didn't see.

Walter started raising the window, making lots of noise and got halfway in when two hornets attacked Walter, stinging him in two different places. Walter worked his way on in and closed the window. Then Luke and Jess came through the front door, laughing. The door wasn't even locked. They knew it and they also knew the hornets were there.

∞

A day or so later, Walter Dixon and Ivan McCoy were standing and talking close to the foot bridge behind Guy Kidd's store. Damon Gibson walked over to see Walter, and it didn't take long for Damon and Ivan to get into an argument. Damon pulled out his pocketknife; Ivan reached down, picked up a chunk of wood, and hit Damon on the side of the head. The wood was half rotten, so it didn't seriously injure Damon, but it likely gave him a headache. Damon stabbed Ivan in the muscle of his arm; the blade went in all the way to the handle. Ivan had to be rushed to Oneida Hospital.

∞

Soon after the excitement of the fight, Walter Dixon and Damon Gibson were sitting on the foot bridge, talking, when a diving bird suddenly swooped across the top of the water and dove in for a fish. The bird misjudged the shallow water near the bank and rammed its beak and head into the mud. Damon eased around and got a hold of the bird with both hands and pulled it out of the mud. The bird, now free, reached up and latched hold of Damon's ear. Damon went to jumping and a squalling. Anyone not knowing would think Damon had started an Indian war dance. Damon stretched that bird's neck as far as his arms would reach, and the bird finally decided to let go. That bird left Damon's ear bleeding — and I'm sure hurting. Damon left for home.

∞

The first day that Walter Dixon helped Guy Kidd deliver groceries, they started early. Guy had a list of items he checked off as they loaded the truck. Guy delivered to customers who lived too far to carry their groceries home, like Bell Farm, Rattlesnake

Ridge, and Bald Knob. They were gone all day. Getting back to the store, the truck bed was empty, and Walter was plumb tuckered out. When Walter got home, he went straight to bed and slept till about noon the next day.

∞

Down below Guy Kidd's Grocery was a good place to swim, and that's where many boys would be on a hot day. When Walter and Tom Dixon pulled their pants and shirts off to swim, both boys would be in their birthday suits. One day while they were there swimming, the water was muddy from past days' rain. Walter's cousins Hobert and Don Dixon came down to swim, and Hobert got to showing off how good he could dive and how far he could swim under water. Hobert dove in with everybody watching. All of a sudden, everyone saw blood in the water. Don and a few others dove in and got Hobert out of the water. Hobert's nose was cut bad. When he dove in, he hit a sharp rock edge that he couldn't see because the water was muddy. Hobert's mom, Rose, hired Guy to take them to Stearns, and from there, the ambulance took them on to the hospital in Somerset.

Walter and Tom decided they'd had enough for one day. But when they got out to put their clothes on, they found they were not where they had left them. When they found them, the pant legs were tied in a knot. Since the pants had been baking in the sun and likely got moist when they were moved by the rascal responsible, the boys had a difficult time getting the knots untied. The Dixon boys figured it was Jess and Luke who'd tied the legs. It took them about an hour to get the pants untangled. They were mad as wet hens and cussed the Watson boys with every breath.

∞

As the summer days leisurely drifted along, the swimming hole remained one of the popular attractions. Another swimming outing on another day ended in more excitement. There was a big sycamore tree close to the bank with a rope tied to one of the limbs, allowing the boys to swing out over the water and drop into the deep part. Walter Dixon had swung out on the rope many times, but on this particular day, things didn't go Walter's way.

To get hold of the rope, you had to climb up the steep bank to the fence and hold on to the rope and fence while turning around to face the water. Walter let go of the fence as his big toe on the right foot got caught—his toenail decided to stay with the fence when he jumped. While Walter was in the air, he knew his toe had a problem. When he hit the water, he felt as though his toe was on fire. Walter got out of the water quickly. Seeing his toenail gone, he headed home as fast as he could.

∞

A few days passed and Walter Dixon's toe got to feeling better. He decided to stay out of the water for a while anyway. He definitely didn't want to get it infected. And what better time than now to go fishing. Walter liked going above the Upper Camp in Co-operative to Copin Camp to catch some crawdads. They made good fish bait.

Walking back to White Oak Junction, behind Guy Kidd's store across the creek on the side where the houses were, Walter took the path that went all the way to Bridge 11 and to the place where he loved to fish, called the Big Beach. Years earlier, a big beach tree had fallen next to the pond, making a good place to sit and fish.

Another good place to fish a little farther up past Big Beach was Big Spring. Going past it and turning left to go around the bank, you'd come out at Mine 15. There at the rocks was a good place to swim, and on past there, going over a hill where it leveled off was Granny Bottoms, where the big rock was—Walter's and the other boys' favorite place to fish. Walter and his brother Tom and Damon Gibson spent many carefree afternoons of quiet enjoyment there; catching a fish was an added bonus.

∞

Another school year in Co-operative got under way. The principal, Mr. Farley, drove a black 1951 Ford and he parked close to the chinning bar on the playground.

One recess, Walter Dixon and several other boys were playing baseball. Walter was up to bat. He hit a line drive, and the ball hit the front of the car's hood, knocking the emblem off. Walter stayed on edge for several days, thinking someone would tell Mr. Farley. After a few days, Walter figured everyone was afraid to say anything, thinking Mr. Farley would paddle every kid in the whole class. Mr. Farley and his paddle had a reputation; he very well might have paddled every kid; he was unpredictable that way.

The next week, Mr. Farley missed a day of school; an old lady took his place. After lunch, Walter and a couple of his buddies didn't go back to class.

They stayed outside but out of view of the windows. What the three were unaware of was that the old lady left a note for Mr. Farley.

The next day Mr. Farley called the boys to his desk, and he read the note out loud for everyone to hear and then proceeded to give each boy five licks with his paddle. I guess you could say, as fate would have it, Walter got paid back for hitting Mr. Farley's car, even if it was an accident.

Another day at recess, several boys were playing on the chinning bar. Each boy was taking a turn, showing what they could do. Mr. Farley had been standing close by watching. When each boy had a turn, Mr. Farley said he wanted a turn. Mr. Farley got on the chinning bar showing off like the boys and doing pretty good until he tried holding his body weight with his toes. He fell and about broke his neck. He was lucky. He could have been hurt badly.

∞

When Walter Dixon was around eight years old, he started taking an interest in his brother-in-law Red's guitar. Walter was left-handed, so the guitar was upside down when he played. He taught himself to play. Walter couldn't read music. (Many people in that area at the time, including my two older brothers and relatives, played several instruments, and not one of them could read music. They learned and played by ear.) He learned by ear and even learned to tune the guitar. When Walter started helping Guy Kidd at the store, Walter found out Guy had a guitar, and Guy's sons had not taken an interest, so Guy didn't mind Walter playing it.

As Walter and Guy spent more and more time together, Guy got to know Walter and invited him to go raccoon hunting with him. Now, that was a pretty big deal for Guy Kidd to ask someone to go hunting with him. Guy asked only those he thought highly of. The first couple of times Walter went hunting, Bull Hines, a friend of Guy's, would go also. Not every time but occasionally, Guy would find a comfortable spot under a tree and enjoy a little White Lightning. Walter and Bull would be walking the roads listening for the dogs to tree a raccoon. Often when they got back to the vehicle, Guy would be asleep. Bull would go straight to the vehicle and get out the food. Guy sometimes put the food in a bushel basket and anything you could think of to eat was in there, and Bull loved to eat. Sometimes Walter thought Bull came on the hunting trips only to do that—eat.

Guy's hunting dogs were well trained. When Guy went hunting for raccoons or squirrels, that's what the dogs treed. They were valuable, and Guy loved them better than anything. The Charlie Gibson family had a dog that showed up at their house one day, played with the kids, and never left. As time went on, Guy's dogs and the Gibson dog were constantly picking fights with each other. When the Gibson kids walked to Guy's store, the dog would follow. The dogs would have to be separated; otherwise they would fight.

One day, Guy drove by the Gibson home with all four dogs in the bed of his truck. They yelped and barked at the Gibson dog. The Gibson dog ran and jumped in the bed of Guy's truck. Guy stopped his truck, hearing the commotion in the truck bed. Guy stepped out in time to see one of his dogs go flying to the ground. Then another dog came out. In short order, another of his dogs hit the ground. When the fourth dog came out, the four stood there barking, looking up at the truck bed. When the Gibson dog jumped to the ground, all four of Guy's dogs went yelping toward home as hard as they could run.

Guy stood there looking at the Gibson dog and reached in his front pocket and threatened to kill the dog. Two of the older Gibson boys, standing on the front porch the whole time, saw what Guy was getting ready to do. One of them said, "Guy, if you do that, you'll be sorry." Guy continued staring at the dog for a long minute. As mad as he was, he decided it was best to let it go. Guy got in his truck and drove on home.

∞

Across from the front of Guy Kidd's store on the mountain lived Frank New, his wife, and their four daughters. The New family then moved off the mountain to a house across the creek behind Guy's store, next door to Lexie Dixon and her children. Not long after they moved, Frank died. This was before the swinging bridge was built. It was around midnight when Frank died.

They couldn't use the dirt road to get the body out because the creek had risen over the road due to recent hard rains. In this situation, everyone crossing the creek used a small paddle boat. Once you started in the boat, you had to paddle like mad to get across the swift water. They put Frank's body in that small boat. With the added weight, they couldn't get a good start, but they pushed it off the bank as hard as they could anyway. Being night made it even harder and they misjudged where the boat would hit the other side. They would have lost Frank's body if not for a couple men on the other side ready to grab the boat. No telling where it would have ended up. It took men with courage to get the job done. Not many days afterwards, relatives from Ohio came. Mrs. New and the four daughters left the area, and Walter Dixon never saw them again.

∞

The next night, Walter Dixon decided to stay with his sister Patsy, who was married to Ledford Clark. They lived behind Guy's store. Walter stayed up with Patsy, waiting for Ledford to get home from work. All of a sudden, Walter thought he heard something and walked to the door and opened it. He then heard somebody yell, "Help!" Then again, "Help!"

Walter ran toward the sound. When Walter got to the edge of Rock Creek, he yelled, "Where are you?" Ledford spoke again in a softer tone as he crawled to the bank way downstream. Ledford had misjudged how fast the water was traveling, which was easy to do in the dark. Plus he'd just worked a shift and had to be tired. The little boat had turned over, and Ledford lost his dinner bucket and was lucky he got out where he did. The next day, Walter Dixon, Damon Gibson, and Mike Kidd, using Guy Kidd's jeep, managed to pull the boat out from where it had lodged against a log downstream. The boat survived in one piece, and they put the boat back in the water and tied it off.

∞

During the school Christmas Break, Guy Kidd gave Walter Dixon, Damon Gibson, and his son Mike some M-80s (large, powerful firecrackers) a couple days before Christmas. M-80s were very loud when they exploded, and they'd go off even under water. On Christmas Eve, they thought it would be more fun if they used their sling shots and shot the M-80s. The boys walked up the road toward Bridge 11 but only for about a quarter of a mile. Across the creek lived Cater Tucker. The boys used trees for cover and, taking turns, fired M-80s with their sling shots at the Tucker house. There was a space from the floor of the porch to the ground and an M-80 rolled under the porch and exploded. The echo through the house must have been something.

That brought Cater out on the porch, holding his shotgun. The boys stayed hidden. They waited several minutes after Cater went back in his house. All three boys started bombarding the house with exploding M-80s as fast as they could send them across the creek. Cater came out on the porch and this time he fired one round up in the air, cussing and yelling, "You get out of here."

The three boys again waited until Cater went back in the house before running toward Guy's store. Only when they got a safe distance away did they start walking, all three laughing and talking about how much fun that was.

When the boys ran out of M-80s, Guy gave them a five-gallon can and a little carbide. You can make quite an explosion with carbide. Here's what they did: First they put some carbide in the can and placed the lid back on. Then they made a small hole in the can and dropped in a couple drops of water on the carbide. They inserted a piece of paper in the hole letting the gas build up inside the can. The last thing they did was light the paper and run fast for cover. When the flame encountered the gas, it exploded, sounding like a stick of dynamite going off. Now that was awesome. Everybody in the area of White Oak Junction heard the explosion and knew it was a bunch of boys just being rowdy.

∞

The holidays came and went. In front of Guy Kidd's store straight up the mountain to the top is where Guy had his television antenna. When the picture would get a little blurred or fuzzy, Guy would ask Walter Dixon to walk alongside the antenna wire to check it. Sometimes Damon Gibson and Mike Kidd would go with him. They had to make sure the power was turned off cause if you accidently touched the wire, it would shock the shit out of you. They also had to walk the whole way to the antenna to make sure nothing was on the wire, such as a tree limb.

Walter never refused to check the TV wire when Guy asked because there was a particular night through the winter when Walter liked watching Guy's TV for a couple of hours. Sometimes Randle, Guy's son, acted like he didn't want Walter to watch TV, so Walter would ask Guy if it was okay for him to watch. Guy always said it was okay, and Guy would walk with Walter into the room where the TV was. That's all it took. Leaving Guy's house at night, especially when the moon wasn't shining, Walter would practically run home.

∞

Another school year ended. Walter Dixon and Damon Gibson were together doing something nearly every day. Damon found out Walter loved to play the guitar; he told Walter he'd been playing around with his dad's guitar. Walter got Red's guitar and Damon got his dad's. They started walking the road toward the White Oak Junction Church to find a good place to practice and almost got to Road 1363, the main gravel road, when Walter happened to look over to his left and notice the huge culvert that was in the dip of Road 1363. Walter looked over at Damon and said, "Come on. This'll be the perfect place."

They went back in the culvert and started playing their guitars. It sounded like the guitars were amplified. The boys played for hours.

When they decided to give the guitars a rest, the boys walked up beside the church house to the big rock. Walter and Damon sat for a long time eating wild blueberries. The vines grew right beside the rock. If the boys had a taste for hazelnuts and beechnuts, all they had to do was walk up close to old Mine 15 and gather up what they wanted and take the nuts home. After the nuts dried, the boys removed the hull and dug out the kernel. Walter often said, "Man, these are good." Going to their perfect place to play their guitars—the culvert—became a habit for them, and they spent many hours and days there.

∞

As the days became hotter, more young people found themselves down at the swimming hole. One day, Walter Dixon and Damon Gibson walked down and were standing on the bank talking when William Gene Clark walked up. It wasn't long before William and Damon had strong words. When Damon called William a bad name, William hit Damon in the jaw. Damon looked all around on the ground but couldn't find anything within reach to use as a weapon. Damon tried hitting William with his fist but never was able to. William managed to land another punch on the side of Damon's head that made him even madder, and Damon's swings continued to come up empty.

Damon's brothers Howard and Hershel, seeing the fight, ran home and each boy came back with a knife. Before Howard and Hershel got back to Damon, William ran up the bank and swam across the creek, headed for Guy Kidd's store.

Damon took a knife from one of his brothers and followed William. William ran inside Guy's store when he saw Damon coming. Damon followed William inside, close behind him. Milliard Young, Damon's grandpa, was in the store and grabbed Damon and held him until William could leave. As mad as Damon was, he might have stabbed William. William was smart enough to stay away from Damon for a long time.

∞

A couple Saturdays later, Walter Dixon helped Guy Kidd straighten up the feed house. When finished, they walked into the store. Guy asked his wife Ada to fix Walter a bologna sandwich and told Walter to get himself a bottle of pop. Guy was likely behind the counter looking through receipts and bills. When Walter finished eating, he asked Guy, "Can I play the guitar?"

Guy said, "Sure, you know where it's at."

Walter had just sat back down with the guitar when Damon Gibson walked in. Seeing Damon, Walter said, "Go get your dad's guitar; we'll play some." It took Damon only a few minutes to run home. He was back in no time with his dad's guitar.

They'd been playing a while when Junior Hill and some of the boys from Bell Farm stopped at Guy's before heading home. They'd been down at the Tennessee State line drinking all day and were well loaded. While Walter and Damon played their guitars, Junior and the boys got to carrying on and dancing all over the store, having themselves a time. Guy over behind the counter seemed to be enjoying himself, watching everybody having fun. It was probably about four hours before Junior and the boys wore themselves down and left. Walter and Damon were ready to give the guitars a rest. Before Walter and Damon left, Guy said, "You boys come back and play anytime you feel like it."

∞

Next to Guy Kidd's store was a scrap iron pile. Damon Gibson rode his bicycle to the store, parked it, and intended on going in the store. Junior Hill was on the porch and walked over and kicked Damon's bike toward the scrap iron pile. Damon walked back, picked up his bike, and told Junior, "Don't be kicking my bike!" Damon started to go inside the store again. Junior walked over and this time picked up the bike and tossed it on the scrap pile. Damon walked over, picked up a piece of iron pipe, and hit Junior on the side of the head. It started bleeding.

Junior reached for Damon, and Damon went running toward home with Junior chasing after him, his head pouring the blood. Damon's dad Charlie was outside and saw Junior chasing Damon. Charlie gave Junior a shove and he stumbled. Junior fell and started rolling down the hill. When Charlie saw how bad Junior was bleeding, Charlie loaded him in his car and drove to Whitley City to the doctor.

∞

One night, Guy Kidd wanted to go raccoon hunting. Two of Guy's sons, Mike and Randle, wanted to go with their dad, so Guy asked Walter Dixon and Damon Gibson to join them. It was already dark when Walter and Damon walked to the store. Guy told his boys to go put some gas in the truck. Guy kept gas in five-gallon cans in the feed house. This was before Guy got a gas pump and started selling gas at the store. Randle got one of the five-gallon cans, and Mike held the carbide light to see by. It's hard to pour gas into a vehicle from a can without spilling a few drops. The carbide light is an open flame, and Mike got too close.

At that moment, Guy yelled from the porch, "Don't get that light too close to the gas." As soon as Guy spoke, the gas around the top of the neck ignited. Guy ran to the truck to put out the flame and the pocket of his pants caught on fire. Guy went to jumping and slapping his leg. If it hadn't been such a dangerous situation, it would have been funny, watching Guy jumping around. He finally got the flame out, and they loaded up and continued to the hunt as they had planned.

Another time, it was just Guy and Walter who went hunting. It didn't matter how tired it made Walter; he never refused when Guy asked him to go hunting. The dogs treed and Guy shot up in the tree and out fell a raccoon into the pond below. However, the shot didn't kill the raccoon, only came close enough to jar him off the limb. The dogs jumped in the water after the raccoon, and the raccoon got a hold of one of the dogs and almost had the dog drowned. Guy jumped in to help the dog. The dog got ripped up pretty bad, so the next morning, Guy took the dog to the doctor. The dog survived to fight another day.

∞

One evening, the sun was setting and Guy Kidd's son Mike, Walter Dixon, and Damon Gibson, walking around outside the store talking, wandered close to the feed house. Mike opened the doors where the bales of hay were kept; the hay made a good place to sit and talk. Mike started positioning some of the bales of hay so they could have a bale to lean back against. As he was doing that, Mike found a half gallon jar of moonshine with about a third gone. Well, the three boys passed the jar around and all three boys got higher than a Georgia pine. When the boys decided they'd had enough, Mike put the jar in the exact place he'd found it.

It didn't take Guy long to find out somebody had been in his White Lightning. The next day, Walter and Damon didn't start moving until afternoon when they decided to walk up to Guy's and talk with Mike. As soon as they walked up, they saw Guy outside by his truck, which was parked close to the feed house, and Guy motioned for Walter and Damon to walk over to where he was standing. When the boys walked close, Guy said, "Boys, if I find out you've been in my moonshine, I'll beat the hell out of both of you." Guy was mad and that's all he said. Guy liked to have some moonshine handy to sip on from time to time. Walter and Damon figured this was a good time to disappear, and they quietly walked away.

They walked back down the old railroad bed past the Gibson home. As they walked, a thought crossed Walter's mind about last night when they were drinking. He thought usually when Damon was drinking, he loved to fight. There had been a couple times he thought he and Damon might get into an argument, but they never had and through it all, they remained best friends.

A short walk down the old railroad bed and over to the left was a swinging bridge. Over the hill from there was where Stearns Company dumped slate. Many a time, Walter and other boys had dug in that area and found lumps of coal. So Walter and Damon thought that's what they'd do. They dug three grass sacks full, which took them just two hours, and put them in the flat bottom boat. The flat bottom boat was the same boat that people once used to get across the creek behind Guy Kidd's Grocery. On the way across the creek, Walter and Damon got to horsing around and started rocking the boat. Well, the weight of the coal was too much, and the boat flipped over. They lost the coal they'd spent two hours digging and were forced to swim the rest of the way across.

∞

The next day, walking up to Guy Kidd's store, Walter Dixon saw Lincoln Troxell sitting on the store porch. Walter said, "How you doing, Link?" Lincoln looked up and smiled. Walter thought, poor Ole Lincoln couldn't afford to buy a quart of moonshine so he was sitting there drinking a bottle of rubbing alcohol. And alcoholics will drink anything as Walter knew from watching his brother Tom; Tom got his nickname "Lightning" from drinking Lightning Hot Drops™.

∞

On the outside wall on the porch at Guy Kidd's store was an old crank phone. It was for anyone in the community to use, because that's all they had. When

Guy heard a certain number of rings, he knew who it was. Ada Kidd's mom and dad, Leo and Ida Dolen, lived across the creek in the community of Fidelity. They were getting on in years and Guy knew he and Ada needed a way to contact them in case of an emergency. Guy bought enough wire to stretch all the way to the Dolen home and he got Walter and Damon to run the wire.

Guy got it all set up, and about two weeks later, Walter, Damon, and Mike got to needing money, probably to buy some moonshine; they were afraid to get into Guy's again. The three boys went to the Dolen house, which was Mike's grandma and grandpa, and took the wire down, rolled it up neat, and brought it to Guy and sold it to him. Guy found out what they'd done when he tried to make a call either the next day or the day after. Boy, was Guy mad when he realized he'd bought the same wire twice. Word got to Walter and Damon via Mike that his dad wanted to see them and he meant now. When Guy got all three boys together, he said, "I could have you boys put in jail and the only reason I'm not is because my son's involved. I still may do it if that wire is not put back where you got it—now!"

∞

After a few days, things calmed back down. When some of the young men who went out of state to find work came home for the weekend, they usually stopped at Guy Kidd's store on the way home. Most often, when they did, they had already been to the Kentucky/Tennessee State line and were pretty well lit.

Walter's brother Tom came home with a friend from up north one weekend. His buddy wanted more beer and they went to Tommy Strunk's place and bought Country Club and came back to Guy's. Walter and Damon got out the guitars and started playing. It didn't take long for some of the guys to start stomping and hollering. Even Ole Guy kicked into a knee-slapping square dance. The fun went on to pert near midnight; that's when Guy stopped the guitar playing and started trying to get people out the door.

Tom Dixon and his buddy had been drinking Country Clubs and Walter had to help Tom's buddy across the bridge behind Guy's store. Earlier in the evening when the boys came in with Country Club, Walter tried to tell Tom to go easy with his drinking, that Country Club was strong. Tom said he could handle it. Well right now, he couldn't walk without help.

∞

One day Walter Dixon and Damon Gibson walked down the gravel road to where White Oak Junction Church was on the hill in the background. Two of Marshall Hall's boys, Linville and Eugene, came down the hill toward Walter and Damon in a pretty car and swerved the car to hit them. When the car passed, Walter picked up a rock and threw it, hitting the trunk lid of the car. It made a big dent, but the boys drove on.

The next day, word circulated that the law was looking for Walter and Damon because Marshall Hall swore out a warrant for the dent Walter had put in the car. So Walter and Damon decided to hide out in the woods, but they didn't go too far away since they planned to go home when it got dark. That went on for a couple of weeks; they generally stayed anywhere someone would take them in through the night until Walter got bone tired and told Damon, "I'm going home so I can lay down in my bed." Damon went home, too.

About 3:00 a.m., the sheriff came and got Walter and put him in the police car. The sheriff then drove to Guy's store and a deputy's car was sitting there. The sheriff stopped alongside the deputy's car and Walter could see they already had Damon. Walter and Damon spent nine days in jail for making the dent in the Hall boys' car, and it didn't matter to the judge that the Hall boys tried to run them over; they had no proof of that. The weekend after Walter was released from jail, relatives from up north (likely Indiana) came home for a visit. Walter left with them and never came back to the area to live, returning only for short visits.

What's written here about Walter and Damon is only a small portion of their lifelong friendship and the good memories they made in White Oak Junction.

∞

MARRIED THIS YEAR (Year Unknown)

James Murphy and Joyce Moore got married. Their children were Luther, Wanda, Jim, Darla, Fuzz, Steve, and Melissa.

Donald Dobbs and Connie Dennis also got married. Their children were Jason, Richard, Greg, Melissa, and Vicki.

∞

BORN THESE YEARS 1963, 1964, 1965, 1966, 1968, 1969, 1970, 1972, 1974, 1976

BORN 1963

Paul Shoopman
Debbie Parks
Mike Coffey
Jov McFall Blevins
Luther Murphy
Lori J. Waters

BORN 1964

Robert Watson
Wanda Murphy
Jane Jones
Billie Cox
Jimmy Dixon

BORN 1965

Wayne Jones
Jerry Dixon

BORN 1966

Kathy Shoopman
Jim Murphy
Michael R. Watters
Libby Waters

BORN 1968

Darla Murphy
Dester Terry

Angelia Dixon
Jayne Waters

BORN 1969

Loretta Douglas
Fuzzy Murphy
Tommy R. Watters
Joanne Jones

BORN 1970

James Blevins
James S. Watters

BORN 1972

Steve Murphy
Melinda Carson

BORN 1974

Melissa Murphy

BORN 1976

Shanna Dixon
Shawa Dixon

FARON CLARK
FAMILY PHOTO

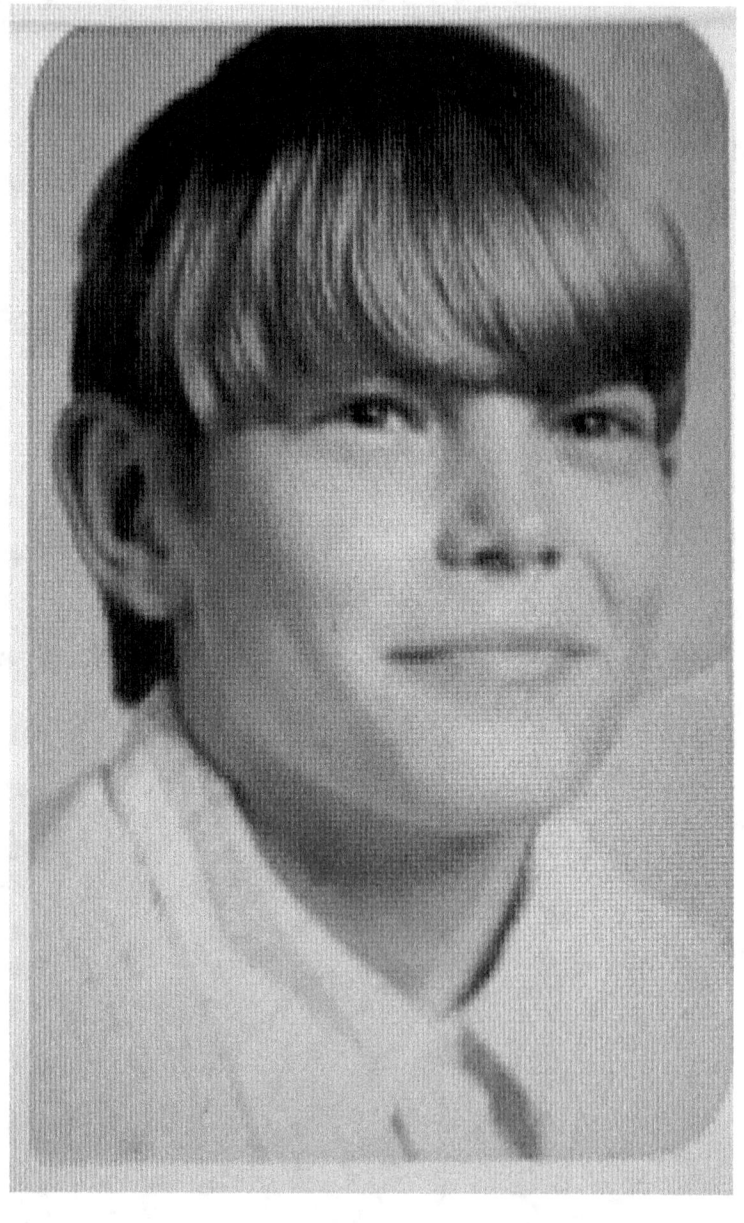

CHAPTER 41

Faron Clark and the Music

In later years, Jewell Kidd's Grocery became the hub for community news and happenings. If something happened in Co-operative or the surrounding communities, folks stopped in at Jewell's to get the scoop. By asking a few questions, they quickly learned the details of what happened.

Even the police often stopped at Jewell's to get the latest news. One time after a shooting at Dobb's Mountain, the deputies stopped at Jewell's to talk about it. Someone was always dropping in to find out the latest. The store had a welcoming atmosphere, and Jewell was always ready to sit down in a rocker beside the potbelly stove in winter or outside on the porch in summer to talk to folks when she wasn't taking care of customers.

∞

Over the years, Jewell trained several girls to work in the store and help her with household duties, such as cleaning the living quarters, cooking, and cleaning and sweeping the floor of the store. These girls also helped her with Jack when he was a toddler. Opal Jones, Joan Chitwood, Wanda Clark, and Ila Clark were a few of the girls who helped Jewell. I'm sure there were others. This help was very important to Jewell, freeing her up to run the store.

∞

Jewell Kidd's mom and dad, Bill and Nettie Bell, lived in the next house as you headed up the holler from Jewell's store. At one point, Jewell's sister Betty and her husband Gib Carson were visiting Bill and Nettie. The family called Bill and Nettie Ma and Pa Bell. One afternoon, Jewell decided to walk over for a quick visit because she couldn't leave the store unattended for more than a few minutes. Gib was sitting on the porch reading a newspaper while Pa Bell was in the garden hoeing. As Jewell stepped upon the porch, she said, "Ain't this a pretty sight. A big strapping man sitting on the porch while his father-in-law is in the garden doing all the work."

Gib said, "What's wrong with a daughter helping?" Jewell walked toward Gib, smacking at him. Gib held up his hands to deflect Jewell's blows. They both fell off the porch, landing in the front yard. Pa Bell dropped his hoe and hurried toward Jewell and Gib. As Pa Bell came near, both Gib and Jewell were getting to their feet, laughing and dusting themselves off.

Pa Bell said, "You two are going to have to stop this before one of you gets hurt."

"Don't worry, Dad, I won't hurt him," Jewell said, quietly laughing as she walked into the house.

∞

Across from the Co-operative School lived the Raymond and Darkie Clark family. The youngest son of the Clark family was Faron. Stepping out on the front porch of the Clark home and looking straight across the gravel road and White Oak Creek, one could clearly see the two Co-operative School buildings. Young Faron thought the White Oak Creek in front of their home was his and he claimed it. Faron was about five years old and not yet old enough to start school; in those days, a child had to turn six prior to the school year starting to enter the first grade. There was no preschool or kindergarten available.

During recess sometimes a school kid might wander over to the creek to throw a stick in the water to see how far it would float. Paper milk cartons worked well floating in the water; two boys might try racing their empty milk cartons. Young Faron would get him a pile of gravel from the gravel road close to his side of the creek bank. Any school kid wandering over close to the creek would receive a hail of rocks from Faron.

Faron was adventurous. It didn't take many days before Faron was walking over to the school playground, and it took him only one day to figure out those kids were not trying to take his creek; they were just looking for something to do for fun. Faron was a smart kid. He started going over to the playground every day to play with the kids. He made friends easily. That first day when the bell rang and recess was over, Faron was all alone on the playground. It was a long wait for the next recess. Faron didn't like that his friends left him and went into the school building. He wanted to keep playing. But more than that, he was curious about what went on inside the buildings.

The next day, Faron walked over to the playground. He'd been playing with the first and second graders since they were close to his age. When the bell rang for class to start again, Faron went into the first and second grade room with the kids. Faron thought he could come and go as he pleased, and he did until one day the teacher, Miss Wood, made Faron stand in a corner. Miss Wood had been lenient at the beginning with Faron, but if Faron was going to be in her class, she had to treat him like all the other kids. Faron learned a valuable lesson that day. Standing in the corner hurt his feelings.

∞

Darkie Clark, Faron's mom, walked down to the Upper Camp in Co-operative to visit Dorothy Dixon. Faron went with his mom. Dorothy's son Johnny and Faron stayed outside to play. The boys wandered over into the yard of the next-door neighbor, the Willis Watson family. The Watsons weren't home, but the boys noticed a bushel of apples on the Watson back porch. Johnny got him an apple and started eating it; so Faron got one too. Darkie saw Faron with an apple, but she didn't say anything until they left the Dixon home and were walking home.

"Faron, where did you get the apple you were eating a while ago?"

"On the porch next door to Johnny's."

"Did someone give it to you?" his mom asked. Faron said, "Nobody was home."

Darkie stopped and on both sides of the road were trees. She broke off a small limb, and Faron watched as his mom stripped off the tiny limbs. She gave Faron a whipping and explained why. Faron learned another valuable lesson: You don't take something that doesn't belong to you.

∞

Time was moving. Growing up in Co-operative, Faron Clark made lifelong friends with Randy Jones, Robbie and Jerry Shoopman, Jack Kidd, and others. After the Co-operative School closed, the boys still living in Co-operative put up basketball goals inside the two vacant classrooms in the smaller building. The local boys spent many afternoons playing basketball in the very building that many who had once lived in Co-operative had made such precious memories.

∞

Jack Kidd, Jewell Kidd's son, got a new bicycle and he wanted Faron Clark to go for a ride with him. So Faron got on the handlebars, and they were cruising along great until Jack said, "Look, no hands." Boy, was that a mistake. Both Jack and Faron went skidding on the gravel road. It took several days to get over that ride.

∞

Growing up in the Clark home was a happy time. Raymond, Faron's dad, drove a dump truck and he had to get up early to start his day. Faron, now in school, naturally wanted to sleep in as long as he could. Raymond would go out and start the truck and come back in to wait on the truck to warm up. Faron wanted to sleep longer, but there was no escaping the idling of his dad's loud dump truck. Faron would get a little frustrated and get up and run to the barrel stove in the living room, their source of heat. He'd go around and around the stove trying to get warm. Raymond got up early even on weekends, and on Sunday mornings, he'd turn on the Mull Singing Convention. But not too loud. If anyone said anything about it, Raymond would say, "It won't hurt you to get up."

While Faron was still at home, he went with his dad, Willie Slaven, and Jimmy T. Coffey to Stearns and they talked to Frank Thomas, CEO of Stearns Coal and Lumber Company. Winter was coming and the few families left in Co-operative needed something to burn in their stoves to stay warm. Mr. Thomas gave them permission to go to Co-operative Mine and get what coal they needed as long as they didn't sell any of it. Reaching the face of the mine, they didn't have to go but a few steps and were able to get all the coal they wanted. So you could say, tongue-in-check, that Raymond, Faron, Willie, and Jimmy were the last coal miners in Co-operative.

Faron Clark, born and raised in Co-operative, never left and still lives in a house up the holler from Jewell Kidd's Grocery. He has the distinct title of being the last man standing.

Faron spoke of his growing up in Co-operative: "We didn't have a lot of material things growing up. But we had wonderful parents and a good time; we were millionaires, really, when it came to growing up in a loving home and didn't know it. We were taught to work hard for what we got."

∞

As time moved along, the neighborhood boys got interested in music. Jewell's son Billy Jay taught himself on the guitar, but he wasn't interested in playing in front of others. Jack, Jewell's youngest son, on drums, Faron Clark on guitar, Robbie Shoopman on bass, and Jerry Shoopman also on guitar organized a band. They played at the old Sullivan and Lucy Smith house in Bell Farm.

On Saturday nights, it was a place to dance and listen to live music. Jewell Kidd loved to dance and for a while was a regular. There were a few times when Jack couldn't play, but Jewell went anyway. One particular night when Jack wasn't there, two men started arguing and were close to fighting. Jewell got between the two men. Jewell told the one man who was much bigger than the other guy to back off, that it wouldn't be a fair fight. Jack got worried that his mom might get hurt, so the band began inviting people to come to Jewell's store. They used Ma Bell's old empty house when they needed a dry place out of the weather. The boys played and Faron's sister Rayma Dean sang.

On warm summer nights, the musicians would gather in and sit on the porch of Jewell Kidd's store, and people could dance on the road in front of the store outside in the wide-open spaces. The mountains all around nestled the store like a mother caressing her child on her lap as the sun disappeared behind the many trees, casting shadows and awakening the fireflies too numerous to count. With the lights inside the store shining through the windows and the

CO-OPERATIVE, KENTUCKY
PHOTOS OF JEWELL BELL KIDD AND
JEWELL KIDD'S GROCERY.
PHOTOS COURTESY OF REBA KIDD.

porch lights on, the whole place in front of the store was illuminated. Folks could easily see the occasional car coming from either direction. After a car passed, they'd go right back to dancing. Around 1971, the gravel road through Co-operative was paved. From then on, dust was not an issue, and dancing was much easier on the pavement.

Jewell's brother, Estil Bell (nickname Leck), would occasionally come home from Ohio for the weekend. All day Saturday, he'd sit at the store and talk to folks as they stopped to get something they needed for home. They'd talk up a get-together for that evening and word would spread. Others who had to move north to find work often came home for the weekend and gathered at Jewell's also. After spending one of those Saturday nights at Jewell's, from then on, every time they came home they'd make a point to be at Jewell's come evening time. Before dark, a small crowd of people gathered in front of the store, ready to enjoy dancing and listening to music. The musicians sat where they wanted to on the porch.

Lots of times there'd be several guys playing on guitars and banjos and at least one on a bass and one on a mandolin; sometimes one or two would sing. Neighbors and friends from Dobbs Mountain, families that lived up the holler from Jewell, and a handful of families that still lived in Co-operative would be at Jewell's. A few regulars like Big Nose and Fannie Coffey, Howard Dobbs, and Bob and Donna Roberts would gather in for an evening of good times and fun on the road in front of Jewell Kidd's Grocery.

Other than having her family around her, Jewell was happiest on those Saturday nights with good friends around her dancing, and Jewell was always the life of the gathering. She might grab the arm of someone she hadn't seen dancing and before the evening was over they'd be dancing every song. Jewell enjoyed having people make a big circle and someone would be pulled into the circle to dance.

CO-OPERATIVE, KENTUCKY
JEWELL KIDD'S GROCERY
PHOTO COURTESY OF REBA KIDD.

Those people in the hills and hollers didn't have to go to an arena to hear live music, and they didn't have to go on a trip to enjoy themselves. They learned long ago as children running and playing outside and enjoying life, with little thought of the material things they didn't have, to be content and thankful for the good friends they shared the day with. Those happy thoughts and memories were carried with them each day they lived, and their enjoyment was simply getting together and making their own fun at Jewell Kidd's Grocery.

Listen…Listen, I can still hear Jewell's laughter. I bet you can hear it, too, if you try real hard. But you have to block out the noise of the world. The echoes of music and laughter can still be heard on the road to Co-operative.

Auf Wiedersehen
Adios
Arrivederci
Ciao
Au revoir

Goodbye

    … until we meet again.

∞

GRATITUDE LIST

(Names are not in any order.)

My gratitude for the people listed below is beyond words. Without you, this book would not exist. Thank you from the bottom of my heart for sharing your time and stories with me. I love each of you. You became family as I talked with you, some in person and many over the phone. You opened the windows of your memory because you believe in what I'm doing. For that, I'm eternally grateful.

    I hope when you see the names below, you will reach out and rekindle your friendships and get acquainted with the people you don't know. We all share something that's worth remembering and holding onto. If you experienced a different coal camp than Co-operative, we share similar feelings for the places we grew up in. You understand why I love Co-operative. Thank you!

RL Terry
Walter Dixon Jr.
Sam Perry
Boris Haynes
Roger Shoopman
Faron Clark
Nathan Nevels
Gloria R. Worley
Lecia Marcum Moreau
Joan Chitwood
Jeff Watson
Gene Maples
Lee Winchester
Stella Smith Winchester
Thelma Keith Abbott
Roger Chitwood
Wanda L. Worley
Eddie Winchester
Clora Watson Fotis
Brandon Worley
Leif Slusher
Noosha Ravaghi
Glenna Clark Parks
Ila Clark Freeman
Wanda Clark Gibson
Lynn Strunk
Reba Coffey Kidd
Lot Coffey Kidd
Kaiton Slusher

Theresa Coffey
Dawn Strunk
Arlena Troxell Jones
McCreary County Record
Barbara Dixon
Lonnie Jones
Donald Dixon Jr.
Jeremy Dixon
Rankin Parks
Carl Jones
Faye Shoopman Jones
Don Slaven
Wilma Douglas Maxwell
Jeremy Pennington
Diane Crabtree Logsdon
Sara King
Darla Murphy
Linda Byrd
Wanda Murphy Worley
Linn Gibson
Angelia Dixon Shaffer
Teresa Lynn Kidd
Richard Dobbs
Jewelene Carpenter
Debbie Freeman McNeil
Lois Dobbs
Phyllis Young Hill
Jeannie Dixon
Linda Winchester Perkins

David Black
Mike Ball
Jim King
Donald Buster Bell
Alvin Jones
Linda Shoopman Hill
Carolyn Crabtree Shoopman
Mary Jones Cummings
Rick Cox
Robert Mercer
Google.com
McCreary County Public Library Staff
The Artisan Shop Staff
Miss T. Gibson
Debbie Trammell
Josh Hines
McCreary County Museum
WHAY Hay 98 (the Little ELVIS Show)
Larry Davis
Wendle Branscum
Junior Keith
Loretta Clark
Denise Branscum
Crystal Mitchell
Veda Pelow Clark
Grady Wilson
Janet Gregory
Reverend Ben Ball
Novella Watson

Patricia Duffey
Judy Wilson
LD Worley
Tammy Leach Shephard
Marsha Blevins Thrash
Greg Gregory
Wanda Coffey
Joyce Gregory
Deena Anderson Swafford
Clara Stephens
Janice Waters Grundy
Jo Kidd
Donald Coffey
Noah King
Jan Lopresti Davis
Vella Davis Johnson
Bobby Thompson
Joyce Hall
Kay Morrow
Mary Hall
Joyce Hardwick
Bob Dixon
Ernie Jones
Barbara Shepherd Dixon
Larry Black
Geneva Watters
Clifford Dobbs
Buzz Duncan
Alma Crisp Moore

Wanda Worley
Fayrene Terry Roberts
Wanda Terry
Gerald Wilson
Gary Bowden
Randle Coffey
Stan Cox
Vic Dobbs
Sue Koger Hatfield
Melinda Manning Clark
Wanda Murphy

∞

Additional names of teachers I discovered since publishing *CO-OP: Coal, Community, & House 52* in 2020

Co-operative   Hobson Stephens
                          John L. Shepherd
                          Wilma Marcum
                          Ms. Murphy
                          Ms. Creekmore

Mt. View   Mr. A. O. Lee
                          Thelma Lovitt

White Oak Junction   Alma Jo Kidd
                          Thelma Lovitt
                          Wilma Marcum

Barthell   Louise Spencer

Yamacraw   Fannie Morgan
                          Thelma Lovitt

∞
WORLEY'S Published Books

CO-OP: Coal, Community, & House 52
Catch a Falling Star

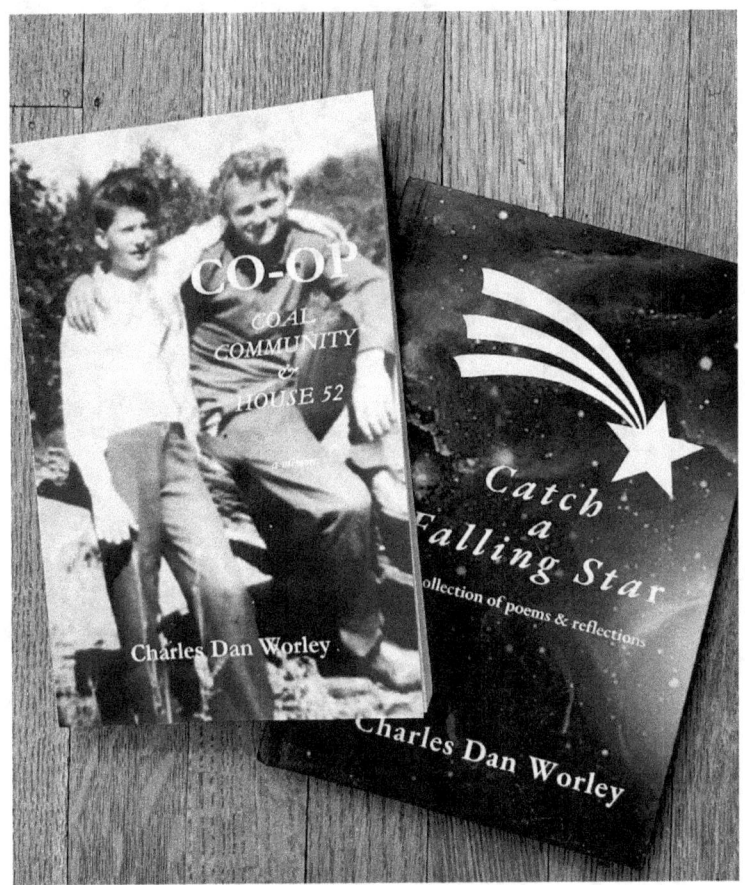

∞
COMING SOON FROM
Charles Dan Worley
∞ Western Novel
∞ Poems & Reflections II

Photo Credit: Brandon Worley

ABOUT THE AUTHOR...

Charles Dan Worley—writer, poet, and artist—lives in Stearns, Kentucky, in the beautiful Appalachian Mountains, still close to the place he was born and raised.

He received his B.S. in Art degree from the University of the Cumberlands (Williamsburg, Kentucky).

His first memoir was released in 2020: *Co-op: Coal, Community, & House 52*. His book of poems and reflections was published in 2021 titled *Catch a Falling Star*. Both of these books were nominated for the 2022 TCK Publishing Reader's Choice Awards.

In addition to his love of writing and art, he has a love of antique cars and has won many first-place awards at car shows in different states.

Visit him on Facebook: @charlesworley

THE ROAD IN CO-OPERATIVE, KENTUCKY
PHOTO BY CHARLES DAN WORLEY

OCTOBER 2022

www.ingramcontent.com/pod-product-compliance
Lightning Source LLC
Chambersburg PA
CBHW050309120526
44592CB00014B/1839